ECOLOGY, JUSTICE, AND CHRISTIAN FAITH

ECOLOGY, JUSTICE, AND CHRISTIAN FAITH

A Critical Guide to the Literature

Peter W. Bakken, Joan Gibb Engel, and J. Ronald Engel

Bibliographies and Indexes in Religious Studies,
Number 36
G. E. Gorman, *Advisory Editor*

GREENWOOD PRESS
Westport, Connecticut • London

Library of Congress Cataloging-in-Publication Data

Bakken, Peter W.
 Ecology, justice, and Christian faith : a critical guide to the literature
/ Peter W. Bakken, Joan Gibb Engel, J. Ronald Engel.
  p. cm.—(Bibliographies and indexes in religious studies,
ISSN 0742–6836 ; no. 36)
 Includes bibliographical references and indexes.
 ISBN 0–313–29073–3 (alk. paper)
 1. Human ecology—Religious aspects—Christianity—Indexes.
2. Christianity and justice—Indexes. 3. Human ecology—Religious
aspects—Christianity—Abstracts. 4. Christianity and justice—
Abstracts. I. Engel, Joan Gibb. II. Engel, J. Ronald.
III. Title. IV. Series.
BT695.5.B35 1995
016.2618'362—dc20   95–36040

British Library Cataloguing in Publication Data is available.

Library of Congress Catalog Card Number: 95–36040
ISBN: 0–313–29073–3
ISSN: 0742–6836

First published in 1995

Greenwood Press, 88 Post Road West, Westport, CT 06881
An imprint of Greenwood Publishing Group, Inc.

Printed in the United States of America

The paper used in this book complies with the
Permanent Paper Standard issued by the National
Information Standards Organization (Z39.48–1984).

10 9 8 7 6 5 4 3 2 1

To Carolyn A. (Chris) Cowap
1935-1988

Program Director, Economic Justice and Environmental Health, and Justice for Women, National Council of the Churches of Christ in the USA

who saw, not separate categories of issues, but one concern for Earth and all its creatures

Contents

Series Foreword

> Who has so 'subjected it', this creation which was made to serve human beings, as their 'garden', that it is now in need of liberation? We human beings have. That is the answer given, among others, by Luther and Calvin. Luther thinks that creation is delivered over to the 'vanity' and the 'perverse enjoyment' of human beings. And Calvin declares that 'all innocent creatures' must 'bear the penalty for our sins'.
>
> *- Alexandre Ganoczy,*
> *"Ecological Perspectives in the Christian Doctrine of Creation"*

As the door begins to swing shut on one century and another door to open on a new, it is clear that humanity will take with it much baggage as it crosses the threshold from the twentieth century to the twenty-first. This baggage includes degradation and destruction of the natural environment partly out of ignorance and partly out of the need for economic development. But there is also some light that will shine through the doorway into the new century, albeit weakly, and that is a growing concern and activism in favor of the environment, not least among individual Christians and their churches. In his summary overview of the ecological perspective in Christianity Ganoczy reminds us that both the Mosaic and the Pauline traditions incorporate awareness of and concern for the environment (or creation), albeit not always sensitively or positively.[1] Such awareness, he maintains, continued among the Fathers and medieval theologians. Ganoczy admits, however, that "it would certainly be wrong and anachronistic to extract a regular ecological doctrine of creation and salvation from the patristic tradition. Its anthropocentrism is indisputable."[2] That is, although humanity may have forfeited dominion over the earth through the Fall, humans continue to "possess" the earth—man raises himself up again in an individual ethical enterprise that ignores the incipient ecological focus first found in Genesis. It is probably accurate to say that the fine balance between ecological sensitivity and anthropocentrism found in the Hebrew Bible was lost by the beginning of the post-Judaic era, if not before, and that early in their history Christians began to interpret God's command in Genesis 1:28 ("Be fruitful and increase, fill the earth and subdue it, rule over the fish in the sea, the birds of heaven, and every living thing that moves upon the earth") as justification for exploiting the environment.

---

[1] Alexandre Ganoczy, "Ecological Perspectives in the Christian Doctrine of Creation," *Concilium* 4 (August 1991): 43-53.

[2] Ibid., 48.

While awareness of the fragility of nature, and humanity's place in the scheme of things, has never been absent from the Christian tradition and its Semitic forebearers, there has been a widely held belief that the dominion theme in Genesis has been responsible for much environmental destruction in countries where the Judaeo-Christian tradition dominates. This belief became particularly pronounced in the 1960s, probably with the publication of Lynn White's influential article, "The Historical Roots of Our Ecologic Crisis" in *Science* 155 (1967): 1203-07, which strongly argued that the environmental crisis brought about by human activity was a direct consequence of the domination theme so clearly stated in Genesis. In Christiansen's view, most theologians of the day with an interest in ecology uncritically adopted White's thesis as the only defensible one.[3] In more recent times there has been a substantial reaction to this view, perhaps best reflected in the important work by Paul Santmire, *Travail of Nature*.[4] As Christiansen summarizes Santmire's thesis, there are two models in theological anthropology: one is a "spiritual motif" in which nature is simply a backdrop for salvation history; the other is an "ecological motif" which assumes a divine and human concomitance with nature.[5] Much theological writing, in this view, can be categorized as either "spiritual" or "ecological"; as with all such arguments, there is a danger of slipping into the comfort of an "either-or" paradigm, but if this can be avoided there is much to be gained from looking at the Christian enterprise in this way.

The trend today I believe is towards the latter, ecological motif, and this is one reason for the present volume. As an example, Roger Burggreave argues convincingly that the natural world in fact is not given to human beings; rather the world issues from God and belongs to him. It is not human property but is given to humanity in stewardship. "This means that if human beings 'take' and 'appropriate' the earth, they are usurpers and robbers. They have no right or privilege; rather, they are the 'last to come.'"[6] More than this, the biblical conception of creation places humanity in an ethical relationship with creation. "Human beings are not just put in the world as a "being among other beings," but created in an ethical relationship to the world: they discover that they stand in an "ethical bond" with creation.[7]

In this move towards recovery of an ecological motif in Christian theology and practice, theologians seem to be approaching the issue from two related perspectives. One is an emphasis on the biblical foundations of respect for nature and on the embodiment of this in the divine-human covenant. Thus it is argued that early in Genesis the covenantal relationship embracing all of creation is established by God: as Granberg-Michaelson maintains, "it is a covenant with 'every living creature', a covenant God describes as 'between me and the earth' (Gen. 9:13).[8] Closely related to this biblical perspective is what one might term an immanental, activist perspective in which individual Christians and the churches intervene in the social, political, and economic processes when the natural environment is threatened. Granberg-Michaelson again: "as the church, our response to God's covenant with creation must certainly place us in stalwart resistance to all that breaks the integrity of creation, all that treats the earth as

---

[3] Drew Christiansen, "Moral Theology, Ecology, Justice, and Development," in *Covenant for a New Creation: Ethics, Religion, and Public Policy*, edited by Carol S. Robb and Carl J. Casebolt (Maryknoll, NY: Orbis Books, 1991), 268.

[4] H. Paul Santmire, *The Travail of Nature: The Ambiguous Ecological Promise of Christian Theology* (Philadelphia: Fortress Press, 1985).

[5] Christiansen, "Moral Theology," 258.

[6] Roger Burggraeve, "Responsibility for a 'New Heaven and a New Earth,'" *Concilium* 4 (August 1991): 110.

[7] Ibid.

[8] Wesley Granberg-Michaelson, "Covenant and Creation," in *Liberating Life: Contemporary Approaches to Ecological Theology*, edited by Charles Birch, William Eakin and Jay B. McDaniel (Maryknoll, NY: Orbis Books, 1990), 30.

an object for our possession rather than God's gift, and all that subjugates the creation to destruction and ruin rather than saving the creation through fellowship with it."[9]

Such perspectives, both biblical and activist, are becoming institutionalized by the churches, as careful reading of such encyclicals as *Gaudium et spes* and *Sollicitudo rei socialis* suggests. The latter, for example, is viewed by Ronald and Joan Engel as a positive and influential step of the Catholic Church towards environmentally responsible theology, for in it John Paul affirms some important ecological principles, especially the importance of acting in recognition that creation is a unified ecological system.[10] And so we are seeing the full development of a conscious, articulated relationship between environmental and social ethics in the Christian tradition—what we have come to call "eco-justice." It is no longer merely public worrying by a few fringe theologians and activists; the institutional church has taken eco-justice on board, and when that happens, for good or ill the issue becomes mainstream. We are now at the stage of seeing some positive responses by government and corporate players in the developed countries to eco-justice concerns expressed by Christian organizations; perhaps similarly positive reactions will occur elsewhere in the near future.

Accompanying this growing concern for the environment among Christians has been a burgeoning literature from within the Christian tradition on environmental matters, ecological ethics, and associated theological issues. Indeed, the volume of writing on these topics in the last three decades or so has been phenomenal. Not only ethicists and practical theologians, but also church historians and systematic theologians, biblical scholars and philosophers have felt compelled to add their perspectives to the debate. Journals and publishers around the world have taken an interest in the range of issues related to eco-justice, and it is rare for a day to pass without noticing a new book or article on the subject. It was thus timely and gratifying to receive from Dr. J. Ronald Engel, Professor of Social Ethics at Meadville Theological School in Chicago, and his colleagues, Dr. Peter W. Bakken of the AuSable Institute at the University of Wisconsin-Madison and Dr. Joan Gibb Engel (co-editor with her husband of *Ethics of Environment and Development*) a proposal for a volume devoted to ecology, justice, and the Christian faith.

Drs. Engel and Bakken clearly possess the combined knowledge and expertise needed to assess the literature on Christian eco-justice—this much is evident from their judicious choice of entries and the quality of annotations in the bibliography. Moreover, their introductory critical survey, "The Struggle to Integrate Ecology, Justice, and Christian Faith," comprehensively analyzes the principal developments and themes in the field, which are carefully delineated and comprehensively referenced in the extensive endnotes. Students new to the study of Christian perspectives on ecology and justice, as well as scholars seeking to order their more extensive knowledge, will find this opening discussion immensely beneficial. Furthermore, the bibliography itself succeeds in covering, in its eleven broad subject categories, all key aspects of the field, from historical and philosophical underpinnings to grassroots activities and institutional structures. In these sections the compilers have thoroughly and objectively annotated a fully representative range of the most important works in this field. Indeed, so extensive is the treatment (extending to some 500 items) that the bibliography will serve as an indispensable resource not only for newcomers to the ecology and faith debate but also for those engaged in advanced study and scholarship.

Putting this volume together has been no simple task for the compilers, yet they have done so competently and professionally—so much so that my task as Advisory Editor of the series has been unusually trouble-free and pleasurable. The result is a carefully structured and judicious survey that is accessible to students and useful to scholars. *Ecology, Justice, and Christian Faith* undoubtedly sets a new benchmark for

---

[9] Ibid., 33.

[10] J. Ronald Engel and Joan Gibb Engel, eds., *Ethics of Environment and Development: Global Challenge, International Response* (Tucson, AZ: University of Arizona Press, 1990), 4.

the bibliographic treatment of eco-justice issues, and I am pleased to welcome it as a valuable addition to Bibliographies and Indexes in Religious Studies.

The Reverend Doctor G. E. Gorman FLA FRSA
Advisory Editor
Charles Sturt University—Riverina
August 1995

Foreword

Many bibliographies are best "grazed" casually or browsed through quickly, but a few definitive annotated bibliographies should be savored for quality that provides perspective, encouraging deeper reflection. *Ecology, Justice, and Christian Faith: A Critical Guide to the Literature* definitely deserves to be savored. This long-awaited overview, covering more than three decades of literature on the subject, should interest scholars in diverse fields: theology, religion, ethics, politics, social and green sciences, environmental and cultural history. The guide is also instructive for leaders of religious or environmental organizations, a new generation of whom are beginning to discern how interrelated ecology, justice, and faith are. Items in this bibliography show how to bring these spheres of thinking together dynamically.

Up to this point, historians of environmental thought and action have given very little attention to the lively corpus of theologically-informed critique and religiously-grounded ethical reflection on this subject. This neglect occurred despite—or perhaps because of—awareness of modern (including fundamentalist) religion's negative environmental potential. But now that the future of Earth community is so threatened by the nature-manipulating intensity and gross social inequity of human activity, every society and institution must reform to fit the needs of natural integrity and humane culture. Toward this end, no major source of spiritual and moral insight can legitimately be ignored.

Ever since Francis Bacon asserted the modern ultra-anthropocentric agenda of conquering nature for human convenience, technologists, economists, politicians and theologians have shown confusion about the human vocation. Are we here for creation's sake, or does it exist for us, particularly our kind? What is our responsibility to future generations, as well as to everykind now alive? For the sake of both human and otherkind, members of this tool-making species that does ethics must learn to revalue the natural world, to welcome diverse human cultures and animal and plant species, while working for just and sustainable community. But for "greener" faith commitment to take hold, many more persons must adhere to normative values and together pursue promising patterns of life that will preserve ecological integrity while counteracting maldevelopment. In short, the eco-*in*justice crisis requires our substantive reflection on a coherent, spirited, ethical framework for response and clarification of its significance for religious, economic, and social life in a world searching for just and sustainable community.

Religiously grounded eco-justice thought, and action consistent with it, contributes significantly by giving ethical focus to public discourse and common pilgrimage to meet the environmental challenge. To what is said so well about that ethic in the Preface and Critical Survey, I would add these observations:

(1) Eco-justice provides a framework for constructive thought and action that concentrates on the link between ecological health and socio-economic justice. For we confront a dual crisis: degradation of the natural environment and impoverishment of low-power people everywhere. Brutal treatment of human beings and the rape of eco-

systems occur in a reinforcing pattern. Authentic responses to eco-injustice attend to both ecological integrity and social equity together—the well-being of human with otherkind in one Earth community over time. As much of the literature shows, such responses encompass both personal and public life, engaging all three levels of moral agency: individual, institutional, and societal.

(2) The motive power for caring deeply about human and other creatures is religious in that it expresses ultimate concern. "The earth is the Lord's, and all that dwell therein." Theological connections and liturgical practices matter a lot in encouraging humans to respect created reality as spirited being intrinsically valued by its Creator. This is the deep basis for eco-justice thinking. Ironically, a perspective that first emerged to reconcile post-Earth-Day competition between social justice and environmental action groups has turned out to offer much more than "tradeoffs." It provides a dynamic framework for philosophical reflection and for refocusing the study of theology and ethics, including environmental ethics, to meet the real needs of Earth community in the twenty-first century. The goal of eco-justice thinking and doing—which is more than eco-centric but appreciative of the need for eco-system integrity—is to equip new generations to live eco-justly, i.e., to worship, work, produce, consume, educate, celebrate, shelter, meet, eat, with environmental integrity. That pattern of living differs greatly from what is proposed in the prevailing economic ideology and idolatry of profit-maximizing, free-market globalism. The standard for evaluating the choices is simple enough: "You shall know them by their fruits."

(3) This theologically resonant, ecologically alert value framework is contextual, not absolutist. Neither an eco-justice ethic nor beliefs shaping it clarifies exactly what humans ought to do about immediate choices faced at any given time and place within a "good" creation. In light of tradition, experience, and reason, the task is to discern afresh the good to be achieved or the path of right relations, and to wrestle contextually with particular options that do not resolve dilemmas of policy and practice but that seem to better serve the common good and the good of the commons. Hint: the deep, practical values that animate the quest for eco-justice inform and qualify each other. Ecological sustainability, basic sufficiency, fair participation, and post-anthropocentric solidarity with Earth and people all matter as mutually correcting and reinforcing core values. A full-orbed understanding of just and sustainable community encompasses these norms as essential, interactive components of a healthy future.

I was the Presbyterian representative to the Eco-Justice Working Group of the National Council of the Churches of Christ in the USA which in 1985 asked Ron Engel, its Unitarian Universalist representative, to put together a critical bibliography on ecology, justice, and Christian faith. Ron, Professor of Social Ethics at Meadville/Lombard Theological School and Lecturer at the Divinity School of the University of Chicago, has long taught courses in the field of environmental ethics and religion. Ron was immediately joined by Peter W. Bakken, whose interest in eco-justice began when a Ph.D. candidate at the Divinity School. Peter is now Research Fellow of the Madison, Wisconsin Outreach Office of the Au Sable Institute of Environmental Studies. Later, Ron and Peter were fortunate to enlist the help of Joan Gibb Engel, Ph.D., editor and author in the fields of nature writing and environmental education. I commend these three friends for their quality achievement—both the many entries and the overview. Thanks to their patient labor of love through many hours reviewing, expanding, and editing specific entries, a host of others can now learn from the rich, previously rather hidden, literature reviewed in *Ecology, Justice and Christian Faith*. This volume is an important product of my joint efforts with Ron Engel to initiate professional development, strategic publication, and educational innovation to meet the environmental challenge. As the bibliography shows, the eco-justice movement has matured in some ways, and in others it has just begun.

Dieter T. Hessel, Director
Program on Ecology, Justice, and Faith

Preface

Throughout the second half of the twentieth century the interlocked problems of global environmental degradation and social injustice have challenged the peoples of the world to reconsider some of the most fundamental questions of human life: How are we to understand our moral obligations to the natural world? And how are these obligations related to our obligations to ourselves and other persons in the communities of which we are also a part?

Since global environment and development issues are complex and involve every facet of life on the planet, any satisfactory answer to these questions requires a normative framework at least as large and complex as the questions themselves. An adequate normative framework must be of sufficient size to embrace the many values of natural, as well as distinctly human, existence and to distinguish and coordinate their diverse, often conflicting, moral claims. It is difficult to conceive of a moral framework adequate to this task that does not eventually make appeal to a comprehensive vision of the order of the cosmos and the proper role of human beings within it. This is one way of saying that it is difficult to conceive of a moral framework adequate to this task that is not religious in quality, if not in name. It is for this reason that persons have, for several decades, searched the great bodies of religious thought and tradition for moral wisdom on how to live responsibly in nature and society.

We have prepared this annotated bibliography of the literature on ecology, justice, and Christian faith in order to help meet the pressing need for critical and systematic ethical and theological reflection on the complex environmental and social issues of our time. The literature treated here—over five hundred articles, essays, and books by some three hundred authors between the years 1961-1993—is the most extensive body of published writing available in the world today on the relationships between environmental and social ethics from the standpoint of a particular religious faith. We believe that it constitutes a major resource for Christians and non-Christians alike.

This bibliography draws from a wide and diverse body of human knowledge and experience. Many different Protestant and Catholic traditions, as well as Eastern Orthodoxy, are represented. Contributions come from Christians of diverse cultural backgrounds. Practitioners of most disciplines of theological scholarship are included-- biblical scholars, church historians, comparative religionists, ethicists, practical, systematic, philosophical, and confessional theologians. The variety of theological perspectives represented embrace foundationalist and hermeneutical, creation-centered and liberationist, theocentric, anthropocentric and biocentric, evangelical and process. A broad range of contemporary ecological and social justice issues are treated, from poverty, hunger, and war to loss of biological and cultural diversity, women's issues, appropriate technology, genetic engineering, land ownership and reform, rural life, animal rights, duties to future generations, simple lifestyles, and population. In addition to the fact that the literature as a whole is informed by disciplined and self-critical study of Christian scriptural and doctrinal traditions, a majority of the writings draw substantially upon knowledge gained through critical inquiry in the sciences and humanities, ecumenical and inter-faith dialogue, and practical efforts to create just and sustainable communities in many parts of the world.

Remarkably, although these writings draw in various ways from centuries of Christian and secular experience and reflection, they were generated in a very short period of time: the three decades since the emergence of widespread public concern for the global *problematique* in the mid-1960s. Moreover, the literature continues to grow at a rapid rate, a fact that repeatedly delayed the publication of the bibliography, and finally required us to set 1993 as an arbitrary cut-off date. Within this approximate time-frame, the foundations were laid for what Alvin Pitcher has called "another Reformation."

The Concept of Eco-Justice

The concept of "eco-justice" is the normative framework that gives coherence (explicit or implicit) to much of this literature and constitutes, in our view, its single most substantive contribution to contemporary moral and religious thought. Eco-justice is the moral claim that ecology and justice belong together, that there is an overarching moral imperative for human beings to pursue what is ecologically fitting and socially just, and to do so in such a way that each is supportive of the other.

Christian writers defend the ideal of eco-justice on biblical, doctrinal, and ontological grounds. They argue that human beings realize their special calling within the divine ordering of creation to the degree that their actions embody caring, just, and sustainable relationships with one another and with the rest of nature. Tragic choices among and between ecological and human values, as well as between individuals and communities, and present and future generations, will always be necessary, but the world is so structured that, if human beings exercise proper moral oversight, such choices are less frequent and may even result in achievements of compensatory value.

Eco-justice writers also find support for the imperative of eco-justice in empirical evidence that the good of human individuals and communities exists in positive and reciprocal interdependence with the good of non-human individuals and systems. They point to the fact that, in an interdependent world, a healthy ecosystem is required for human life to flourish, and justice between humans is required if human communities are to sustain flourishing environments. The most telling empirical evidence, of course, is the contrary: degradation of the natural environment and impoverishment of oppressed people often go hand in hand and can be traced to the same cause.

Christian theologians and ethicists have provided substantial biblical, moral, historical, economic, social, political, theological, and other content for the concept of eco-justice, and delineated many of its implications for public policy and public moral witness. The concept of eco-justice is not a Christian invention, however; it is open to a variety of religious and philosophical interpretations and may be called by a variety of names. Some form of the notion that the welfare of the human community and the welfare of the ecosystem are reciprocally related and require an integrated societal ethic may be found in many cultures throughout the course of human history, as well as in modern secular efforts to think through our duties to society and nature. The literature reviewed in this bibliography is important, therefore, not only for the light it sheds on the various traditions of Christian thought and action, past and present, but for the models it provides for eco-justice criticism, construction, and practice in other faith traditions and in society at large.

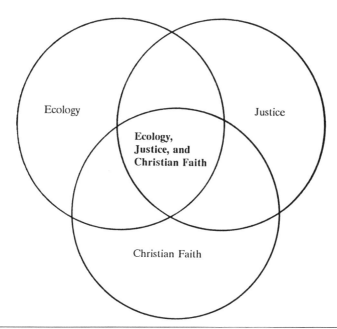

Fig. 1. Venn Diagram Showing Relationships of Ecology, Justice, and Christian Faith.

The Scope and Limits of the Bibliography

The normative center of the bibliography is the concept of eco-justice; its scope, however, is broader. Our aim is to include the most important literature since 1960 that addresses the intersections of the three fields of ecology, justice, and Christian faith regardless of how they are or are not specifically related to one another (see Fig. 1). We focus on works that include all three of the following:

(1) Attention to ecological values, such as the integrity of organisms or ecosystems, or the sustainability of evolutionary processes, and to ecological issues such as biodiversity, agriculture, resource limits, or land use

(2) Attention to social justice values, such as liberty, equality, or the common good, and to justice issues such the distribution of economic wealth, political oppression, racism, or sexism

(3) Attention to Christian theology, history, ethics, institutions, and public witness as they relate to ecological values and issues, on the one hand, and social justice values and issues, on the other

"Ecology" and "justice" are terms that require definition because of their diverse uses in the literature. "Ecology" typically denotes the many values and processes—intrinsic, instrumental, systemic—of a flourishing natural order, local, planetary, cosmic; although it is often used interchangeably with "environment," we assume that it refers to the world of nature beyond human reach as well as those particular portions of the non-human world with which humans interact. Ecology is sometimes employed to refer to a field of normative values and at other times to a scientific discipline. Justice likewise refers to a plurality of values—liberty, equality, community, wisdom—and a plurality of forms—distributive, material, procedural.

In sum, the subject matter of this bibliography is both broader and narrower than the concept of eco-justice. It is broader because the works annotated here were selected on the basis of whether they address the relationships between Christianity and ecology and justice—not by whether they see that relationship in a particular way. It is narrower because it only treats works that develop a Christian theological perspective on the relations between ecology and justice. The reader will find an extended discussion of the spectrum of values considered in this literature and in the fields of environmental ethics and social ethics generally, and the variety of kinds of relationships that are posited to hold between them, including those views that consider ecology and justice to be antithetical in one or more respects, in part one below.

A creative and integrated theological approach to the connections and tensions between ecological wholeness and social justice defines our ideal bibliographical entry. Such a work would include a theological interpretation of humanity's place in the cosmos, an empirical reading of our socio-ecological context, ethical principles and values defining right forms of social organization and right relations between human groups and between human beings and nature, and an analysis of, and prescription for, one or more issues affecting both society and the environment. In practice, of course, not every annotated work gives equal attention to theology, ethics, and policy, just as few equally meet the ecological, justice, or Christian theology criteria spelled out above.

Clearly, there is an immense body of literature that is relevant to discussion of the relationships between ecology, justice, and Christian faith. In principle, virtually all the literature on environmental ethics, social ethics, Christian theology and the environment, and Christian theology and social ethics is contextual to this bibliography. Our work has been made manageable because our criteria have required us to omit works that treat only two of the three fields of ecology, justice, and Christian faith. However, this also means that we have had to leave out many important and relevant works. We especially regret the omission of those works that focus exclusively on the relation of the Christian faith to ecology—including the substantial body of work on the theology of nature and natural theology, and on the history of Christian attitudes toward the natural world. These works constitute critical background to the development of eco-justice thinking. The reader will be helped by citations to this literature within the works annotated, and by following up bibliographical references in the annotated works.

There are other notable limitations to this bibliography. Most obvious is the fact that we are limited to works first published, or later translated, in the English language, and to English-language literature of primarily North American origin. The growing attention by theologians in Asia, Africa, Europe, and South America to the subject of eco-justice is not adequately represented here. A second limitation is that most church statements and their supporting materials have been left out, except for a few that we have judged particularly significant, and most religious education materials are likewise omitted. For some omissions we can only plead finitude. Writings on ecology, justice, and Christian faith constitute, in a sense, an "invisible literature." There is no bibliographical index heading for this subject, and it is hard to tell from titles alone whether a particular book or article meets our criteria for inclusion. Because of these limitations, this bibliography is neither exhaustive, nor fully representative of Christian thought on ecology and justice over the past three decades. Nonetheless, the works included are prominent and influential writings and serve as important signposts to the range of ideas, issues, and materials that must be grappled with in order to advance the integration of ecology, justice, and Christian faith.

We have tried to be consistent in applying our three criteria, but have occasionally stretched them to include representatives of important or influential perspectives. For example, we felt we could not leave out the influential work of Thomas Berry even though his attention to social justice issues and specifically Christian teachings is slight compared to most of the other works included. Similarly, the work of Lynn White Jr. is so seminal for the discussion that we felt we could not omit his classic 1967 essay, although it only touches upon the issue of justice. We have also stretched the 1993 cut-off date in order to include several essays from the Global South (most of which were written earlier but were not easily available), a context that we felt needed more adequate representation.

The Organization and Use of the Bibliography

The bibliography is divided into two major parts. The first is a critical introduction to the eco-justice movement in Christian theology; the second, divided into eleven chapters, is the annotated bibliography proper. Since the subject matter of many annotated works does not fall exclusively into any single category, it is important for the reader in search of works on a particular topic to refer to the end of each chapter for cross-references to related items, and to consult the general subject index.

In general, the annotations in this bibliography are longer than those found in most other annotated bibliographies. We have tried to summarize the general argument of the book or essay while lifting out for special emphasis the implications of the work for the norm of eco-justice. The reader should keep in mind that annotations are highly condensed generalizations, and cannot do justice to the richness of an actual book or essay.

The bibliography is addressed to anyone with an interest in relating justice, ecology, and Christian faith—whether it is out of concern for the historical paths the discussion has taken, problems arising at practical and theoretical levels, resources for teaching and research, or the spectrum of positions that has so far emerged. It is intended for use in a wide range of institutional contexts: religious education; college, university, and seminary teaching; church programming and administration; parish ministry; academic research; liturgical renewal; public policy analysis and advocacy; social witness; and personal life-style transformation.

This bibliography documents the fact that there exists a strong eco-justice movement in Christian communities throughout the world, and that this movement is supported by significant eco-justice inquiry in all fields of Christian theology. Our ultimate hope is that the bibliography will contribute to the further institutionalization of disciplined study on the relations of ecology, justice, and faith, Christian and non-Christian, in universities, seminaries, institutes, churches and educational associations of all kinds, and that this study will lead, in turn, to increased awareness of the moral significance of action in pursuit of eco-justice.

Acknowledgments

Work on this bibliography began in the fall of 1985 under the auspices of the Eco-Justice Working Group of the National Council of the Churches of Christ in the USA. Since 1985, it has benefited from the generous support of a goodly company of scholars, students, and friends. Principal among these are Bill Gibson and Dieter Hessel. Without their steadfast faith in the project and repeated acts of personal and scholarly assistance, it would never have been completed. Other scholars who helped at critical stages include Don Browning, Carl Casebolt, Heather Eaton, Bill French, Dana Horrell, Fred Krueger, David Larsen, Robin Lovin, Owen Owens, Larry Rasmussen, Joseph Sheldon, and Holmes Rolston III.

Nor could the project have been successfully completed without the help of several generations of Meadville/Lombard research assistants, including Kent Burbank, Wanda Kothlow, Joan Montagnes, Ken Olliff, and Barbara Jo Sorenson; the support of Meadville/Lombard faculty secretaries Amir Tarik and Dinah Wallace; and the help of librarians Neil Gerdes and Christine Mitchell at Meadville/Lombard, and Emilie Pulver and Ken Sawyer at Jesuit Krauss McCormick Library at the Lutheran School of Theology at Chicago.

The project was launched by two grants from the Presbyterian Church (U.S.A.), an initial grant from the Presbyterian Church program agency, and a grant in 1988 by the Presbyterian Committee on Social Witness Policy. Additional funding came at a critical time from an anonymous member of the Rockefeller Family. A grant in 1992 by the World Environment and Resources Program of the John D. and Catherine T. MacArthur Foundation to the Program on Ecology, Justice, and Faith at Meadville/Lombard enabled the bibliography to be expanded to a book-length publication. Institutional support has been provided by Meadville/Lombard Theological School and the Au Sable Institute of Environmental Studies.

Irreplaceable personal support has come from Martha Nack. It has been an instructive and pleasurable experience for the authors to work with Greenwood Press, its series editor, Gary E. Gorman, acquisitions editor, Alicia Merritt, and production editor, Jane Lerner.

The authors wish to thank all of these persons, and many others unnamed, for their generous help in this long labor of love.

Critical Survey: The Struggle to Integrate Ecology, Justice, and Christian Faith

Critical Survey

The struggle to integrate ecology, justice, and Christian faith that began in earnest in the 1960s has every indication of being a permanent part of Christian thought and practice for many years to come. The story of this many-faceted attempt to transform Christian self-understanding is one of the most remarkable stories in modern Christian history, even as it is also one of the most difficult to fully understand and evaluate. The fact is that in a very short period of time the aim of a small band of theologians and church activists to incorporate a concern for the natural environment with longstanding Christian witness for social justice has become the espoused purpose of numerous church bodies, ecumenical coalitions, scholars and church leaders.

In 1960, few persons, Christian or non-Christian, considered Christianity to have anything substantive, or positive, to contribute to the environmental issues that were pressing themselves upon public consciousness, or believed that the environment was an essential ingredient in Christian commitment to justice and peace. Three decades later Pope John Paul II broadcast to the world his conviction that the Christian faith requires stewardship for the planetary ecosystem (108), and an ecumenical coalition of Protestant, Roman Catholic, Orthodox, and Anglican leaders, meeting at Baixada Fluminense, parallel to the United Nations Conference on Environment and Development (UNCED) in Rio de Janeiro, urged fellow Christians throughout the world to make "strong and permanent spiritual, moral, and material commitments to the emergence of new models of society, based in deepest gratitude to God for the gift of life and in respect for the whole of God's creation" (445).[1] As the Bibliographic Survey documents, these pronouncements were backed by solid, often revolutionary, achievements in theological scholarship and religious leadership.[2]

Yet in 1995 the struggle to integrate ecology and justice is far from won, in principle or in fact, within, much less outside, the Christian community. The movement continues to encounter tough resistance both to the notion that the life-systems of the planet are in jeopardy, and to the notion that care of the environment and justice to the oppressed are one single "struggle for life" (492). One comprehensive review of the response to environmental issues in American Protestantism from 1970-1990 found overall "a major shift toward environmental concern within Protestantism, especially within Protestant thought."[3] It also found Protestant environmentalism to be internally divided, unclear about its "community" model of the ethical life, lacking in philosophical and scientific rigor, and politically naive and uninformed. Meanwhile, veteran leaders of the movement faced the same apathy, and the same issues, that confronted them in the 1960s—vastly inequitable distributions of wealth; unsustainable patterns of economic development, population growth, and land use; pollution of air, land and water; little recognition of the beauty or needs of other creatures or the natural world as a whole (431). As the 1992 "Letter to the Churches" from Baixada Fluminense confessed, "We have come to our senses only very late, and do not do so even yet."[4]

The critical survey that follows is designed to serve as an interpretative framework for the better understanding of the literature covered by this bibliography and for the better use of its annotations. It consists of four parts. The first is historical. It identifies the principal parties and basic trends in the post-World War II struggle to integrate ecology, justice, and Christian faith and provides a narrative of the landmarks in the development of the eco-justice movement in international and North American ecumenical life and thought. The second is contextual. It describes several major fields of study that contributed in significant ways to this literature. The third is analytical. It distinguishes the diversity of social justice and environmental values found in the literature, analyzes the primary ways Christian theologians and ethicists whose work is annotated in this bibliography have sought to relate them to one another, and identifies the primary factors that have inhibited or aided such integration. The fourth is evaluative. It provides a brief summary of the achievements of the eco-justice movement to date.

In the following discussion, the numbers within parenthesis indicate entry numbers of works annotated in the bibliographic survey. They are intended to be illustrative, not exhaustive, of the points at issue.

HISTORICAL OVERVIEW

The Central Debate

Most participants in the Christian ecumenical movement during the last several decades have assumed, if they have not explicitly addressed, the importance of human well-being and just social relationships within the great drama of creation and redemption. The major tension was and is between those views that assert the primacy of the struggle for our full humanity to the neglect or exclusion of serious attention to environmental issues and relationships, and those that reflect an ecologically-informed understanding of the struggle for human liberation. We shall call the first the "justice perspective" and the second the "eco-justice perspective" in the discussion that follows.

Although this bibliography screens out the literature of the justice perspective except as it engaged the challenge of eco-justice, the interplay between these two perspectives dominated most systematic theological and ethical reflection, as well as the ecumenical programs, studies, and public activities that addressed the issues of ecology and justice between 1961 and 1993.[5]

The Justice Perspective

Those who hold the justice perspective affirm the primacy of the struggle for social justice in human history. They begin with either a particular ideal of justice, or the problem of injustice to a particular group—defined by class, race, gender, or culture. Environmental issues, if and when acknowledged, are dependent variables. As C. S. Lewis wrote in 1947: "What we call Man's power over Nature turns out to be a power exercised by some men over other men with Nature as its instrument."[6]

Proponents of the justice perspective typically draw upon the biblical liberation narratives and the social sciences, together with some form of social or moral philosophy, to define the human condition and the telos of human moral responsibility and fulfillment. They tend to make a positive assessment of the technological capacities of human beings to marshal the powers of nature for human welfare. Although proponents vary considerably in their views regarding the degree and kind of economic and social transformation required to achieve justice, most have supported economic and technological expansion as a primary means to the achievement of the common good.

The justice perspective has found a variety of philosophical and theological expressions over the last half-century. It may be seen in liberal views of justice as freedom of opportunity; in social democratic views of justice as equality of benefits; in Marxist views of justice as equality of participation in the community of labor; in the revelation-through-history view that dominated Christian social ethics and biblical theology at mid-century; in the theological secularism that emerged in the 1960s; and in the "emancipatory theology of history" views of European, Latin American, Afro-American, political, and liberation theologies of the 1970s and 80s.

The Eco-Justice Perspective

Those who take the eco-justice perspective seek to pursue the struggle for justice and for a healthy environment together. They begin with an inclusive understanding of the values of social justice and ecological wholeness, or with the inter-related problems of injustice and environmental degradation in a particular community or issue. Justice for people and care for the rest of life are considered dependent and independent variables. It is not possible to adequately address one without also addressing the other; yet each also needs to be addressed on its own terms. William E. Gibson defines eco-justice as "respect and fairness toward all creation, human and non-human" and says that "it means social justice in the context of ecological realities; and it means ecological harmony or balance maintained in the context of social justice."[7] John B. Cobb Jr. writes that "the term 'eco-justice' expresses the determination to hold together the concern for justice as a norm for human relations and the awareness that the human species is part of a larger natural system whose needs must be respected."[8]

Both the prophetic and creation biblical traditions, as well as both the social and natural sciences are important to those who hold this position, as are philosophical and theological understandings of the unique place and responsibilities of human beings in the natural order. Although eco-justice proponents share with justice proponents a positive assessment of the capacities of human beings to be subjects of their own history, they tend to be more critical of the way these capacities have been organized and used in the development of technology, industry, and urban settlements, and of the commitment to ever-expanding economic and population growth. Advocates of this perspective have increasingly come to the conclusion that major reforms and redirections in the dominant patterns of global economic and social development and in the worldview and value priorities of contemporary societies will be needed if justice is to be achieved and the environment restored to health.

There are various interpretations of eco-justice, and a similar variation in the terms used to describe it. The majority of persons concerned for the positive integration of social justice and ecological ethics do not use the term "eco-justice" itself. Sometimes they use an alternative term to describe the idea. "Ecological justice," for example, was used by the National Council of the Churches of Christ in the USA (NCC) in the 1970s to mean "equity for all members of the community of life within the sustainable boundaries of the biosphere" (417).[9] Recently, the term "environmental justice" has come to be used by some authors to describe the basic idea of eco-justice. For example, Jim Wallis writes: "Environmental justice means the establishing of right relationships in the whole of creation."[10] More typically, however, the term "environmental justice" or "environmental racism" is used to refer to a particular field of eco-justice concern—the disproportionate burden of environmental degradation often borne by poor and minority communities. Other writers have used such terms as "public environmental ethic" or "ecological social ethic" (177).

Some eco-justice proponents use the term "eco-justice" but give it a special meaning that it does not necessary hold for others. An example of this is the use of the hyphenated "eco-" in "eco-justice" to signal both the ecological and economic aspects of justice. This usage continues to be important to many of those who first introduced the term into ecumenical discussions in North America. Still other writers use the term "eco-justice" but give it a more restricted meaning than we are assuming here. For example, eco-justice and especially "ecojustice" (without the hyphen), are sometimes employed to mean justice to the nonhuman (183). But this neglects the social justice side of the concept. Most writers who use the term do so to refer to how taking account of the needs of non-humans relates to, or interacts with, doing justice to human persons and groups.[11]

The concept of eco-justice is shared not only by those who first crafted the terminology in the early 1970s as a way of speaking of "ecological wholeness and social justice," but also in the emerging concern for just and sustainable development, or the "sustainable society," in the mid-1970s, which tended to view the environment as a critical condition, limit, or means to the pursuit of economic and social justice; in applications of covenantal and stewardship theologies and ethics to the dual challenge of justice and ecology; in the ecofeminist view that the oppression of women by men is integral to the hierarchical, dualistic societal relationships and ideologies that have also oppressed the earth and the human body; in the ecological systems view, which sees humans as unique members of relational networks inclusive of other creatures and natural systems and values the health and viability of the biosphere as a whole and its constitutive bioregional communities; in the view that the circle of moral considerability needs to be widened to include the intrinsic values, "rights," or welfare of animals as well as persons; in the affirmation that ecology needs to be added to the key values of justice and peace, as seen in certain interpretations of the World Council of Churches' (WCC) program on Justice, Peace, and the Integrity of Creation in the 1980s; in the emergence of concerns for "environmental justice" in the 1980s; and in certain interpretations of creation spirituality that also came to prominence in the 1980s.

International and Regional Developments

There have been two basic loci of ecumenical discussion—international and regional. International ecumenical attention to ecology and justice was anticipated in theological discussions in the Faith and Order Movement in the early part of the century, taken up by the World Council of Churches in 1948 after its founding in 1948, passed from Faith and Order to the Church and Society subunit of the WCC under the leadership of Paul Abrecht in the mid-1960s, and then, in ever expanding circles, encompassed an increasingly broad spectrum of Protestant and Catholic ecumenical participation, eventually involving representatives of most of the world's religious faiths. The first recognized appearance of regional ecumenical interest in the environment was within a group of Christian theologians, scientists, and church leaders who formed the Faith-Man-Nature Group in North America in the mid-1960s. Over the course of the following decades Christians in most other nations of the world became involved in similar kinds of regional discussions. Although the preponderance of initial interest in ecology was in the churches of Western nations, early eco-justice movements also emerged in Cuba, the Philippines, Korea, and Brazil (439).

Interactions

International and regional initiatives interacted in complex ways throughout the post-World War II period. Critical to the success of this interaction was the role played by lay, clerical, and staff leaders of the World Council of Churches—among them, Paul Abrecht, Charles Birch, David Gosling, Wesley Granberg-Michaelson, Douglas John Hall, D. Preman Niles, Roger Shinn, and Paul Verghese (later Paulos Mar Gregorios)—and by similar leadership in national and other ecumenical and denominational church organizations. In North America, the staff of the National Council of the Churches of Christ in the USA and the national staffs of the American Baptist, Lutheran, Methodist, Presbyterian, and United churches, and the United States Conference of Catholic Bishops played key roles. Also critical were innovative institutes and para-church centers, such as Appalachia—Science in the Public Interest, Au Sable Institute, Ecojustice Project at Cornell, Institute of Creation Spirituality, Land Stewardship Project, and the Riverdale Center for Religious Research; and ecumenical and inter-faith networks, including the Eleventh Commandment Fellowship, North American Conference on Christianity and Ecology, and the North American Coalition on Religion and Ecology.

Stages in the Struggle

In retrospect, it is possible to see similar issues and ideas being debated throughout the world at similar times, and international and national communities undergoing a similar evolution.

Three major stages in the struggle to integrate ecology, justice, and Christian faith in the international and North American ecumenical movements may be discerned. The first consists of the emergence of the eco-justice movement in the mid-1960s and its first promising expressions in theological, ethical, biblical, historical, and public policy studies in the early 1970s. The second consists of the mixed results of efforts to implement the theme of the World Council of Churches program on "Just, Participatory, and Sustainable Society" over the following decade. The third stage, dominated by the WCC conciliar process of covenanting on "Justice, Peace, and the Integrity of Creation," was marked by a widening and deepening of the eco-justice movement as it became a truly global and cross-cultural movement.

The Emergence of the Eco-Justice Movement

The Debate Begins

If there is one event that can be said to mark the beginning of the post-World War II struggle to integrate ecology, justice, and Christian faith it is the address "Called to Unity" delivered by Lutheran theologian Joseph Sittler at the third Assembly of the World Council of Churches in New Delhi in 1961 (151). Declaring that "a doctrine of redemption is meaningful only when it swings within the larger orbit of a doctrine of creation," and Christology is irrelevant unless related to our earthiness—including hunger, war, and the care of the earth, Sittler claimed, with a directness and urgency unequalled by anyone before him, a theological basis for an ethic that joined ecology, justice, and peace, and placed it squarely on the agenda of the ecumenical movement.[12]

The heightened awareness of the finite and fragile beauty of planet Earth in the face of the threat of nuclear holocaust struck Sittler and others of his generation with the force of revelation. As Sittler said, "When atoms are disposable to the ultimate hurt then the very atoms must be reclaimed for God and his will."[13] The sense of a new revelation of God's Word speaking through the inter-related environmental and social crises of the age, and through the Earth itself, calling humanity to new responsibility for creational survival and planetary citizenship, was to be a constant factor in the Christian eco-justice movement for the rest of the century, and a vital source of its moral and spiritual authority.[14]

The prevailing theological currents in the 1960s were not, however, well poised to receive a new revelation of Earth as a "theater of grace." For all their differences, they were united in what H. Paul Santmire subsequently called their "the-anthropocentric" focus on God's saving acts in history, and in their rejection of the doctrine of creation as a basis for, or significant concern of, Christian ethics. The 1966 World Council of Churches' conference in Geneva on "Christians in the Technical and Social Revolutions of Our Time" illustrated the reigning intellectual climate. The secular theologies of Arend van Leeuwen, Hendrikus Berkhof, and Harvey Cox were important touchstones of discussion.[15] There was considerable optimism about the human capacity to understand nature through the physical sciences, to control nature through technology, and to guide the use of technology by means of the social sciences; in fact, the report of the conference described human power over nature as having no limits and asserted that this was the biblical view.[16] Not surprisingly, persons holding these views reacted negatively to the rising interest in the environment, and were skeptical, if not antagonistic, to arguments such as those of the Club of Rome that the planet could not sustain perpetual economic and population growth. In North America, the most scathing attack on the environmental movement came from the pen of clergyman Richard John Neuhaus who, at a conference seeking reconciliation between those seeking environmental quality and those seeking social justice, characterized environmentalism as a crypto-fascist, racist attack on the poor and non-White populations of the United States (301).

Paths to Eco-Justice

In the 1960s and early 1970s several parallel paths led in the direction of eco-justice. The first, animated by Philip N. Joranson, was taken by the Faith-Man-Nature Group, which grew out of a 1963 seminar of the Faculty Christian Fellowship associated with the National Council of the Churches of Christ in the USA.[17] The evolution of this group is instructive. Whereas its initial work was directed to remedying specific environmental problems and changing religious attitudes toward nature, and its members were among the first to publish on the need for a Christian environmental ethic (429, 430), by the late 1960s it had determined that a careful delineation of the technological-economic and social-political character of the environmental crisis was necessary. Daniel Day Williams set forth the group's emerging eco-justice vision when he declared at a 1969 conference: "Nature and man are bound together in a fateful history where responsibility of man for his life and for his world meets the demands of a new order where basic justice is required."[18]

A second path in North America was taken by Christian clergy and scholars active in inner city parishes, campus ministries, and industrial missions, or in anti-poverty, civil rights, anti-war, women's liberation, and other social change movements of the 1960s. Many in this group were strongly affected by the clash between their allegiance to the reigning ecumenical justice perspective and their awareness of the seriousness of the environmental crisis. They responded by seeking ways to turn what appeared to be opposing moral imperatives into mutually reinforcing ones.[19] A good example is the work of Owen D. Owens and his colleagues on the staff of the Board of National Ministries of the American Baptist Churches in 1971. When confronted by two staff reports, one on justice and the other on ecology, that had to be reconciled if the Board were to achieve consensus on its mission, they chose to integrate them by focusing on their common ethical and theological principles—reverence, inter-dependence, and stewardship. As a result, the term "ecojustice"—the joining of "ecological wholeness and social justice"—was born (501).[20] Another example is the ministry of Bill Gibson who was moved by a conference on "Coming to Terms with the Limits to Growth" to co-found with Frank Snow the Eco-Justice Project and Network (EJPN) at Cornell University and to begin publishing one of the most influential journals of the eco-justice movement, *The Egg* (later the *EcoJustice Quarterly*).

A third path to eco-justice was taken by the sub-unit on Church and Society of the World Council of Churches when it initiated a five year study, beginning in 1969, on "The Future of Man and Society in a World of Science-Based Technology" (253). Serious challenges to the reigning justice perspective appeared for the first time in 1970 when Australian biologist and process thinker Charles Birch joined the study and spoke of the need for an ecological ethic (266). Further challenges came when Norwegian physicist Jørgen Randers presented the conclusions of his work with the Club of Rome project at MIT, and when University of Chicago theologian Langdon Gilkey argued that a theology of history must be conceived within a theology of nature, and that this required rethinking the doctrines of God, providence, and liberation, and constructing a new theology of hope. Meanwhile, arguments in support of the desacralization of nature, the technological dominion of humankind, and the moral goal of "humanization" continued to be voiced by Charles West, Wolf-Dieter Marsch, and Thomas Derr (174). The culminating report of the five year study, adopted at Bucharest in 1974, was a remarkable affirmation of the ideal of eco-justice. It accepted the thesis of nature's limits, presented a theology of "cosmic solidarity" inclusive of human solidarity, and called for a society that is both just and sustainable (092).

The 1972 United Nations Conference on the Human Environment at Stockholm was decisive for the future of the eco-justice movement because it disclosed that the struggle to integrate ecology and justice was a struggle of geo-political proportions. Stockholm marked the birth of the notion that environmental protection must become an essential element in social and economic development and the beginning of widespread recognition among conscience constituencies that the North had moral obligations to rectify its neo-colonial exploitation of the South. It thus helped conceive the concept, if not the terminology, of "just and sustainable development." Many members of the ecumenical movement attended the conference, and two Catholic lay persons, economist Barbara Ward and microbiologist René Dubos, were influential in shaping it. They also jointly authored the conference's independent report of consulting experts to the United Nations Conference Secretariat.[21]

Early Eco-Justice Literature

The groundswell of interest in the relationships between ecology, justice, and faith was expressed in books and articles that set basic directions for eco-justice thinking for the rest of the century. One of the leaders of the Faith-Man-Nature group, Paul Santmire, must be credited with the first book-length treatment of these relationships in 1970 (144).[22] Santmire was also one of the first to follow the lead of Sittler and pursue how biblical metaphors, in this case the political symbol of the "Kingdom of God," could be interpreted as pointing to theocentric ethical principles inclusive of both societal and environmental relationships. A year later, Rosemary Radford Ruether began her distinguished career as the leading ecofeminist theologian by authoring one of the first papers to link the oppression of women with the oppression of the earth, and arguing that neither could be overcome until the whole hierarchical, dualistic structure of Western and Christian patriarchy was transformed (249). The same year, Kenneth Cauthen offered his vision of "Christian biopolitics," a comprehensive eco-justice paradigm based on process theology (071). Pioneering work in eco-justice theology in the first half of the 1970s also came from the pen of John Cobb, who soon emerged as the best known process theologian in the world and one of the most prominent eco-justice theoreticians as well (075); from Paulos Gregorios of the Syrian Orthodox Church, who drew on the Patristic tradition to argue that the human vocation is the priestly vocation of mediating between creation and Creator, and whose manuscript for *The Human Presence* was influential in World Council of Churches' discussions well before its publication (097); and from Norman Faramelli (180, 348) and Robert Stivers (220), who explored the ethical and policy implications of the "limits to growth" thesis for economic justice and ecological wholeness.

The Just, Participatory, and Sustainable Society

Any hope that an integration of justice and ecology might constitute the basis for a new consensus on the meaning of Christian mission was short-lived. Conflicts broke out among members of the ecumenical movement in the mid-1970s. In the World Council of Churches, the conflicts were primarily between eco-justice advocates from Europe and the United States and spokespersons from the global South who shared the outlook of the new theologies of liberation. In the National Council of Churches, the conflicts were primarily between eco-justice advocates and politically conservative church leaders. However, as scholars such as Bruce C. Birch and Larry L. Rasmussen pointed out, in addition to these differences, there was the plain reality that it is easier to achieve an initial consensus on broad principles and ends than to agree on strategies for placing those principles into practice, especially in a situation where significant change requires major transformations in the economic, political and ideological structures of Western civilization, and major sacrifices on the part of the primary beneficiaries of that civilization (034). Nonetheless, in spite of, or perhaps because of, these conflicts important strides were made during this period in translating the eco-justice vision into a practical ethical approach that spoke forcefully to leading issues of the time, and effectively guided innovative strategies for change.

From Nairobi to MIT

The second stage in the struggle to integrate ecology, justice, and Christian faith began auspiciously. The fifth Assembly of the World Council of Churches meeting in Nairobi accepted the call of Bucharest and established a Council-wide program emphasis on the "Just, Participatory, and Sustainable Society" (JPSS). In his plenary address, comparable in historic importance to that of Sittler in New Delhi, Charles Birch sought a unification of liberation and ecological themes:

"There is a connection between human justice and renewal of the earth, and between human injustice and environmental deterioration. . . It is a cock-eyed view that regards ecological liberation as a distraction from the task of liberation of the poor. One cannot be done without the other. It is time to recognize that the liberation movement is finally one movement. It includes women's liberation, men's liberation, the liberation of science and technology, animal liberation, plant liberation, and the liberation of the air and the oceans, the forests, deserts, mountains and valleys" (333).[23]

Discussions at Nairobi seemed to confirm Birch's outlook. Concern for "quality of life" replaced "humanization" as the telos of earthly salvation, a vision of "hope" replaced technological optimism, and the importance of "sustainability" was clearly recognized.

But it was quickly evident in post-Nairobi discussions that the predominant reading of sustainability did not embrace what Birch and others hoped for—an ecological ethic that affirmed the intrinsic values of other creatures as well as humans. The meeting of the Church and Society Working Group in 1976 defined sustainability as social justice within ecological constraints, and thus ecology as an instrumental, not intrinsic, value (015). Subsequent work in the Advisory Committee on JPSS and the Commission on the Churches' Participation in Development failed to draw the implications of sustainability for political and economic organization. Prominent in these discussions was Argentinian liberationist José Miguez Bonino who argued that ecological problems result from unequal exploitation of natural resources.

In 1978 at Zurich, the idea of a "dominant social paradigm" was introduced into WCC deliberations. On the one hand, this provided an opening for eco-justice thinkers such as Abrecht, Herman E. Daly and Gregorios to argue for a new paradigm inclusive of both justice and ecological values. On the other hand, it exacerbated differences as each of the contending parties found a different culprit responsible for the dominant global system—either Euro-American imperialism, the growth-system common to East and West, patriarchy, Hebrew monotheism, the mechanistic worldview, or some other factor.

The principal follow-up to the JPSS theme adopted at Nairobi was the WCC Conference on "Faith, Science, and the Future" at MIT in 1979 (254, 255, 497). Attended by over 900 theologians, scientists, and church leaders from throughout the world, it mirrored most of the perplexities and conflicts that had surfaced in the previous decade regarding the roles of science, technology, and faith in achieving a just and sustainable society. Gone from the debate was the technological optimism of the 1960s; and the conference quickly reached consensus on the need for disarmament. Agreement was reached on very little else. While some stressed the positive benefits of scientific understanding in spite of its abuses, others saw science as simply an instrument of power. Sharp clashes occurred over nuclear energy and genetic experimentation. The North-South fissure at Stockholm re-erupted as the environmental concerns of "developed" nations and the economic interests of "less developed" nations were sharply juxtaposed. While both sides of the liberationist vs. eco-justice debate had opportunities to present their case, each side felt the conference was biased in the other direction. C. T. Kurien of India attacked the idea of sustainability as an ideology of a "pampered minority," and liberation theologian Rubem Alves and thirty other participants staged a "Third World Protest" (328, 358, 378). Yugoslav economist Ernest Petric, Orthodox leader Vitaly Borovoy, and German pastor Gerhard Liedke joined Birch, Daly, Shinn and others in arguing the necessity for "ecological realism" (050, 061, 262, 341).

Fruits of JPSS

In 1974, the same year that the WCC conference in Bucharest issued its historic call for a "just and sustainable society," the division of Church and Society of the National Council of the Churches of Christ in the USA launched a committee of inquiry, chaired by Margaret Mead and René Dubos, on use of plutonium as a commercial nuclear fuel. The next year the committee proposed a policy statement condemning such use of plutonium, and in so doing sparked a sharp rebuke by U.S. nuclear industry interests. In response, the NCC Governing Board mandated a study of the ethical implications of energy production and use. The resulting study, *Energy and Ethics*, directed by Chris Cowap, argued that the JPSS triad of equity, sustainability, and participation required the adoption of a soft energy path entailing conservation, renewable energy, synthetic fuels, and lifestyle change (407, 417). After heated debate, in which the study was attacked for being "antitechnology and antigrowth; insensitive to the poor; against the free market, probably socialist, perhaps anarchist; . . . and beyond the church's competence," the NCC Governing Board voted in 1979 to support a national energy policy which did not utilize nuclear fission, and to support a ban on commercial use of plutonium (386).[24] These and other studies of energy production and use from an eco-justice perspective established Christian ethics as a legitimate disciplinary partner in the global energy debate, and prepared the ground for the application of JPSS criteria to subsequent studies by U.S. and Canadian churches and the WCC on acid rain and global warming (428).

The JPSS theme also may be discerned in the attention that C. Dean Freudenberger, John Hart, and others began to pay to the issue of world hunger and the development of new patterns of sustainable food production and consumption (393, 403). This included efforts to reduce crop monocultures, pesticide use, and meat consumption, and nurture community-based agriculture in North America and elsewhere (220, 379, 418). As chapter 9 indicates, the concern of both Protestant and Catholic church coalitions for hunger and sustainable agriculture and land-use, especially in the Midwest, continued from the 1970s into the 1990s. Eco-justice analysis and prescription also began to be applied during this period to personal lifestyle assessment, which meshed well with the simple-living and voluntary conservation movements that were emerging in many North American churches at the time (184, 349, 441).

Although JPSS largely disappeared from the agenda of the ecumenical movement after MIT, the triad of justice, participation, and sustainability proved enormously fruitful for eco-justice reflection. It provided the ethical framework for constructive efforts by eco-justice theoreticians in the late 1970s and early 1980s to systematically relate theological, ethical, biblical, and doctrinal norms with scientific and historical analyses of the global situation to yield eco-justice promoting policy prescriptions for economics, politics, technology, community and church life, and it continued to be refined and expanded throughout the 1980s. The publications of Ian Barbour (257, 258), Birch and Cobb (065), Daly and Cobb (343), Albert J. Fritsch, (183), Jeremy Rifkin (366), Shinn (271), Loren Wilkinson and the Fellows of Calvin College (387), and the Presbyterian Eco-Justice Task Force (465) are especially noteworthy in these respects.

Widening and Deepening the Struggle

The third period in the struggle to integrate ecology, justice, and Christian faith spans the years between the early 1980s and the early 1990s. It was marked by an increasing number of viewpoints and constituencies in the Christian eco-justice movement, and an expanding understanding of the resources and capacities each of these viewpoints and constituencies bring to the common task. The widening and deepening of the struggle led to new integrations as well as new fragmentations within the movement, while tensions between the movement and those who regard environmental concerns peripheral to the main task of human salvation and liberation continued.

The sixth Assembly of the World Council of Churches in Vancouver in 1983 called for a "conciliar process of mutual commitment (covenant) to justice, peace, and the integrity of creation" (JPIC) and this became the overarching Protestant ecumenical context for the pursuit of eco-justice for the next decade. The theme was advanced through numerous processes and events, including consultations at Amsterdam in 1987 and at Annecy in 1988, culminating in a world convocation in Seoul in 1990; galvanized by Wesley Granberg-Michaelson, WCC program secretary for Justice, Peace and Creation, it continued to play an important role at the seventh WCC Assembly in Canberra in 1991, "Come, Holy Spirit—Renew the Whole Creation!," and in WCC participation at UNCED in 1992 (445, 479, 492, 493). Unlike JPSS, JPIC has not faded from sight; the WCC continues to wrestle with its meaning and to ponder the future of the process (474).

Increasing Pluralism

Soon after assuming the reins of the Church and Society sub-unit of the WCC at Vancouver, David Gosling noted that the JPIC conciliar process required the participation of a variety of cultural perspectives (093); this in fact happened. Native peoples from North America (023), Australia and the South Pacific, as well as Africans (015), Asians, and other groups not previously represented, brought new perspectives to the process. The most vivid expression of the increasing cultural and religious diversity within the WCC was the speech delivered by South Korean Chung Hyun Kyung in Canberra comparing the Holy Spirit to *Kwan In*, a female *bodhisattva* (074).

The WCC discussions are only one indication of a rapidly growing appreciation for theological, cultural, and social *pluralism* within the eco-justice movement as a whole. The trend is clearly evident in anthologies published in the early 1990s that interpret the meaning of eco-justice from different theological, ethnic, gender, racial, confessional and cultural standpoints (066, 103, 104), and in the number of publications that began to appear on eco-justice by African, Asian, and Latin American writers (019, 416, 451). Diversification was apparent regionally as well. In North America, Canadian churches and theologians began to assume a more self-conscious cultural identity. Not only new theological and cultural perspectives, but new issues, such as concern for animal rights and welfare (206), and for the relation of gay rights and ecology (284), appeared on the eco-justice agenda.

New developments within the Catholic community offer a good example of the widening of the eco-justice movement. Although there was early Catholic involvement in ecology and justice concerns through pioneering individuals such as Fritsch and Ruether, and through church involvement in farm and hunger issues, the distinctiveness and variety of approaches within the Catholic tradition were not visible until the 1980s. The early *aggiornamento* of Roman Catholic theology and mission of the early 1960s codified in Vatican Council II, followed by vigorous forms of liberation theology, expressed a more ethically-demanding vision of human unity, but neglected environmental issues.

Official Catholic teaching about environmental stewardship began during Pope John Paul II's 1979 trip to the Americas (451) and continued in the 1980s through a series of encyclicals and messages, such as "Sollicitudo rei socialis," that stressed responsibilities to future generations, the need for redistribution of wealth, and the environmental responsibilities of human dominion (108, 201, 355, 467). Some regional groups of Catholic bishops tended to take a more radical stance with regard to economic and ecological dimensions of the issue (157, 384, 426).

The most original contribution of the Catholic tradition to the ecology, justice, and faith discussion during this period came from persons working out of various forms of the creation spirituality perspective. One of the founders of this approach, Thomas Berry, a Passionist priest, long-time president of the American Teilhard Association, and self-ascribed "geologian," began in the early 1970s to share papers on how the natural world constituted the primary revelation of the divine in our time, but his work was not widely available until the 1980s (119, 273, 331). Matthew Fox, a Dominican, began a retrieval of previously neglected creation-centered themes in the Catholic mystical tradition (009).[25] In a series of influential books beginning in 1983, Fox argued the *priority* of the creation tradition over what he called the fall/redemption tradition, including the capacity of humans to be co-creators with the divine in the creation of eco-justice for all beings (088, 087). The creation spirituality perspective has inspired persons working for eco-justice goals in many parts of the world, as the writings of Sean McDonagh, who works with T'boli tribes of Philippines, indicates (011, 458); it also overlaps the new Orthodox (117), and Protestant sacramental approaches that appeared during this period, including Gibson Winter's sophisticated explication of the "artistic process" through which divine and human powers may collaborate to liberate creation (224).

Deepening Understanding

The second major trend was a *deepening*, or intensification, of theological understanding by persons working within one or more of the variety of particular approaches to eco-justice, a trend that yielded increasingly rich disclosures of the spiritual and practical implications of these perspectives.

A considerable expansion of attention to Christian ecofeminist thought began in the early 1980s with work by Denise Lardner Carmody (23) and Elizabeth Dodson Gray (235), bolstered by ground-breaking cultural studies by Carolyn Merchant (013). By the early 1990s, feminist theologians such as Sallie McFague were systematically addressing questions of the theology of nature (125), the distinctive character of feminist eco-spirituality was under intense discussion (225), ecofeminist approaches had spread to other parts of the world (231), and to groups not previously involved in the discussion, such as Afro-American women (245, 252), and there were challenging reflections on feminist approaches to the treatment of animals (226).[26]

A parallel deepening of understanding occurred within the family of neo-Reformation theologies, whose primary theological departures for eco-justice ethics have been revised doctrines of God's sovereignty, human dominion, covenant, and stewardship. Evangelical interest in the environment, that began in 1970 with the publication of Francis Schaeffer's *Pollution and the Death of Man*, became increasingly prominent in the discussion through the outreach of the Au Sable Institute and its director, Calvin B. DeWitt, the public advocacy of Jeremy Rifkin (422), as well as new work by Susan Power Bratton (281), Ronald J. Sider (499), Howard A. Snyder (470) and others (503).[27] At other points on the theological spectrum, James M. Gustafson published his major theocentric revisioning of Christian ethics and began to draw its implications for eco-justice issues (188, 290), and Jürgen Moltmann made a major shift in his theological approach and published a series of highly creative works expounding a trinitarian understanding of human responsibility for creation (128-32).[28] Other examples of mainstream Protestant thinkers pursuing an increased depth of theological understanding of their own traditions include John Douglas Hall's expansion of his work on stewardship (100), the work of James A. Nash on the Christian doctrine of love (204), and work on covenant by Charles S. McCoy (120).

Deepening theological understanding was accompanied by a deepening practical understanding of the requirements for the work of eco-justice in church and society. Leaders of the ecumenical movement in North America such as Dieter T. Hessel turned their attention during this period to the specific challenges of embodying eco-justice ethics and values in congregational life, including church covenants, preaching, ritual, education, and building-design (442, 448, 461).[29] They also intensified their previous efforts to influence public policy, and to build coalitions with environmental and community groups. In 1984 the National Council of the Churches of Christ in the USA formed an inter-denominational Eco-Justice Working Group which addressed issues of air pollution, toxic substances and energy, and critically engaged the failure of mainstream environmental lobbies in Washington, D.C. to be accountable to the full eco-justice agenda. In 1986, the Working Group held a consultation "For the Love of Earth and People" that launched a decade of collaborative work between the NCC and grass-roots organizers working in poor and ethnic minority neighborhoods around environmental justice issues such as toxics.

New Integrations

It is possible to see how, over the course of this period, the gradual widening and deepening of interest in ecology, justice and Christian faith, when coupled with the practices of ecumenical dialogue, led to an organic unfolding of the eco-justice movement and to more fluid forms of interaction among its components. The conciliar process of JPIC modeled this process because it was a deliberate search for consensus among many different constituencies and viewpoints. Overlapping, multiple meanings of the term "integrity of creation" resulted—some having a more forthrightly ecological meaning, with specific reference to God's *natural* creation, others a more cosmological meaning, and still others suggesting a more eschatological vision towards which all human enterprise must strive. At the Amsterdam consultation Hall interpreted "integrity" as an abstract quality akin to "justice" and "peace" and inclusive of society, culture, and the ecosystem (150).

The increasing rapprochement between liberation theology and eco-justice theology during this period is especially notable. Thinkers on both sides of the debate found resources within their own particular approaches that enabled them to embrace much of the substance of the other's position. The tendency of some eco-justice theologians, beginning with Charles Birch's address at Nairobi, to articulate the ways in which they could affirm the rising emphasis on liberation is a good example of this theological strategy, and it flourished in the 1980s in the many volumes devoted to some variation of the theme "liberation of life." Eco-justice ecumenists also adopted methods of liberation theology, beginning their reflections, for example, with the stories of victims, including the victims of nature (492). In response, liberation thinkers such as Leonardo Boff (068), Enrique Dussel, and Juan Luis Segundo began to include panentheistic views of the relations of God and the world in their theologies.[30]

Integration in perspectives was also furthered by process thinkers, such as Cobb and Jay B. McDaniel, who were hospitable to dialogue with alternative perspectives, either incorporating what they considered positive contributions of these perspectives into their own positions (076, 121), or carefully clarifying their differences (078, 241). Cobb was also critical of an over-emphasis on the many "theologies of" (434). Feminist theorists were similarly prone to draw in eclectic fashion from biblical, Asian, modern, goddess and indigenous peoples' beliefs, on the assumption shared with process thinkers that eco-justice spirituality need not be limited to any particular faith, and that whatever promotes the full humanity of women and men and the preservation of the Earth is a bearer of authentic religious meaning (154, 237, 248). Similar integrative tendencies were evident among persons working out of the creation spirituality perspective.

New and Continuing Divisions

It is likewise possible to see how the gradual widening and deepening of interest in ecology, justice, and Christian faith led, in many cases, in the opposite direction, toward increasing *fragmentation*, evident not only in continuing conflicts between justice and eco-justice advocates, but new conflicts within the eco-justice movement itself.

Continuing conflicts between justice and eco-justice proponents might not be expected given the fact that "justice, peace, and the integrity of creation," adopted at Vancouver in 1983, confirmed in principle the prophetic call of Sittler at new Delhi. The JPIC covenant adopted after seven years of international discussion at Seoul in 1990 included as one of its four goals "building a culture that can live in harmony with creation's integrity" (510). Nonetheless, there were repeated eruptions throughout the JPIC process, and in other fora, of the differences that had appeared so dramatically at MIT in 1979. Few among those who charged that women's issues were not sufficiently central to the JPIC process, such as Jane Cary Peck and Jeanne Gallo (242), or those who composed the "Justice Forum" at Seoul (482), were happy with the process or outcomes of the JPIC. But neither were those who lamented the last minute withdrawal of the report on ecological issues from the final report of Seoul, or worried that the JPIC discussion had shifted attention away from sustainability as a norm for social and economic organization and toward a manner of Christian thinking *about* the Earth and to norms for the church alone (474, 483).

New conflicts also began to emerge in recent years between eco-justice advocates and religiously conservative Christian thinkers, such as E. Calvin Beisner or Richard C. Chewning, who interpret economic justice as the right to property and profit and deny environmental limits (330, 335). In these views, "eco-theology" of any kind is unbiblical or heretical in its view of God, humanity, and nature.

Also during this period fissures appeared *within* the eco-justice movement. These differences sometimes repeated the debate between justice and eco-justice advocates, now seen as differences in emphasis within the eco-justice perspective—those, for example, who put a greater stress on the ecological side of eco-justice, such as Thomas Berry, versus those who put more stress on the justice side of the equation, such as Gregory Baum (278); or those who placed a greater stress on broad ecumenical national efforts within the NCC versus those who focused on local community organizing around specific issues of environmental justice.

From some perspectives, integration was itself becoming a problem. The North American Conference on Christianity and Ecology split into two groups over the issue of whether it should or should not restrict itself to specifically "Christian" religious bodies. Evangelicals like Wilkinson argued that syncretistic Earth-based ideas such as those of Fox drive evangelicals away from environmental concerns (160, 326), and Christian feminists such as Carmody were critical of ecofeminists such as Ruether for similar reasons (230). The very fact that many efforts during this period tried to achieve meaningful consensus *within* particular church communities sometimes led to accentuation of confessional and theological differences.

CONTEXTUAL STUDIES

A number of scholarly discussions and inquiries are pertinent to attempts by Christian theologians and ethicists to integrate ecology, justice, and faith. These disciplines and fields of study comprise distinct bodies of literature; several of the most important are noted here.

Social and Natural Sciences

Both the social and natural sciences, and increasingly, efforts to integrate the findings of both, have served as crucial intellectual background for the eco-justice movement. In many cases, scientists bore the mantle of modern prophets, and their findings and predictions materially influenced the course of events. Since the late 1940s natural scientists, such as Harrison Brown, Aldo Leopold, Fairfield Osborn, Karl Sax, and William Vogt, had tried to alert the Western world to the environmental impacts of unbridled industrial and population growth.[31] In the 1960s, these warnings increased, as did the heed the media and the public paid them. In 1962, Rachel Carson effectively illustrated how unrestricted use of chemical pesticides was disrupting "the web of life" and the environmental movement of the 1960s was launched.[32] It was not long before debates broke out among scientists regarding exactly what *kind* of a problem the environment presented, and which of the several factors influencing environmental deterioration—population, technology, economic organization, political and other power relationships—was most critical.[33]

As the decade progressed, it became increasingly clear that the environmental and social problems being faced in the West were not only related to one another but to similar problems appearing in many other parts of the world, as well as to the problems appearing *between* different parts of the world—especially the increasing gap in wealth between the so-called "developed" countries of the North and the "developing" nations of the South. Systems theory and computer technology offered the possibility of making sophisticated empirical studies of the interactions between global technical, social, economic, and political trends and their consequences for the planetary environment. The first major study of this kind, conceptualized by the Club of Rome and implemented by a team of international scientists at Massachusetts Institute of Technology, concluded that the rates of increase in a *combination* of factors (population, agricultural production, natural resource consumption, industrial production, and pollution) were leading the world to overstep its biophysical "limits to growth," and that this was responsible for what they termed the "global *problematique*"—"the complex of problems troubling persons of all nations: poverty in the midst of plenty; degradation of the environment; loss of faith in institutions; uncontrolled urban spread; insecurity of employment; alienation of youth; rejection of traditional values; and inflation and other monetary and economic disruptions."[34] This general form of analysis set the terms of debate on the relationships between environment, equity, and economics from the first international conference on the human environment at Stockholm in 1972 to the United Nations Conference on Environment and Development in Brazil in 1992, and as we saw earlier, played a key role in the thinking of the ecumenical eco-justice movement.

The social scientific discipline of economics has played a critical and controversial role in the struggle to come to terms with the relations between ecology and justice, as the works annotated in chapter 8 indicate. Economic justice has been a central concern of the eco-justice movement since its inception, and it has drawn heavily upon the work of those members of the economics profession who have dissented from the prevailing neo-liberal, growth-centered assumptions of the discipline, providing as well an important forum for their ideas. The steady-state economic theory of Herman Daly stands out as especially influential in this field.

Theology and Philosophy

Most theological work in the field of ecology, justice, and Christian faith has been done by persons who have explored the resources of one or more previously established school or method of theological study. This means that the theological approaches from which they draw remain important contextual factors in ecology, justice, and faith discussions.

Theological Forerunners

Among the progenitors of post-World War II discussions of Christianity and ecology were theologians and metaphysicians who took upon themselves the task of making the Christian witness credible in light of the new knowledge of humanity's evolutionary origins and interdependence with the rest of the natural world gained through the natural sciences. Important early influences on the eco-justice movement include Catholic evolutionary scientist and philosopher Pierre Teilhard de Chardin; Protestant theologians William Temple and Paul Tillich; and philosophers and theologians who developed the school of process theology on the basis of the metaphysics of Alfred North Whitehead—especially the "Chicago School" of process thought, led by Charles Hartshorne, Bernard Meland, and Daniel Day Williams.[35] Notable among a number of early twentieth-century theologians and philosophers of religion to more directly anticipate the post-World War II struggle to construct a unified ecological social ethic is Albert Schweitzer, who proposed a holistic ethic of "reverence for life" (218). Martin Buber, H. Richard Niebuhr, Dietrich Bonhoeffer, and Walter Rauschenbush likewise saw the need to speak in one unified moral and religious voice about the relationships of human beings to one another and to otherkind.[36]

Theological Approaches

Some major twentieth-century schools of theology have tended to neglect the intrinsic values of nature and the seriousness of environmental issues, whereas other approaches have deliberately sought to construct theologies of nature supportive of such values and issues. Debates between these two orientations concerning the shape and possibility of a Christian theology of nature vs. a theology of history, the proper relationships between Christian theology and natural theology, the role of metaphysics and cosmology to theology, and the relations of religion, science, and technology, have had a continuing influence on efforts to integrate ecology, justice, and Christian faith in the 1961-1993 period.[37] Many leaders of the eco-justice position, such as Cobb, Gilkey, Gustafson, McFague, Moltmann, and Sittler have been important contributors to these discussions.

The first group may be called "theologies of salvation history." The best known figure in this group, Karl Barth, was the leading theologian of mid-century Neo-orthodoxy. He conceived of creation as principally a stage for the historical unfolding of the drama of God's address to humanity in Jesus Christ.[38] The founding manifesto of Neo-orthodoxy, the *Barmen Declaration* of 1934, boldly asserted the primacy of Christology in the face of Fascism, but cast an atmosphere of suspicion around the doctrine of creation due to its association with racist ideology under the Nazi regime.[39] Other post-World War II movements took a more positive view toward the possibility of achieving justice in history, but retained, and in some cases intensified, the nature/history dualism of Neo-orthodoxy. These movements included historicist interpretations of biblical theology, the so-called "secular" theologies that emerged in the early 1960s in North America and Europe, and Catholic liberation theology that first achieved visibility at the Medellín meeting of Latin American bishops in 1968 and in the writings of the Peruvian priest Gustavo Gutierrez. The secular, political and "death of God" theologies popular in progressive Christian circles in Europe and North America in the 1960s celebrated the "desacralization" of nature and repudiated any form of metaphysical or essentialist thought that related Christian ethics to the general order of nature. These theologies shared with liberation theology the view that secularization is continuous with the meaning of biblical salvation history for it enables humans to "come of age," assume their rightful autonomy and dominion, and use the power of technology to alleviate human suffering, especially the suffering of the poor.[40]

The second group of theological approaches constitutes the background for much of the eco-justice literature. The most influential types are:

(1) Protestant neo-Reformation theology, with its strong theocentric premise and stress on basic biblical motifs and doctrines, of several kinds, depending upon the confessional and disciplinary commitments of the author (Gustafson, Hall, Moltmann, Nash, Rasmussen, Rifkin, Santmire, Shinn, Wilkinson);

(2) Catholic theology, again of several types, all building on some understanding of the Catholic natural law tradition, but some working more directly out of the official positions and actions of Catholic church leaders (Charles M. Murphy, the encyclicals and proclamations of Pope John Paul II); others out of reinterpretations of Thomas Aquinas (William C. French), and still others more concerned for cosmology and creation spirituality (T. Berry, Fox, McDonagh);[41]

(3) process theology, an especially prominent school of thought in North American discussions (Barbour, Cauthen, Cobb, Daly, McDaniel);

(4) liberation theology, known for its radical critique of the received Christian tradition and its insistence that praxis, or liberating action, be put before theological reflection, also of several kinds, depending upon the primary community of concern: European political theology (Soelle), feminist liberationist thought (Adams, McFague, Ruether), eco-womanist thought (Riley, Williams), Latin American liberation theology (Boff, Hedstrom), Native American theology (Tinker);

(5) theology and animals, an interdisciplinary field composed of work by theologians such as Jay McDaniel and Andrew Linzey, and scientists such as Michael W. Fox, specifically directed to the welfare, rights, and care of animals.[42]

Developments in the field of religion and science have also been a significant influence in these discussions. Since the mid-1960s, *Zygon: A Journal of Science and Religion,* under the leadership of Ralph W. Burhoe and his successor Philip J. Hefner (105), has explored a new relationship between science and religion and its implications, among other things, for attitudes to nature. In the 1980s, the Center for Theology and the Natural Sciences at the Graduate Theological Union in Berkeley also began work in this area.[43]

Environmental Philosophy and Ethics

Another rapidly evolving body of thought that made major intellectual contributions to the struggle to integrate ecology, justice and Christian faith is the field of environmental philosophy and ethics. Emerging in the mid-1970s in North America, and promoted through the journal *Environmental Ethics*, edited by Eugene Hargrove, the field has rapidly spread to many other parts of the world. Although most Christian writers are not well acquainted with its technical literature due to the sharp disciplinary separations between secular philosophy and most forms of Christian social ethics, its key ideas and approaches have been influential factors in the eco-justice movement.

Some environmental ethicists, such as Holmes Rolston III, a former Presbyterian minister, have made important inter-disciplinary contributions (142, 214).[44]

Biblical Studies

No sub-discipline of theological study has undergone more substantial revision in the past several decades than the field of biblical studies. At the beginning of this period the dominant perspective in biblical theology was represented by Gerhard von Rad, who viewed creation as a derivative extrapolation of belief in salvation with only marginal significance in the Hebrew scriptures. It was generally thought that a fore-grounding of history and God's acts in history differentiated the religion of Israel from that of the surrounding peoples of Mesopotamia, Canaan, and Egypt. This "God who acts" view, so-called from the title of an important work by biblical scholar G. Ernest Wright (152), or the "mighty acts" view, from the writings of Karl Barth, provided considerable credibility for the position of those who held the ecumenical justice perspective and neglected environmental issues.

In the 1960s and early 70s, however, biblical scholars began to revise this view, von Rad himself being among the first to do so. In 1964 he wrote, "the greater part of what the Old Testament has to say about what we call nature has simply never been considered. . . . we are nowadays in serious danger of looking at the theological problems of the Old Testament far too much from the one-sided standpoint of an historically conditioned theology."[45] Lynn White Jr's article appearing in 1967 (see below) was an impetus to biblical scholars to continue in this direction. For a long time after White's entry into the biblical arena, scholars, beginning with James Barr, tended to focus on the Genesis creation account, as White had, particularly on the *imago Dei* and on the commandment that humans are to have dominion over the earth.[46] Bernard Anderson argued that the language of Genesis 1 is royal language and shows its priestly author beginning to "democratize" theology. Anderson also sought to show that being made in the image of God entails a moral imperative for humans to be responsible stewards of nature (028). Terence E. Fretheim, working with both the creation and Exodus accounts, showed nature to be an integral component of a story in which moral actions have natural consequences (044, 045). Concentrating a lifetime of biblical scholarship on the daily contact of persons and land, Walter Brueggemann came to the conclusion that the symbolism and treatment of the land are central concerns to the Hebrew Bible (035-039). Of the many others who have importantly elucidated the eco-justice connections of Hebrew bible studies, we have included a limited selection in chapter 2.

New Testament studies bearing on eco-justice have been most fruitfully pursued in a manner differing from the close textual analysis associated with Hebrew bible studies, and it is consequently necessary to include generalists in the list of those who have made significant contributions.[47] The tendency has been to dwell on overall themes, such as redemption and the Kingdom, and to draw out the consequences of these for ecology and justice. Jesus' life is seen to exemplify the proper relationship of humans to creation, as for instance in Hall (190), Birch and Rasmussen (034), Mihoc (051), and Schillebeeckx (034). As the primacy of justice has become a focus of New Testament studies, eco-justice has been included as one of the linked dominations against which Jesus stands, as for instance in Walter Wink (059) and Ivone Gebarra (046). Redemption of humanity and nature together has been a particularly strong focus. Fox posits a conflation of Christ's life, death, and resurrection with Earth's creation, exploitation, and ultimate restoration in *The Coming of the Cosmic Christ* (087).

Historical Studies

Since the late nineteenth century a substantial body of scholarship has been devoted to understanding the historical development of the social teachings of the Christian churches, and the interplay between Christian beliefs and institutions and the values and structures of social, political and economic life, including the ways in which Christianity has variously motivated, embodied, and thwarted struggles for justice in virtually every part of the world. Beginning in the 1950s, a small but significant body of research by Allan Galloway, Clarence J. Glacken, Perry Miller, George Huntston Williams and others began to uncover the equally long and complex history of the ecological dimensions of the teachings of the churches and the impact of Christian beliefs regarding nature on society and culture, including their influence on the emergence of scientific, literary, artistic, and social reform movements sensitive to the need to protect animals, plants, and ecosystems.[48]

In 1967, Lynn White Jr.'s "The Historical Roots of Our Ecologic Crisis" fanned into flames long smoldering resentments of Christianity's excessive anthropocentrism and failure to value the natural world (026). It is not accidental that the article was published at the height of the influence of the secular theology of the 1960s and at a time when environmental issues were claiming increasing public attention. White laid the blame for environmental degradation at the door of late medieval Latin Christianity and the biblical doctrine of dominion.[49] The controversy that erupted around his essay directed attention to the religious sources of environmental attitudes and spurred a great deal of research by scholars on the links between Christian belief and the treatment of the environment.[50] It also served as an important reference point for eco-justice advocates in their efforts to get Christian theologians and the churches to pay more attention to environmental issues, and motivated early members of the movement to search for ecologically positive themes in the Christian tradition, such as John Black's retrieval of the medieval doctrine of stewardship (002).

In the 1980s this field of research began to overlap the new field of secular environmental history, and substantial works by Santmire, Bratton, Fox, Roger D. Sorrell, and others on the ecological views of early Christian figures and movements began to appear.[51] Subsequently, the story of the "greening" of Christianity in the twentieth century began to be told. Roderick Frazier Nash published the first historical overview of the emergence of concern for environmental ethics among Christian thinkers in the nineteenth and twentieth centuries.[52] In the 1990s historians such as Robert Gottlieb began to publish studies of how environmental and social justice movements were intertwined in American and world history, but the history of the relationships between the social and ecological aspects of Christian life and doctrine remain largely unexamined.[53]

THE CONCEPT OF ECO-JUSTICE

Eco-justice rests on an unshakeable belief that ecology and social justice are inseparable. Yet, as the hyphen reminds us, eco-justice is a response to the fact that our world has pulled these values and realities apart. In the following analysis we distinguish the social justice values that constitute eco-justice from the ecological values that also constitute it, focusing in the first case on how ecology enters into relationships of justice and injustice among human beings, and in the second case on what it might mean for human societies to do justice to the nonhuman beings and systems that make up "the environment."

The Social Justice Values of Eco-Justice

Of the many ways of differentiating types or forms of justice, one helpful typology, proposed by Christian social ethicist Douglas Sturm, speaks of justice as liberty, equality, community, and wisdom.[54] Each of these forms of justice is relevant to environmental issues in a distinctive way, and each is prominent in the literature surveyed by this bibliography.[55] Depending on the situation, and how the value in question is interpreted and applied, each of these forms of justice can reinforce or be at odds with particular ecological concerns.

Liberty

Liberty is often seen as antithetical to, or at least limited by, biophysical constraints—especially as respect for those constraints is codified in public laws enforced by public authority. While it is true that environmental protections restrict the liberty of persons to do certain things, biophysical integrity is also an essential condition for the exercise of freedom: not only because free action presupposes life and health, but also because nature provides meaningful content for choice in the sense of "freedom for" (317). Freedom exercised only in a degraded or highly artificialized environment is emptier and more impoverished than freedom in a healthy environment that includes a variety of landscapes and degrees of "naturalness." Environmental protections thus can enlarge liberty by giving persons and communities the freedom to engage their environments in more satisfying and meaningful ways.

Liberty also includes protection from having one's life determined by others' control over one's environment. Community self-reliance and self-determination in the production of essential goods and services—rather than integration into a network of global trade which undercuts local autonomy and increases economic pressures to exploit the environment—is thus a priority for some eco-justice theorists (277, 303, 343). At the personal level, simple lifestyles are urged as a way of gaining freedom from the incessant drive to work more to earn more to consume and possess more (164, 270, 366, 379, 422).

Equality

Justice as equality, or at least as opposition to arbitrary, unnecessary, or extreme inequalities, has also been an important concern for environmental ethics and policy. In some quarters there is fear that environmentally-motivated "no growth" policies will freeze existing unequal distributions of income, wealth, and privilege (300, 302). So too, rapidly industrializing nations resent already-industrialized nations telling them to slow their development in order to protect tropical forests or prevent climate change (503). At the national level, the costs and benefits of environmental protection are often unjustly distributed—but, as the environmental justice movement has made clear, so are the costs and benefits of toxic pollution and environmental degradation (294). Persons concerned about *both* the massive disparities in wealth between nations *and* the health of the biosphere argue that wealthy nations must reform the global economy or provide money and technology to poorer nations so that they can increase incomes while protecting their natural resources. If resource limits constrain economic growth, then distributive justice must be more aggressively pursued if present inequalities are not to be frozen in place (294, 312, 325, 333, 365). The affluent are urged to adopt more frugal lifestyles, to reduce their disproportionate environmental impact, and to release resources needed by the poor (349, 418, 441).

Thus, an ecological sensibility can be combined with a commitment to equity, expanding and enriching the latter's meaning. "Distributive justice" can be understood to include not only the right distribution of political power, wealth, or social services, but of environmental goods also. Equality may be thought to encompass equal rights to environmental goods or necessities, equal sharing of the burdens of environmental degradation or regulation, and equal opportunity to participate in decisions affecting one's environment (203, 379, 387).

Community

While rights to liberty and equality can be applied to groups, the value of community is itself a distinct meaning of justice. The social value of community comes into play as societies must make collective decisions about land and resource use, when, for instance, communities and ways of life that depend on forests or fisheries are threatened by resource depletion or the necessity of setting legal limits on harvests. An "elitism" that secures environmental amenities for some at the expense of the legitimate needs of others violates the norm of community, as does a paternalistic or authoritarian approach to solving environmental problems.

On the other hand, an ecological worldview can enhance social solidarity by showing the intimate connections between factions and even very distant peoples which result from their sharing "only one Earth" (189, 325). In that worldview, community and solidarity also extend through time, giving rise to responsibilities to future generations, or what is sometimes called "intergenerational justice" (002, 189, 345).

The texture of meaning of the word "community" in the present and at the local level also becomes thicker and richer when embraced by an ecological worldview. In traditional societies—those of indigenous peoples, and of agricultural and nomadic populations—the life of the community is intimately intertwined with the land on and by which it lives (004, 012). While technological advances do not make us any less interdependent with the rest of nature, the loss of community in urban and industrial society is linked by some to the loss of closeness to nature and participation in its cycles and rhythms (033, 332, 379).

Wisdom

Sturm's fourth term is justice as wisdom. This principle points to the role of knowledge of the good, of the place of humanity in the cosmos, in adjudicating the conflicting demands that are made in the name of justice, and in discerning the limitations of all existing efforts to embody justice. Justice as wisdom may be less familiar than the previous three forms, but it is suggestive for eco-justice.

In the first place, wisdom is what directs politics to transcend the self-seeking pursuit of individual and group interests and to pursue a common good which is not reducible to an aggregate of individual goods (197, 201). When the focus is on human-human relations in an ecological context, wisdom can be likened to prudence. The social order must fit into the requirements of the natural order so that the good for human beings—including justice in the other senses of the term—can be achieved and sustained. The ability of existing political processes to deliberate about and formulate just and effective environmental policies is a critical issue for many eco-justice writers (295, 311, 471).

But wisdom is related to eco-justice at an even more profound level. While the basic meanings of liberty, equality, and community are relatively independent of the question of humanity's relationship to nature, part of wisdom's role *is* that of defining the human-nature relationship. The notion of a higher order of being and value embracing humanity and nature to which human beings are responsible, or into which human projects and purposes must fit, has traditionally been expressed in Christian theology through concepts of the "orders of creation" or "natural law." The extension of natural law thinking to cover eco-justice issues characterizes the writings of Pope John Paul II in this bibliography (070, 108, 291, 355, 452). Yet even when traditional natural law thinking is rejected as too static or hierarchical, natural law constitutes an important foundation for a significant portion of eco-justice literature which grounds respect for human beings and nature in a cosmological vision (136, 182, 273).

The question of how to define humanity's position in the cosmic order is, however, a sharply contested one in the ecology-justice-faith literature. Ideas of humans' unique dignity and status have traditionally undergirded commitment to human rights and justice for all persons (188). Does a sense of humanity's embeddedness in nature call these convictions into question, reducing humans to merely one species among others? Some fear that an ecological perspective does undermine the sense of human transcendence and uniqueness (300, 309), but for others the opposite is true. In theologies of responsible dominion or stewardship, wisdom means recognizing humans' distinctive role in nature as the basis of both human rights and human accountability for our treatment of the rest of creation. In these theologies, ecological consciousness enlarges and enriches one's sense of what it means to *be* human, with distinctive capacities to understand and care for the earth (062, 101, 160, 327).

The Ecological Values of Eco-Justice

In the preceding section, ecological or environmental values have meant the value that ecological systems or components of the environment can have *for human beings*. For some ethicists and theologians, this is the only way that plants, animals, rocks, rivers, landscapes, ecosystems—or cities, cars, pollutants and other human transformations of the environment—can be involved in questions of morality and justice. Such thinkers recognize only those values in nature that have instrumental or aesthetic value for persons—which serve, as "natural resources" or "environmental amenities," the physical or psychological needs of human beings.

Arguments within this framework arise over how environmental costs and benefits are to be distributed among human beings; what ways present modes of production, consumption, and behavior must be changed to accommodate environmental limits and fragile ecosystems; and how to balance competing values of freedom and safety, present and future needs, artificial and natural amenities, aesthetics and economic prosperity, and so on. At this level, "eco-justice" means doing justice to humans with respect to environmental goods and within resource limits. In Christian ethics, such environmental concern arises from love for neighbor in the light of human embodiedness and embeddedness in nature. Effective love of neighbor requires attention to the ecological context that sustains the physical, psychological, and cultural life of one's fellow human being.

However, the normative paradigm of Christian eco-justice in its fullest or most comprehensive expression considers not only the value *of* nature for human beings, but also the value (positive or negative) of human actions *for* individual organisms and ecological systems. In environmental ethics, this distinction is referred to as that between the "intrinsic" value of nature or nonhuman beings and their "instrumental" value. To recognize the intrinsic value of otherkind is to recognize that not only human needs but also the needs of nonhuman nature are of primary, irreducible moral concern. Destruction of species, disruption of ecosystems, and animal suffering are morally important as direct harms to nonhuman beings, not just because of possible indirect harms to human beings that might result. Differences in this perspective have to do in part with *which* aspects or components of the natural world ought to be respected in this way: sentient animals? all living organisms? species? ecosystems? the earth as a living "superorganism"? inanimate natural objects such as rocks, rivers, or geological features?

God's care for plants and animals apart from their utility to humans is attested at various points in Scripture. God admires and blesses creation prior to the appearance of human beings; Noah is charged to preserve creatures that are "unclean" (and therefore useless to humans) as well as the creatures that are "clean";[56] Israel's sabbatical laws allow rest for domestic animals and forage for wildlife;[57] Psalm 104, God's challenge to Job from the whirlwind,[58] and Jesus' Sermon on the Mount[59] stress God's care for nonhuman creatures in and for themselves. Absolute value-distinctions between human and nonhuman are undercut by the common origin of humans and other creatures,[60] and their common destiny in "a new heaven and a new earth."[61]

This form of ecological concern can be seen as an extension of traditional social justice norms and values.[62] And, in fact, the humane movement, especially in the nineteenth century, had close connections to the movements for women's rights and the abolition of slavery.[63] It is also possible to see the intrinsic values of nature as a subset, parallel to the values of social justice among human beings, of more inclusive or universal moral norms. In either event, we can again use Sturm's typology to consider what justice to nonhuman individuals or systems might mean. It is at least possible to ask about our obligation to respect the "freedom" of nonhuman creatures and processes, to allow them their fair share of life-sustaining resources, to acknowledge them as fellow members of the earth community, or to treat them in accordance with their proper place in a new creation.

Liberty for Living Beings and Systems

For some eco-justice theologians, justice as liberty also includes the "liberation of life" or the "liberation of creation" (065, 224, 436). Few would argue that nonhuman entities, systems or processes are capable of the kind or degree of conscious freedom that human beings have, but it is not hard to see how human actions can limit the ability of nonhuman beings to fulfill the particular potentialities with which they have been created. In theological discourse, the image of Rom. 8 of "the whole creation [groaning] in travail as it awaits the glorious liberty of the children of God" is a key biblical warrant for the liberation of nature (148).[64]

Inter-Species Equity

The application of "equality" to relations with nonhuman beings raises difficult and contentious issues. Some extreme forms of environmental ethics argue for a "biocentric egalitarianism" although it is not always clear what this means (013, 235, 237). Animal rights or "biotic rights" need not mean equal treatment of humans and nonhumans (which would lead to many absurdities when applied to beings with radically different natures and needs). It may mean "equal consideration of interests"[65] that is, a human interest may take priority over a nonhuman interest, but only because it is an intrinsically greater or more vital interest (for example, involves a greater degree of suffering). Human interests are not privileged because they are *human* interests.

Even without claims of strict equality of beings or their interests, affirming the intrinsic value of nonhuman beings implies at least that *some* vital nonhuman interests can override less vital human interests in comfort, convenience, recreation, etc. Finding the appropriate "exchange-rate at the species-barrier"[66] between human and non-human interests is a daunting but necessary ethical task if the intrinsic value of nonhumans is to be taken seriously. Theological warrants for giving nonhumans "a place at the table" can be located in biblical passages such as Psalm 104 and the conclusion to the book of Job, in which it is made clear that God's concern for the rest of creation is not merely derivative of God's concern for humanity (048, 134, 202).

Ecological Community

Again, the attribution of intrinsic value to nonhuman beings adds a new dimension to justice, extending the boundaries of community in yet another direction. In many indigenous worldviews, an individual's identity is constituted by belonging to a community which includes the land and its nonhuman "peoples" (019, 155), not just the human neighbor. Ecologically informed concepts of the "biotic community"[67] or the "earth community" (261) have been proposed as means to a post-modern recovery of more organic, holistic, and inclusive understandings of persons and society that have been submerged in Western societies by post-Enlightenment individualism and anthropocentrism (077, 141, 178). Here, the biblical theme of covenant—especially the Noachic covenant with "all flesh" and the Levitical laws and prophetic oracles which link distortions in human relations to the disruption of nature—is relevant, as are the metaphors of the church as the body of Christ and the cosmic Christ as the one "in whom all things cohere" (182, 199, 221).

Ecological Wisdom

The extension of justice as wisdom to cover human-nonhuman moral relations may define wisdom as harmonious participation in an inclusive cosmic process directed toward the good in nature and history (065, 071, 122, 273, 331) or in a pattern of right relationships among humans and other creatures (100-101, 152-53). Here the biblical linkage of social and cosmic orders is again an important theological warrant (044, 053). Some theologians, including ecologically oriented feminists, stress the need for an appropriate humility regarding the place of human beings in nature; they view the elevation of humans above the rest of creation as an anthropocentric extension of the same false consciousness that legitimates the domination of one human group by another (104, 234-35, 412).

Obstacles to Eco-Justice Thinking

The works we have surveyed testify to a variety of ways of positively relating ecology and social justice within the overall eco-justice paradigm. That paradigm has had to make its way against powerful countervailing forces in twentieth century thought. We cannot, in this survey, identify all the conceptual factors that have impeded the integration of environmental and social justice concerns, but we can offer a few suggestions to contextualize current struggles to reunite them.

Justice or Ecology Viewed as Irrelevant

One obstacle is the widespread tendency to *avoid* looking at the relationship between justice and environmental issues: to focus on one area while ignoring or dismissing the other as irrelevant. Much writing in both environmental theology and Christian social ethics seems authored by those oblivious to the ecology-justice relation (and thus does not appear on this bibliography). This need not be a symptom of indifference, hostility, or suspicion toward "rival" concerns; it may simply reflect the difficulty of addressing all aspects of an issue.[68] However, such neglect can indirectly aid and comfort those who see environmental and social justice concerns running in different directions.

Among the factors contributing to this neglect is the habit of thinking about "humanity" and "nature" as *en bloc* abstractions without internal structure or differentiation—forgetting differences in race, culture, gender, power, and economic status that fracture "humanity," or neglecting the diverse, complex systems that constitute "the environment." Thus some eco-justice writers point to the ease with which environmentalists speak of "humanity's relationship to nature" without attending to the differences between how rich and poor, powerful and powerless, majority and minority, or male and female human beings relate to their natural environments (055, 477). By the same token, it has been too easy for advocates of social justice to see nature as an undifferentiated stockpile of resources to be efficiently transformed into useful products to be justly distributed, or to focus on the societal structures required to meet human needs while ignoring the ecological systems that support those structures.

The habits of professional specialization, especially those separating the social sciences from the natural sciences and social service from natural resource management, add to the difficulty of seeing both the ecological and social dimensions of public problems and policies. The theories and preoccupations of different disciplines and professions strongly affect judgments about what problems are important, what causal factors are most significant, and what solutions are desirable and feasible (257, 271, 343).[69] Natural and social scientists often operate in very different time- and space-frames when defining problems and projecting consequences (487). Economists and ecologists in particular tend to make different assumptions about limits to natural resources, the impact of population growth, and the value of biological diversity and ecosystem integrity (281, 343, 344).

Social location can also affect one's perception (or lack of perception) with regard to eco-justice linkages. The diversity of ethnic groups and economic classes in an urban context fosters sensitivity to a wide range of social justice issues, while the predominance of the built environment can obscure awareness of dependence upon and responsibility for nonhuman nature. In a rural context, connections between at least some kinds of social injustice and the natural environment may be more clearly seen. Intellectual activity in the modern West has been centered in the cities, and urban bias dominates and skews interpretations of history, politics, civilization, and work (078). Nor is it surprising that more remote, indirect, or long-term environmental problems should be of greater concern to relatively affluent, educated persons than to those who must struggle to meet their own immediate, short-term needs (297, 348); or that blue-collar workers whose livelihood depends directly on heavy industry will perceive its environmental impacts differently than professionals for whom factories are most immediately experienced as sources of air and water pollution (204). Conversely, the predominantly White, upper-middle-class leadership and membership of environmental organizations have drawn up agendas that often do not address the environmental problems of poor and minority groups.

Finally, these mutually reinforcing biases and assumptions have tended to promote widespread ignorance of the actual links between ecological integrity and social well-being. An oversimplified and incomplete understanding of the relationship between nature and society gives little impetus for taking the time to trace out their complex causal connections and feedback loops.

Justice and Ecology Viewed as Antagonistic

For some authors in the literature surveyed in this bibliography, the relationship between social justice and environmental protection is adversarial. Those who define justice primarily in terms of individual economic freedom tend to view environmental regulations as unjust by definition. The fact that liberals and conservatives alike assume that rising affluence, economic expansion, and technological progress are the *sine qua non* of the good society means that both liberals and conservatives have seen environmentalism as a roadblock to the economic and technological development needed to raise people and nations out of poverty, or as an elitist luxury unrelated to the interests of the poor (300-301, 330, 358). A few environmental advocates sound almost as if they consider social justice concerns an irrelevant distraction in the face of ecological threats to survival.[70]

The following factors in political experience and intellectual history help to explain how such dualistic views of justice and ecology have arisen and persist.

Western thought since Kant and Hegel has tended to set nature in opposition to history and space in opposition to time. Nature has been seen as a collection of objects governed by deterministic laws in a static or cyclic order; history as a dynamic, even progressive realm of self-conscious subjects capable of freely responding to moral laws. Such a view has contributed to an either-or mentality regarding ecology and justice, making it difficult to see the dependence of history on nature, to situate the human self fully in its ecological context, or to apply moral concepts to human transactions with nature (018, 078, 109,143).[71]

The use of "the laws of nature" and "the order of creation" to justify social inequalities and the social institutions that support them has made the terms "nature" and "creation" anathema to many persons passionately committed to social justice. "Nature" has been invoked to justify the subordination to elite White males of women, nonwhite races, and lower economic classes; social Darwinists and Marxists alike have appealed to the laws and order of nature to defend exploitative capitalism or oppressive Communist regimes. Conservative and totalitarian political theories have often used biological metaphors such as "organism" to describe society (217). In twentieth century Protestantism, especially after the Barmen Declaration of 1934, ethical appeals to "creation" have been tainted by the use of the theology of the "orders of creation" to support the nationalistic Nazi ideology of "blood and soil." Under these circumstances, the affinity of ecological concern for the doctrine of creation and the theology of nature has been seen as a political liability for those dedicated to changing the status quo, and there are fears that environmental concerns will increase existing prejudices and resentments against the poor, minorities, and immigrants (005, 208-9, 300, 439).[72]

Finally, many proposed "solutions" to environmental problems could create or worsen social problems. Environmental regulation, like environmental degradation, often places a heavier burden on the poor in the form of restricted access or higher costs. Expensive pollution controls might raise the price of necessities like food and energy, making them unaffordable for the poor; urban "green space" plans could block low-income housing; limits to industrialization and economic growth threaten to freeze inequalities between "developed" and "developing" nations; population control raises the specters of involuntary sterilization and forced abortion, "triage," or "lifeboat ethics"; and so on (174, 348). Social justice advocates have seen in the pattern of such proposals not-so-thinly-veiled expressions of racism and class interest. Thus the (real or apparent) insensitivity of some environmental proposals and policies to values of equality and freedom helps to reinforce the belief that the pursuit of ecological integrity and the quest for social justice are radically divergent or opposed (222, 300-302, 498).

Factors Encouraging Eco-Justice Thinking

The concept of eco-justice has emerged as an attempt to respond constructively and creatively to these actual and assumed tensions without reducing caring for people and caring for the earth to a simple either/or alternative. As we have seen, activists committed to both the environment and social justice but critical of the effects that some environmental proposals would have on the poor have sought to build bridges between the two movements, to make them mutually critical correctives, and to develop strategies that would address both poverty and pollution.

Over against the centrifugal forces pushing ecology and justice apart, centripetal impulses have also been at work, which these bridge-builders could draw upon. One set of impulses is intellectual: ways of conceiving the relationships between God, human beings, and nature which avoid sharp spirit/matter oppositions and do more justice to the roles of creation and the biophysical world in theology and human experience. Another set of impulses comprises the actual causal connections between social institutions and ecological processes. As events force recognition of how unjust social practices affect the environment, and how environmental use and protection impact society, the concrete meanings of justice and ecology become more complex and interdependent. These impulses have perhaps never been wholly absent, but in the period covered by this bibliography their force has been increasingly felt.

Theological and Philosophical Frameworks

Those in the churches who believe in the ultimate coherence between environmental and justice concerns find crucial theological support in deeper and more sensitive readings of Scripture and Christian traditions. An important general theological theme from the perspective of radical monotheism is the recognition of the unity of human beings and nature in creation: God is the source, goal, and guide of *all* that is, the God of nature *and* history (153, 175, 290).[73]   Incarnation and sacrament point to God's intimate involvement with and redemption of human beings and the earthy, material stuff in which they are embodied and embedded; matter and spirit are distinct but inseparable. (009, 020, 064, 087-88, 097, 107, 124-25, 151, 191). The story told in the Hebrew and Christian scriptures is one in which creation and liberation, providence and redemption, form a single trajectory (443, 466). This story radically undercuts the modern tendency in Western Christianity toward a dualistic separation of nature from history, creation from redemption, and cosmos from liberation.

Of great importance have been biblical themes that more specifically relate justice and environment. Many eco-justice writers draw heavily on the linkage of justice for the poor and vulnerable and the health and fertility of the land in God's covenant with Israel. The unity of social justice and ecological integrity is also expressed in laws relating to land ownership and use, Sabbath, and Jubilee. The prophets call the nation to accountability to the creator-God who liberated Israel, and speak in concrete terms of how violence and injustice disrupt the natural order and destroy the land's fruitfulness (030, 035-38, 053, 055, 184, 248, 349).

Further support for a more integrated view is found in forms of evolutionary and ecological philosophy—from Whiteheadian process metaphysics (065,134), to Teilhard's evolutionary Christology (090), to Ernst Bloch's philosophy of hope (130), to the more poetic and intuitive ontology of communion of Joseph Sittler (100, 153)—that bring nature and history, society and ecology, closer together. These views, which stress the continuity between humans and nonhuman nature, and the dynamic, open character of the latter, have had a major impact on some theologians, who have found in them a common framework for environmental and social justice values. These philosophies also provide vocabularies and rationales for bridging the inclusive theological themes mentioned above and the contemporary insights and concerns of natural scientists and environmentalists.

Patterns of Conceptualization

These theological and philosophical perspectives provide backing for a variety of ways of conceiving a positive relationship between social justice and environmental integrity.

Minimally, they can be seen as equally valid, parallel concerns—affirmed together, not so much because of any intrinsic connection between justice and the environment, but because each is, for its own reasons, an important thing to be concerned about (260).[74] How one concern might actually lead to or require the other at a theoretical or practical level, or how the two concerns might come into conflict over a particular issue—much less how that conflict is to be sorted out or adjudicated—are questions not always asked by writers who address both environmental and social justice issues in the same work.

Ecological and justice concerns can be united by a mutual enemy when environmental degradation and social injustice are traced to a common source. This may be a specific political and economic institution, such as colonialism, capitalism, growth-oriented economics (whether market-driven or centrally planned), or the military-industrial complex (099, 256, 287, 348, 394, 437). It may be a cultural ideology, such as Enlightenment individualism, rationalism and progressivism, or hierarchical and dualistic cosmologies which support patriarchal, anthropocentric and ethnocentric value-systems (067, 125, 143, 235-36, 246, 248-51, 269). The ultimate causes may be located in the human self or psyche: in selfishness, greed, anxiety, fear of death (017, 062, 219). Or, it may be some combination of the above.

The intersection of ecology and justice can also be developed ethically and theologically. Particular ethical and policy issues can be analyzed using a single norm or set of norms that apply to humans and nonhumans, or which include both social and environmental values. Such norms tend to be either teleological or deontological. Process theologians, for example, speak of the *telos* of ethical action as "maximizing the richness of experience," and argue both that the ecological context is an essential contributor to the richness of human experience, and also that the experience (or analogues to experience) of other beings must also be taken morally into account (065). In more deontological interpretations, the "justice and peace" of the World Council of Churches' formula "Justice, Peace, and the Integrity of Creation" may be seen as an expression of the more fundamental and general concept of "the integrity of creation" (023, 155). Another possible unitary principle is the common good in its widest sense (182, 197). Norms at this level of generality and inclusiveness, however, need additional, more specific norms to be usefully applied.

Groups or sets of norms have also been interpreted as applying to humans and nonhumans, or to the "mixed community" of humans and nonhumans as a whole: freedom, equality, community (177); love and justice (204); love as *eros*, *philia*, and *agape* (216); homeostasis, holism, and creativity (263). Some writers employ a set of norms—such as "interdependence, participation, beauty" (501), "the just, participatory, and sustainable society" (065, 220, 255, 257-8, 288, 369, 392, 497), or "sustainability, participation, solidarity, and sufficiency" (398, 443)—which as a whole express the conviction that environmental and social issues cannot be separated, even though some norms (e.g., justice, participation) tend to be applied to the treatment of humans and others (e.g., sustainability) to human impacts on nonhuman nature.[75]

Yet another way of uniting social and environmental values is by orienting them toward a common goal or ideal. This way has obvious affinities with the teleological (goal-oriented) ethics described above. However, its main interest is in projecting a vision of a world in which the values sought by teleological ethics are realized and the obligations laid down by deontological theories are met. The goal can be described programmatically, as the project of liberating all beings from all forms of oppression and domination (065-66, 224, 443), or creating the "Just, Participatory and Sustainable Society," the "life-oriented and life-affirming society" (256), or a flourishing and harmonious "earth community" (064, 261).

Scripture provides a storehouse of images for states of being which realize the good of all creatures. These include the covenantal community dwelling faithfully and justly in God's fertile land (030, 033, 036, 332, 379) and righteousness as "right order" in creation (053). Eschatological visions of the ultimate goal of nature and history have been expressed using the symbols of the Kingdom of God (144); *shalom* as wholeness as well as peace (034, 041, 056); and the Sabbath of creation (130, 128, 146).

Such goals of divine and human action are more inclusive than recent human-centered formulations of Christian hope that have guided social activism—humanization, the spiritual kingdom of ends, the classless society, the responsible society—yet they also take up the commitment to justice that has been integral to those visions.

Causal Connections

The quest for a unified eco-justice theology and ethic has found empirical support in discussions by scientists and policy analysts and the experiences of oppressed and marginalized peoples around the world that have highlighted causal connections between environmental degradation and social injustice.

Theologians and ethicists who are deeply concerned and well-informed about either global environmental or global justice issues cannot easily ignore the environmental ramifications of such issues as international trade and debt, the export of Western technology and economies, and economic dependency. But the most passionate and moving pleas for realizing ecological wholeness and social justice together come from the experience of oppressed groups that have been historically or ideologically linked to environmental degradation: women, indigenous peoples, landless peasants, minority communities, bankrupt farmers, workers exposed to environmental hazards or threatened by the loss of their industry's natural resource base, communities sited on or near toxic waste dumps, and countless others (156, 231, 267, 396, 423). The ministry of the church and other religious groups among these people can hardly address their pain without seeing its linkages to a wounded and threatened Earth. Moreover, those who view modern Western history from the outside (indigenous peoples) or the underside (the poor and the oppressed) are the bearers of traditions and perceptions that have been neglected or suppressed by the dominant and dominating scientific-technological worldview. Such traditions carry not only ecological knowledge and techniques for sustainable living, but also values that offer critiques of and alternatives to the cultural distortions and blind spots that have helped create current problems of social injustice and environmental degradation (004, 272, 388, 414, 510).

Specific cases in which environmental wholeness and the welfare of particular groups are both violated show how interdependent social justice and ecological values can be. Often, both land and people are enmeshed and degraded by the same policy. Large-scale agribusiness practices degrade the land, abuse animals, concentrate ownership, and undermine rural community (379, 394, 400, 413). Poor and ethnic minority groups in the U.S. are more likely to live near a hazardous waste site than are other residents (187, 294).

Numerous examples of causal connections between injustice and environmental degradation can be cited. Some show how environmental degradation creates or exacerbates injustice. The poor suffer the most from pollution and resource depletion and contribute to it the least. Indigenous peoples suffer with the destruction of the ecosystems on which their livelihood, religion and cultural identity directly depend (118, 385). Those most directly involved in exploiting nature—miners, farm workers, slaughterhouse workers—suffer from the unhealthy effects of a degraded environment as well as from low wages (226, 380). Rural women in the Global South must walk farther for wood and water and work harder to raise food as the environment deteriorates (233, 281).

Other examples show how injustice increases environmental degradation. Unjust distribution of land and financial resources force the poor to eke out the barest existence on marginal lands that cannot tolerate such intensive use (408). Military expenditures, political corruption, inequitable trade arrangements, and crushing international debt drain the funds needed for nations of the Global South to protect their national ecological heritage or to invest in more environmentally benign technologies, leading them to overexploit their natural resources in order to raise cash (365, 416, 507). Lack of grassroots participation in development decisions often results in schemes that are economic, social, and environmental disasters. High infant mortality, lack of economic security, and low social status of women help increase rates of population growth (281, 296). Nuclear war threatens, and conventional war devastates, both nature and human society (283, 289).

These issues and others like them will continue to provoke reflection on the varieties of social and environmental values and challenge Christians to develop and refine their frameworks for exploring the complex relations between ecology and justice.

ACHIEVEMENTS OF THE ECO-JUSTICE MOVEMENT

Although the attention of the Christian ecumenical community has remained focused primarily on justice concerns throughout the second half of the twentieth century, and the eco-justice perspective remains a minority perspective within the churches and the academy, the overall trend of scholarly and ecumenical debate since the 1960s has been toward acknowledgment of humanity's responsibilities for the well-being of creation as well as for justice and peaceful coexistence among its own kind. In other words, the *trend* has been toward one or another version of the eco-justice perspective.

On repeated occasions studies and discussions of the relations between ecology, justice, and Christian faith have resulted in a movement by justice proponents toward inclusion of considerations of resource constraints, ecological relationships, and intrinsic natural values into their thinking, and often into their understanding of the meaning of "justice" or "liberation" itself. This has happened in the case of individuals as well as groups. Thus theologians, such as Moltmann and Boff, who previously neglected or downplayed ecological matters, have come to author vigorous statements of eco-justice theology and ethics; other authors, originally hospitable to eco-justice thinking, have become more so.[76] There is comparable evidence that church bodies throughout the world are increasingly willing to use the doctrine of creation as a basis for progressive stands on both ecological and social policies (439), and in North America the "eco-justice" principle has been adopted as the basis for the multi-denominational National Religious Partnership on the Environment. However muddled the MIT conference results, environmental issues, resource limits, and critical questioning of the impact of the technological society were far more prominent in 1979 than at the WCC conference that addressed similar themes in Geneva in 1966.

This overall trend toward acceptance of the need to integrate ecology, justice, and Christian faith, or at least to add ecology to long-standing Christian concerns for justice and peace, must be considered the most significant achievement of the eco-justice movement. The trend is the cumulative result of a number of more particular achievements, each of which is important in its own right:

(1) In 1979 Rifkin noted that "'dominion,' which Christian theology has for so long used to justify people's unrestrained pillage and exploitation of the natural world, has suddenly and dramatically been reinterpreted [as stewardship] . . . and one would be hard pressed to find a leading Protestant scholar . . . who would openly question the new interpretation . . . "[77] The change in the meaning of dominion is but one example of how the eco-justice movement has been able to transform a fundamental biblical or Christian doctrine or symbol in a way that expresses God's intention for the non-human as well as human creation. These interpretations have found acceptance in the Christian community. The doctrine of creation has been resuscitated and moved to a position of primary theological and ethical importance for many Christian theologians, scientists, and church persons, and the doctrine itself has been reinterpreted in keeping with the ecological worldview of reality-as-relation that Sittler proposed in 1970 as the new *principium* of Christian self-understanding (153). Thus was the foundation laid for sweeping hermeneutical transformations in the root metaphors of the tradition, and as

the preceding survey has suggested, for the development of an impressive number of new constructive theologies of the Christian faith itself.

(2) The Christian eco-justice movement has succeeded in making a good case for Christianity's capacity to address the moral and spiritual dimensions of the ecological crisis. Remarkably enough, it has made this case to the secular as well as the Christian community, both of which doubted it previously—the one largely skeptical that Christianity had resources for the task, the other largely indifferent to the need for them. We have noted the spark that White's 1967 article lit under the long-smoldering controversy in Western thought regarding the attitudes of Christianity toward the natural world. The success of the eco-justice movement in responding to White, himself a Presbyterian layman, may be gauged by recent works such as those of environmental philosopher Max Oelschlaeger, who argues that the admonition of the biblical tradition to "care for the earth" is the single most important cultural basis for a new environmental ethic in the West.[78]

(3) Time and again the members of the Christian eco-justice movement have borne witness to their moral conviction that to see the moral truth one must keep one eye fixed on ecology and the other eye fixed on justice. Chris Cowap used the metaphor of "bifocal vision" to suggest that eco-justice means to "look at economic issues through the lens of environmental sustainability, and. . . environmental issues through the lens of economic justice."[79] It is their loyalty to this two-in-one affirmation that has distinguished members of this movement from many of their friends and colleagues in both the environmental and liberation movements. Seldom has it been easy to maintain this balanced vision—to speak on behalf of social justice and the oppressed in the face of overwhelming environmental degradation, or to speak on behalf of ecological integrity and the need for environmental protection in the midst of overwhelming human need. Although, as we have seen, the idea of "eco-justice" comes in many languages and editions, most accept the view that Christian faith requires more than simply *adding* ecology to the list of important social and spiritual concerns, or even, as Roderick Nash suggests in the *Rights of Nature*, "widening the circle" of community to include non-human members. It requires a unified religio-ethical response to the one Creative/Redemptive reality.

(4) The eco-justice analysis and prescription has proven immensely fruitful for thought and action regarding environmental, economic, population, consumption, social, political, and gender issues, especially issues of agriculture (394), animal welfare (206), climate change (428), economics (343), energy (407, 426), land use (450), lifestyle (184), and population (281).

(5) The Christian eco-justice movement has made intellectual, institutional, and personal contributions to the common struggle of persons and groups of many nations, cultures and faiths to put contemporary world civilization on a more authentic and sustainable spiritual foundation (077, 178).[80] Trenchant moral criticism and determined moral resistance to the continued hegemony of the world "growth system" has come from scores of Christian eco-justice thinkers and activists (377). The late twentieth-century movement to build a new world ethic would not have developed as it did without the resources and backing of the World Council of Churches and other organizations within the Christian ecumenical movement. Persons drawing upon the resources of the Christian tradition have played an important role in making the *idea*, if not the terminology of eco-justice, prominent in many of the declarations of common moral purpose adopted by interfaith and international groups since Stockholm (141, 178, 310).

(6) The body of literature, community of scholarship, and network of institutional practices that have emerged in the course of the struggle to integrate ecology, justice, and Christian faith are large enough and coherent enough to constitute a new field of religious action and study.[81] If the literature generated in the past half-century were gathered in one library there would be more than sufficient material for a program of university studies. This fact is slowly making itself felt in the institutionalization of eco-justice thinking in theological schools, colleges and universities, and in religious education.[82]

NOTES

[1] "Letter to the Churches," in Wesley Granberg-Michaelson, *Redeeming the Creation: The Rio Earth Summit: Challenges for the Churches* (Geneva: WCC Publications, 1992), 71.

[2] In addition to the present bibliography, see Carl Mitcham and Jim Grote, "Selected Bibliography of Theology and Technology" in *Theology and Technology: Essays in Christian Analysis and Exegesis*, edited by Carl Mitcham and Jim Grote (Lanham, MD: University Press of America, 1984): 323-516; Joseph K. Sheldon, *Rediscovery of Creation: A Bibliographical Study of the Church's Response to the Environmental Crisis* (Metuchen, NJ: Scarecrow Press, 1992); Fred Van Dyke, "Annotated Bibliography on Planetheonomics," paper presented at the 1986 Forum, Au Sable Institute of Environmental Studies, Mancelona MI, June 17-21, 1986; and Joint Appeal by Religion and Science for the Environment, *A Directory of Environmental Activities and Resources in the North American Religious Community* (Kutztown Publishing Company: Kutztown, PA, 1992).

[3] Robert Booth Fowler, *The Greening of Protestant Thought* (Chapel Hill: University of North Carolina Press, 1995), 175. Although there is some evidence that biblical literalism may be linked to negative environmental attitudes, little consensus has so far emerged in the results of empirical studies of the relationships between religious and environmental attitudes. See Douglas Lee Eckberg and T. Jean Blocker, "Varieties of Religious Involvement and Environmental Concerns: Testing the Lynn White Thesis," *Journal of the Scientific Study of Religion* 28 (1989): 509-17; Andrew Greeley, "Religion and Attitudes Toward the Environment," *Journal for the Scientific Study of Religion* 32 (1993): 19-28; James L. Guth, Lyman A. Kellstedt, Corwin E. Smidt, and John C. Green, "Theological Perspectives and Environmentalism Among Religious Activists," *Journal for the Scientific Study of Religion* 32 (1993): 373-82; Conrad L. Kanagy and Fern K. Willits, "A Greening of Religion—Some Evidence from a Pennsylvania Sample," *Social Science Quarterly* 74 (1993): 674-83; Eric Woodrum and Thomas Hoban, "Theology and Religiosity Effects on Environmentalism," *Review of Religious Research* 35 (1994): 193-206.

[4] Granberg-Michaelson, *Redeeming the Creation*, 72.

[5] For the history of this debate see Joseph Earl Bush Jr., "Social Justice and the Natural Environment in the Study Program of the World Council of Churches, 1966-1990," (Ph.D. Diss., Drew University, 1993); Dana K. Horrell, "Reclaiming the Covenant: The Eco-Justice Movement as Practical Theology", (Ph.D. Diss., University of Chicago, 1993); Martti Lindqvist (487); and references cited in the narrative below.

[6] C. S. Lewis, *The Abolition of Man* (New York: Macmillan Co., 1947), 69. See also William Leiss, *The Domination of Nature* (Boston: Beacon Press, 1972).

[7] William E. Gibson, "Eco-Justice: Burning Word: Heilbroner and Jeremiah to the Church," *Foundations* 20 (October/December 1977), 318.

[8] John B. Cobb Jr., *Sustainability: Economics, Ecology, and Justice* (Maryknoll, NY: Orbis Books, 1992), 21.

[9] National Council of Churches, *Energy and Ethics: The Ethical Implications of Energy Production and Use* (New York: National Council of Churches, Division of Church and Society, 1979), 12.

[10] Jim Wallis, *The Soul of Politics* (Maryknoll, NY: Orbis Books, 1994), 179.

[11] It is likely that "eco-justice" will follow the tendency of other hyphenated and compound terms and, as soon as acceptance warrants, the hyphen will be dropped but the double meaning of ecology + justice will be retained. This tendency is to be noted in the writings of Cobb, cited above.

[12] Joseph Sittler, "Called to Unity," *Ecumenical Review* 14 (January 1962): 178. At the time of his New Delhi address Sittler was a member of the faculty of the Divinity School of the University of Chicago. He began to address environmental concerns in "God, Man and Nature," *Pulpit* 24, (August 1953): 16-17, and in "A Theology For Earth," *Christian Scholar* 37 (September 1954): 367-74. See Conrad Simonson, *The Christology of the Faith and Order Movement* (Leiden: E. J. Brill, 1972) for the theological and ecumenical context for Sittler's address (500).

[13] Simonson, *Christology*, 182.

[14] Some eco-justice leaders, such as John B. Cobb Jr., underwent "a kind of conversion experience" through the revelation of the environmental crisis (075). The revelation of Earth is an important theme in the work of Gerald Barney (431), Brian Swimme and Thomas Berry (273), and Alvin Pitcher (463). On the related subject of the uses and abuses of "green apocalypticism" see Anne Primavesi (243), and John Pawlikowski, "Theological Dimensions of an Ecological Ethic," in *The Ecological Challenge*, edited by Richard Fragomeni and John Pawlikowski (Collegeville, MN: Liturgical Press, 1984).

[15] Wrote Berkhof in his background paper for the conference: "The God who historicizes human existence frees man from entangling bondage to the powers of nature, and tells him to come of age and to become the master of the powers whose slave he previously was." Hendrikus Berkhof, "God in Nature and History," *Study Encounter* 1 (1965): 157. See Arend van Leeuwen, *Christianity and World History* (Edinburgh: Edinburgh House Press, 1964); and Harvey Cox, *The Secular City* (New York: Macmillan Co., 1965).

[16] Bush, "Social Justice and the Natural Environment," 37.

[17] For the history of the Faith-Man-Nature Group see H. Paul Santmire (494); Philip N. Joranson, "The Faith-Man-Nature Group and a Religious Environmental Ethic," *Zygon* 12 (June 1977): 175-79; Roderick Frazier Nash, *The Rights of Nature: A History of Environmental Ethics* (Madison: University of Wisconsin Press, 1989), 102-4. The F/M/N Group held six conferences and published several books: Glenn C. Stone, eds., *A New Ethics for a New Earth* (New York: Friendship Press, 1971; Alfred Stefferud, ed., *Christians and the Good Earth* (New York: Friendship Press, 1972); Philip N. Joranson and Alan C. Anderson, eds., *Religious Reconstruction for the Environmental Future* (South Coventry, CN: Faith-Man-Nature Group, 1973); Dave Steffenson, Robert S. Cook, and Walter J. Herrscher, eds., *Ethics for Environment: Three Religious Strategies* (Green Bay: University of Wisconsin-Green Bay, Ecumenical Center, 1973); Donald Scherer, ed., *Earth Ethics for Today and Tomorrow: Responsible Environmental Trade-Offs* (Bowling Green, OH: Bowling Green State University Environmental Studies Center, 1974).

[18] H. Paul Santmire, "The Struggle for an Ecological Theology: A Case in Point," *Christian Century* 87 (4 March 1970): 276.

[19] Some of the most influential contributions to eco-justice theology, ethics and social practice in the United States were to come from members of this group, among them, Calvin B. DeWitt, Norman Faramelli, Albert J. Fritsch, Dieter T. Hessel, William E. Gibson, James Parks Morton, James A. Nash, Owen D. Owens, Larry L. Rasmussen, Jeremy Rifkin, Rosemary Radford Ruether, H. Paul Santmire, and Gibson Winter.

[20] See also the 1970 study prepared for the Lutheran Church in America by H. Paul Santmire, Joseph Sittler, and others (193).

[21] Barbara Ward and René Dubos, *Only One Earth: The Care and Maintenance of a Small Planet* (New York: W. W. Norton, 1972). Ward also wrote several pioneering essays on Christianity, ecology, and justice during this period (323-25).

[22] In 1970 Frederick Elder also published one of the first books in the field but it was not as directly aimed at the ecology-justice interface as Santmire's (082).

[23] Charles Birch, "Creation, Technology, and Human Survival: Called to Replenish the Earth," *Ecumenical Review* 28 (January 1976): 76.

[24] Dieter T. Hessel, *Energy Ethics: A Christian Response* (New York: Friendship Press, 1979), 113.

[25] See William C. French, "Subject-Centered and Creation-Centered Paradigms in Recent Catholic Thought," *Journal of Religion* 70 (1990): 48-72.

[26] See Carol J. Adams, *The Sexual Politics of Meat: A Feminist-Vegetarian Critical Theory* (New York: Continuum Publishing Company, 1991).

[27] Francis Schaeffer, *Pollution and the Death of Man: The Christian View of Ecology* (Wheaton, IL: Tyndale House, 1970). For a recent adoption of the eco-justice perspective by a progressive Evangelical thinker, and editor of *Sojourners* magazine, see Wallis, *The Soul of Politics*.

[28] See also James M. Gustafson, *A Sense of the Divine: The Natural Environment from a Theocentric Perspective* (Cleveland: Pilgrim Press, 1994); William C. French, "Ecological Concern and the Anti-Foundationalist Debates: James Gustafson on Biospheric Constraints." *The Annual of the Society of Christian Ethics (1989).*

[29] See, for example, Shantilal P. Bhagat, ed., *God's Earth Our Home: A Resource for Congregational Study and Action on Environmental and Economic Justice* (New York: Environmental and Economic Justice Hunger Concerns Working Group of the National Council of Churches of Christ in the USA, 1994).

[30] Enrique Dussel, *Ethics and Community*, translated by Robert R. Barr (Maryknoll, NY: Orbis, 1988), 194-204; Juan Luis Segundo, *Faith and Ideologies* (Maryknoll, NY: Orbis, 1984).

[31] Harrison Brown, *The Challenge of Man's Future* (New York: Viking, 1954); Aldo Leopold, *Sand County Almanac* (New York: Oxford University Press, 1949); Karl Sax, *Standing Room Only* (Boston: Beacon Press, 1955); Fairfield Osborn, *Our Plundered Planet* (Boston: Little Brown, 1948); William Vogt, *Road to Survival* (New York: William Sloane Associates, 1948).

[32] Rachel Carson, *Silent Spring* (New York: Houghton Mifflin, 1962). See Robert C. Paehlke, *Environment and the Future of Progressive Politics* (New Haven: Yale University Press, 1989) for an overview of the 1960s environmental movement in North America.

[33] See Barry Commoner, *The Closing Circle: Nature, Man and Technology* (New York: Alfred A. Knopf, 1971); Paul Ehrlich, *The End of Affluence: A Blueprint for Your Future* (New York: Ballantine Books, 1974); Garrett Hardin, *Exploring New Ethics for Survival: The Voyage of the Spaceship Beagle* (New York: Pelican Books, 1973).

[34] Donnella H. Meadows, Dennis L. Meadows, Jørgen Randers, William W. Behrens III, *The Limits to Growth* (New York: New American Library, 1972), x. A more differentiated global model characterized the second report of the Club of Rome by Mihajlo Mesarovic and Eduard Pestel, *Mankind at the Turning Point* (New York: E. P. Dutton and Co., 1974). Global systems studies continued to exercise considerable influence on the thinking of the eco-justice movement after 1972. See Gerald O. Barney and the Council on Environmental Quality and the Department of State, *The Global 2000 Report to the President* (New York: Penguin Books, 1980); Donella H. Meadows, Dennis L. Meadows, Jørgen Randers, *Beyond the Limits: Confronting Global Collapse, Envisioning a Sustainable Future* (Post Mills, VT: Chelsea Green Publishing Co., 1992).

[35] See Teilhard de Chardin, *The Phenomenon of Man*, translated by Bernard Wall (New York: Collins and Row, 1959); William Temple, *Nature, Man, and God* (London: Macmillan and Co., 1935); Paul Tillich, "Redemption in Cosmic and Social History," *Journal of Religious Thought* 3 (1946): 17-27; Paul Tillich, "The Redemption of Nature," *Christendom* X (1945): 299-305; Paul Tillich, "Nature and Sacrament," and "The Idea and the Ideal of Personality," in *The Protestant Era*, trans. James Luther Adams (Chicago: University of Chicago Press, 1948); Alfred North Whitehead, *Science and the Modern World* (New York: Macmillan Co., 1925); Charles Hartshorne, *Beyond Humanism: Essays in the Philosophy of Nature* (New York: Willett, Clark and Co., 1937); Tyron Inbody, *The Constructive Theology of Bernard Meland: Postliberal Empirical Realism* (Atlanta: Scholars Press, 1995); Daniel Day Williams, *God's Grace and Man's Hope* (New York: Collins and Brothers, 1949).

[36] Martin Buber, *I and Thou* (New York: Charles Scribner's Sons, 1970); H. Richard Niebuhr, in collaboration with Daniel Day Williams and James M. Gustafson, *The Purpose of the Church and Its Ministry: Reflections on the Aims of Theological Education* (New York: Collins and Row, 1960); H. Richard Niebuhr, "The Center of Value," in *Radical Monotheism and Western Culture* (New York: Collins and Row, 1960), 37-39; Dietrich Bonhoeffer, *Creation and Fall: A Theological Interpretation of Genesis 1-3*, translated by John C. Fletcher (New York: Macmillan Co., 1959); Dietrich Bonhoeffer, *Temptation*, edited by Eberhard Bethge, translated by Kathleen Downham (New York: Macmillan Co., 1959); Walter Rauschenbush, *Christianizing the Social Order* (New York: Macmillan Co., 1912), 25-53, 253-54.

[37] Gordon Kaufman's defense of the priority of history (109), Gustaf Wingren's defense of the priority of creation in *The Flight From Creation* (Minneapolis: Augsburg Publishing House, 1971), and the special edition of *Concilium* (148) are examples of this kind of discussion. See H. Paul Santmire, "Studying the Doctrine of Creation: The Challenge," *Dialog* 21 (Summer 1982): 195-200; Harold H. Oliver, "The Neglect and Recovery of Nature in Twentieth Century Protestant Thought," *Journal of the American Academy of Religion* 60, 3 (1992): 379-404.

[38] See H. Paul Santmire, *The Travail of Nature: The Ambiguous Ecological Promise of Christian Theology* (Philadelphia: Fortress Press, 1985), 146-54.

[39] See Mark Ellingsen, *The Cutting Edge: How Churches Speak on Social Issues* (Geneva: WCC Publications, 1993), 3; James M. Gustafson, *Can Ethics Be Christian?* (Chicago: University of Chicago Press), 95.

[40] See Alasdair I. C. Heron, *A Century of Protestant Theology* (Philadelphia: Westminster Press, 1980).

[41] See John Carmody, *Ecology and Religion* (New York: Paulist Press, 1983); Richard N. Fragomeni and John T. Pawlikowski, eds., *The Ecological Challenge: Ethical, Liturgical, and Spiritual Responses* (Collegeville, MN: The Liturgical Press, 1994); Albert LaChance and John E. Carroll, eds., *Embracing Earth: Catholic Approaches to Ecology* (New York: Orbis Books, 1994).

[42] See Andrew Linzey, *Christianity and the Rights of Animals* (New York: Crossroad, 1987); Jay B. McDaniel, "Land Ethics, Animal Rights, and Process Theology," *Process Studies* 17 (1988): 88-102; Michael W. Fox, *On the Fifth Day: Animal Rights and Human Obligations* (New York: Acropolis Press, 1977).

[43] See John Dillenberger, *Protestant Thought and Natural Science* (Garden City, N.Y.: Doubleday, 1960); A. R. Peacocke, *Creation and the World of Science* (Oxford: Clarendon Press, 1979); Holmes Rolston III, *Science and Religion: A Critical Survey* (Philadelphia: Temple University Press 1987).

[44] The following bibliographical surveys are helpful introductions to this immense body of literature: Mary Anglemeyer, Eleanor R. Seagraves, and Catherine C. LeMaistre, *A Search for Environmental Ethics: An Initial Bibliography* (Washington, DC: Smithsonian Institution Press, 1980); Mary Anglemyer and Eleanor R. Seagraves, eds., *The Natural Environment: An Annotated Bibliography on Attitudes and Values* (Washington, DC: Smithsonian Institution Press, 1984); Donald Edward Davis, *Ecophilosophy: A Field Guide to the Literature* (San Pedro, CA: R. and E. Miles, 1989); Eric Katz, "Environmental Ethics: A Select Annotated Bibliography, 1983-1987," in *Research in Philosophy and Technology*, edited by Frederick Ferré (Greenwich, CT: JAI Press, 1989) 251-85; Eric Katz, "Environmental Ethics: A Select Annotated bibliography II, 1987-1990," in *Research in Philosophy and Technology*, edited by Frederick Ferré (Greenwich, CT: JAI Press, 1992) 287-324; Joseph A. Miller, et al., *The Island Press Bibliography of Environmental Literature* (Washington DC: Island Press, 1993). For representative discussions of the relation of ecology and social justice in contemporary philosophical literature see Murray Bookchin, *The Ecology of Freedom: The Emergence and Dissolution of Hierarchy*, rev. ed. (Montreal: Black Rose Books, 1991); Norman Faramelli and Charles W. Powers, "Environmental Ethics: II. Questions of Social Justice" s.v. *Encyclopedia of Bioethics*, edited by Warren T. Reich (New York: Free Press, 1978); Tom Regan, ed., *Earthbound: New Introductory Essays in Environmental Ethics* (New York: Random House, 1984); K. S. Shrader-Frechette, *Environmental Ethics* (Pacific Grove, CA: Boxwood Press, 1981); Peter S. Wenz, *Environmental Justice* (Albany: State University of New York Press, 1988).

[45] Gerhard von Rad, "Some Aspects of the Old Testament World View," in *The Problem of the Hexateuch and Other Essays,* translated by E. W. T. Dicken (New York: McGraw-Hill Book Company), 140.

[46] See James Barr, "Revelation Through History in the Old Testament and in Modern Theology," *Interpretation* 17 (1963): 193-205.

[47] See Calvin B. DeWitt, ed., *The Environment and the Christian: What Can We Learn from the New Testament?* (Grand Rapids: Baker Book House, 1991).

[48] See Alan Galloway, *The Cosmic Christ* (New York: Collins and Brothers, 1951); Clarence J. Glacken, *Traces on the Rhodian Shore: Nature and Culture in Western Thought from Ancient Times to the End of the Eighteenth Century* (Berkeley: University of California Press, 1967); George Huntston Williams, *Wilderness and Paradise in Christian Thought* (New York: Collins, 1962); George Huntston Williams, "Christian Attitudes toward Nature," *Christian Scholars Review* 2 (Fall 1971, Winter 1972): 3-35, 112-26;. There is also an important body of early and continuing historical research focused on the relationships between Christian belief and American attitudes toward nature. See Perry Miller, *Errand Into the Wilderness* (Cambridge: Harvard University Press, 1956). Christian history is also closely bound up with the history of the humane movement. See Charles D. Niven, *History of the Humane Movement* (London: Johnson, 1967).

[49] Similar arguments were advanced by D. T. Suzuki, "The Role of Nature in Zen Buddhism" in *Zen Buddhism: Selected Writings,* edited by William Barrett (Garden City, NY: Doubleday, 1956): 229-58; Ian McHarg, *Design with Nature* (Garden City,

NY: Natural History Press, 1969); Arnold Toynbee, "The Religious Background of the Present Crisis" in David and Eileen Spring, eds., *Ecology and Religion in History* (New York: Collins and Row, 1974), 137-49.

[50] For a recent review of the immense body of literature generated on this question and an evaluation of the discussion see Elspeth Whitney, "Lynn White, Ecotheology, and History," *Environmental Ethics* 15 (Summer 1993): 151-70. See Yi-Fu Tuan, "Discrepancies between Environmental Attitude and Behaviour: Examples from Europe and China," in Spring and Spring, eds., *Ecology and Religion in History*, 48-75; René Dubos, "Franciscan Conservation versus Benedictine Stewardship," in Spring and Spring, eds., *Ecology and Religion in History*, 91-113; and references in Mitcham and Grote, "Selected Bibliography of Theology and Technology," 396-97, for critiques of White's argument.

[51] The first and so far only major historical study of the place of nature in the Western theological tradition is H. Paul Santmire, *The Travail of Nature: The Ambiguous Ecological Promise of Christian Theology* (Philadelphia: Fortress Press, 1985). See also Susan Power Bratton, *Christianity, Wilderness, and Wildlife: The Original Desert Solitaire* (Scranton, PA.: University of Scranton Press, 1994); Matthew Fox, *Historical Roots, Ecumenical Routes* (Santa Fe, NM: 1981); Roger D. Sorrell, *St. Francis of Assisi and Nature: Tradition and Innovation in Western Christian Attitudes toward the Environment* (New York: Oxford University Press, 1988).

[52] Nash, *The Rights of Nature*.

[53] Robert Gottlieb, *Forcing the Spring: The Transformation of the American Environmental Movement* (Washington, DC: Island Press, 1993); Jim Schwab, *Deeper Shades of Green: The Rise of Blue-Collar and Minority Environmentalism in America* (San Francisco: Sierra Club Books, 1994).

[54] Douglas Sturm, "On Meanings of Justice," in his *Community and Alienation: Essays on Process Thought and Public Life* (Notre Dame, IN: University of Notre Dame Press, 1988).

[55] Other standard typologies are not as useful in this context: discussions of retributive and procedural justice are rarely encountered in this literature; "substantive justice" is too broad. Distributive justice is a central concern, but it does not capture the full range of justice issues considered, and is represented by equality in Sturm's typology.

[56] Gen. 1:20-25; 7:2.

[57] Exod. 23:10-12

[58] Job 38-41.

[59] Matt. 6:26-30.

[60] Gen. 2:7; 19.

[61] Rom. 8:18-23; Rev. 21:1; 2 Peter 3:13.

[62] As noted earlier, terms such as "ecological justice" or "ecojustice" have been used to denote this way of extending the idea of justice to encompass our transactions with non-human beings. However, simply widening the circle of beings to which "justice" applies does not constitute the fullest kind of integration of ecological wholeness and social justice. Attention must be paid to the various ways that the demands of justice to humans and to nonhumans are not merely parallel, but intersect.

[63] See Roderick Frazier Nash, *The Rights of Nature: A History of Environmental Ethics* (Madison: University of Wisconsin Press, 1989).

[64] Biblical citations as used here are not intended to be "proof-texts" or exhaustive, or to apply exclusively to one or the other aspect of justice, but as a shorthand way of indicating the kinds of connections that can be made between these aspects of eco-justice and Christian theology (and, where ancient Hebrew themes and passages are involved, to Jewish theology as well).

[65] Peter Singer, *Animal Liberation: A New Ethics for Our Treatment of Animals* (New York: Avon Books, 1975), 2-3, 223.

[66] Mary Midgley, *Animals and Why They Matter* (New York: Penguin Books, 1983), 26.

[67] Aldo Leopold, *A Sand County Almanac and Sketches Here and There* (London: Oxford University Press, 1949), 204 and passim.

[68] See the introduction to Peter DeVos, et al., *Earthkeeping in the Nineties: Stewardship of Creation* (Grand Rapids: William B. Eerdmans Publishing Co., 1991).

[69] Bush in *Social Justice* argues that the inclusion of natural scientists in World Council of Churches' consultations was an important factor in putting environmental issues on the ecumenical agenda, and that later disagreements over resource limits to economic growth were due in large part to clashes between theories arising from the social sciences or the natural sciences.

[70] See Gregory Baum's critique of Thomas Berry (278), as well as the varied critiques of environmentalism by Derr (174), Faramelli (477), Ruether (055), and Santmire (017, 147, 217).

[71] French, "Ecological Concern and the Anti-Foundationalist Debates," 113-30.

[72] See Santmire, "Studying the Doctrine of Creation."

[73] H. Richard Niebuhr, *Radical Monotheism and Western Culture* (New York: Collins and Row, 1960).

[74] Other examples—not included on this bibliography—are Rex Ambler, *Global Theology: The Meaning of Faith in the Present World Crisis* (London: SCM; Philadelphia: Trinity Press International, 1990); and "The Oxford Declaration on Christian Faith and Economics, *Transformation* 7 (April/June 1990): 1-8. The World Council of Churches' formulations, "Just, Participatory, and Sustainable Society" and "Justice, Peace, and the Integrity of Creation" could be read this way; and at one level, they are umbrellas under which a global, ecumenical body has tried to gather the distinct concerns of different constituencies.

[75] This tendency may reflect the persistence of dualistic modes of thought, but it may also point to deeper issues. Philosophers Rolston and Ferré have noted the problems that arise when one attempts to subsume our relations to nature and to other human beings under the same moral categories.

[76] The growing recognition of the eco-justice perspective is evident in Rebecca S. Chopp and Mark Lewis Taylor, eds., *Reconstructing Christian Theology* (Minneapolis: Fortress Press, 1994).

[77] Jeremy Rifkin, *The Emerging Order: God in an Age of Scarcity* (New York: G. P. Putnam's Sons, 1979), x.

[78] Max Oelschlaeger, *Caring for Creation: An Ecumenical Approach to the Environmental Crisis* (New Haven: Yale University Press, 1994).

[79] Chris Cowap, "Not Just Ecology—Not Just Economics: Eco-Justice," *Egg* 6 (Fall 1986): 3.

[80] See Joel D. Beversluis, ed., *A Sourcebook for the Community of Religions* (Chicago: The Council for a Parliament of the World's Religions, 1993).

[81] See J. Ronald Engel, "Environment and Religion," s.v. *Encyclopedia of Bioethics,* edited by Warren T. Reich (New York: The Free Press, 1994).

[82] Thomas Berry has written about the need for the reform of university education in an ecological age in *The Dream of the Earth* (San Francisco: Sierra Club Books, 1988), 89-108. Daly and Cobb discuss the need to reform university disciplines, with special attention to economics, in order to attend to the value and faith dimensions of the environmental crisis, in Daly and Cobb, *For the Common Good* (Boston: Beacon Press, 1989), 25-43. Steven C. Rockefeller has created model syllabi for college instruction in "Religion and the Ecological Conscience," in *Greening the Curriculum: A Guide to Environmental Studies in the Liberal Arts*, edited by Jonathan Collett and Stephen Karakashian, (Covelo, CA: Island Press, 1995). Descriptions of four innovative programs of study in Christian theology and the environment may be found in Philip N. Joranson and Ken Butigan *Cry of the Environment* (Santa Fe, NM: Bear and Co., 1984), 441-56. As of 1995, six North American centers for Christian theological education (Appalachian Ministries Educational Resource Center, Lutheran Northwest Theological Seminary, United Theological Seminary, Seattle University Institute for Theological Studies, St. Thomas University, and the School of Theology at Claremont) had agreed to work together under the auspices of the Program in Theological Education to Meet the Environmental Crisis to further the study of eco-justice. The programs of these institutions, and the ways each theological discipline is pursuing the subject, are reviewed in Dieter T. Hessel, ed. *Theology for Earth Community: A Field Guide* (Maryknoll, NY: Orbis Books, 1996).

Bibliographic Survey: 1961–1993

1

Historical and Cultural Studies

Cultures and their histories form the contexts for eco-justice issues and are sources of both problems and solutions. Works in this section are primarily descriptive analyses of environmental attitudes and their origins and development as they have influenced or been influenced by religious beliefs and touch on social-justice concerns. Lynn White Jr.'s classic essay "The Historical Roots of Our Ecologic Crisis" and the varied responses to it are central to this section, but descriptions of historical figures, historical case studies, and the beliefs and practices of non-Western cultures are also included in this section.

001 Baer, Richard A., Jr. "Ecology, Religion, and the American Dream." *American Ecclesiastical Review* 165 (1971): 43-59.

> Baer claims that modern Americans have become trapped in the Protestant work ethic; they glorify, but do not enjoy God. Only those who experience the grace of God can radically transform their environmentally harmful lifestyles to lifestyles which give life. Environmentalists need to be wary of simple explanations for the environmental crisis and of separating the environmental crisis from other socio-political crises.

002 Black, John. *The Dominion of Man: The Search for Ecological Responsibility.* Edinburgh: Edinburgh University Press, 1970.

> This remains an informative historical study of important (and somewhat neglected) concepts for eco-justice—those of property rights, the role of the state, and the relation of both of these to Jewish and Christian tradition. Identifying the notion of human dominion as central to the Western worldview and rooted in the Judeo-Christian scriptures, Black, Professor of Natural Resources at Edinburgh, explores the means by which its exploitative and self-destructive potential has been held in check. Important among these is the idea of stewardship—humanity's accountability to God for its management of creation. Throughout the Middle Ages stewardship included responsibility for the social effects of the acquisition and use of property, but with the rise of capitalism religious restrictions were relaxed and the state came to be the guarantor of private property rights. Today there are increased state ownership and regulation of property for the sake of the public good. Black explores the histories of related ideas pertaining to population increase, progress, and posterity. He holds that concern for the future good of all humanity is the only motive that can moderate

the effects of human dominion. He concludes by arguing that we face, not sudden crisis, but continuous change and increasing instability as a result of population growth and its effects on ecological diversity and stability.

003   Coleman, William.   "Providence, Capitalism, and Environmental Degradation." *Journal of the History of Ideas* 37 *(1976):* 27-44.

Responding to Lewis W. Moncrief's critique (014) of Lynn White Jr.'s "Historical Roots" argument (026), Coleman locates Christianity's contribution to environmental degradation, not in its encouragement of medieval technology, but in the use of the doctrine of God's providence over nature and society to support the values of economic individualism, freedom, and growth that became dominant in Europe during the commercial and industrial revolutions of the late seventeenth century.

004   Cooper, Rob.   "Through the Soles of My Feet: A Personal View of Creation." In *Eco-Theology: Voices from South and North*, edited by David G. Hallman, 207-12. Geneva: WCC Publications; Maryknoll, NY: Orbis Books, 1994.

A Maori of Aotearoa-New Zealand expresses his people's sense of being "people of the land," participants in God's purpose for creation, responsible for loving and cooperating with the earth, and united with all other people in God. Cooper describes the Maori as "a politically powerless colored minority within our own country," subject to racial prejudice and at odds with the values of White culture. He nevertheless believes that they and other indigenous peoples may become catalysts for changing the self-destructive Western way of life.

005   Cuppitt, Don.   "Nature and Culture."   In *Humanity, Environment, and God*, edited by Neil Spurway, 33-45.   Oxford, and Cambridge, MA: Blackwell Publishers, 1993.

In a provocative post-modernist approach, Cuppitt contends that nature and culture have become indistinguishable: "nature" is a cultural construct and culture is part of the "natural" environment. This recognition is part of a broader shift from a Cartesian-existentialist to a Hegelian-environmental view of the self: the self is not independent of, but constituted by, its environment. Thus environmentalism belongs, not to the doctrine of creation which supports hierarchical value distinctions based on power and gender, but to the doctrine of redemption in which these distinctions are reversed and reconciled. This transition can mean the renewal of Christianity.

006   Derr, Thomas Sieger.   "Religion's Responsibility for the Ecological Crisis: An Argument Run Amok." *Worldview* 18 (January 1975): 39-45.

Following a thorough and careful review of Lynn White Jr.'s "Historical Roots" argument (026), its acceptance by environmentalists, and earlier arguments relating Christianity and technology (including White's earlier writings), Derr claims that the orthodox Christian position—and our only practical option—is "a responsible anthropocentrism, the dominion of man as trustee." While arguing that "Historical Roots" is not entirely hostile to Christianity, Derr believes White's rejection of traditional attitudes ultimately supports brutal, romantic, and antidemocratic environmental values.

007 Engel, J. Ronald. "Christianity, Democracy, Ecology." In *Earth Ethics Report*, vol. 1, no. 1, edited by George Bortnyk, 235-40. Seminole, FL: Earth Ethics Research Group, 1991.

In this paper written for the Earth Ethics Forum '91 held at Saint Leo College, Florida, Engel reflects on the lack of democratic citizenship displayed in the Gulf War and asks, "what is responsible for the loss of the moral content of the democratic ideal in Western society, and what will it take to redeem the promise of democracy as a vision of planetary citizenship?" His answer locates the problem in the conflicts among the democratic ideal, the Christian tradition, and the ecological movement. He enumerates many historical reasons for the conflict, including church repression of democratic movements, fear of a humanist or naturalistic faith replacing Christian teachings, withdrawal by Christian leaders from public life, and the ecologically based critiques of Christian domination. But, says Engel, these are "quarrels between members of the same family." The rest of the paper uncovers the mutual indebtedness of Christianity and democracy, the contributions of democracy to ecological thought, and the influence of ecology on the development of the democratic ideal in America. Engel believes that hope for "a transformed understanding of the democratic ideal lies in its further and more intense integration with the Christian and ecological myths."

008 Engel, J. Ronald. "Teaching the Eco-Justice Ethic: The Parable of Billerica Dam." *Christian Century* 104 (13 May 1987): 466-69.

Engel points out that the churches' success in teaching an eco-justice ethic depends on an ability to celebrate parables of eco-justice gathered from public civic traditions of participatory democracy. One such parable is Thoreau's story of Billerica Dam, which fosters a new perception of reality by drawing an analogy between the human struggle for liberation and nature's struggle for fulfillment. A slightly different version of this essay appears in *The Egg* 7 (Spring 1987): 8-11.

009 Fox, Matthew. "Creation-Centered Spirituality from Hildegard of Bingen to Julian of Norwich: Three Hundred Years of an Ecological Spirituality in the West." In *Cry of the Environment: Rebuilding the Christian Creation Tradition*, edited by Philip N. Joranson and Ken Butigan, 85-106. Santa Fe, NM: Bear and Co., 1984.

Fox, a Dominican scholar and Director of the Institute in Culture and Creation Spirituality at Holy Names College, Oakland, champions four Western medieval "Rhineland mystics"—Hildegard of Bingen, Mechtild of Magdeburg, Meister Eckhart, and Julian of Norwich—whom he finds to share six ecological themes: the goodness of creation, the goodness and blessing that Earth itself is, cosmic awareness, panentheism, the motherhood of God, and compassion understood as interdependence and justice-making. This tradition of spirituality, drawn from scripture, Celtic culture, and women's experience, contrasts with the dominant anti-ecological tradition stemming from St. Augustine.

010 Mastra, Wayan. "Environment and the Christian Faith: A Holistic Approach from Bali." *Evangelical Review of Theology* 17 (April 1993): 259-68.

Mastra, former Bishop and Chair of the Protestant Christian Church in Bali, lyrically describes the harmonious relations in Bali between human beings and nature and between different religious groups—relations he attributes to the island's benign environment. There, missionary activity is carried out by all groups but with a spirit of mutual respect, reflecting indigenous democratic values of agreement and consensus rather than Western ideas of majority rule. Contemplation, gratitude to God, compassion, and preservation of the integrity of creation are, for Mastra, hallmarks of the Balinese Christian's attitude toward nature.

011 McDonagh, Sean, and Vincent Busch. *Our Future a Mirage: Theological Reflections on Philippine Ecology.* Introduction by Brendon Lovett. Quezon City, Philippines: Claretian Publications, 1986.

Following Lovett's introduction, which criticizes the anthropocentric bias of most liberation theology, two Columban missioners working among tribal peoples describe and reflect on the exploitation of nature and people in the Philippines. McDonagh recounts the threats to the survival of tribal Filipinos, including loss of lands, militarization, "development," and assimilation. The destruction of indigenous societies and their habitat impoverishes the earth, human society, and the body of Christ. An adequate Christian response must be culturally appropriate to tribal peoples. In chapter 2 he argues that the "New Story" of the universe (T. Berry, Teilhard de Chardin) and a more adequate theology of creation drawing on Eastern and primal religions as well as Christianity, is needed to halt environmental destruction. The book's most original eco-justice contribution is the chapter by Vincent Busch who recounts how first Moses, then Israel, learned through wilderness experiences to live in harmony with the land and in solidarity with the poor and oppressed. Busch applies this pattern to the struggle for sustainability, self-reliance, political sovereignty, and debt relief for the people of the island of Mindanao.

012 McKay, Stan. "An Aboriginal Perspective on the Integrity of Creation." In *Eco-Theology: Voices from South and North*, edited by David G. Hallman, 213-17. Geneva: WCC Publications; Maryknoll, NY: Orbis Books, 1994.

McKay, a Cree who serves as moderator of the United Church of Canada, develops themes from Native North American spirituality that support the renewed ecumenical emphasis on creation. Because of their central notion of relationship to the whole creation and of sharing in the fullness of life, native peoples are in conflict with European ideas of ownership of land, individualistic Christian notions of salvation, and the pursuit of short-term economic gain. McKay elaborates on the key symbol of "the circle of life" as representing "the inclusive caring community in which individuals are respected and interdependence is recognized" and on associated ideas of cosmic order and faithful living as moving in creation's rhythms.

013 Merchant, Carolyn. *The Death of Nature: Women, Ecology, and the Scientific Revolution.* San Francisco: Harper and Row, 1980.

Bringing together an impressive body of research, this influential history of philosophy examines the transition from organicism to the machine as the dominant metaphor determining the modern worldview. It traces the progress of differing views of nature, seeing historical change as a consequence of both environmental change and of these views of nature interacting with culture. The linkage of both women's liberation and the ecology movement to egalitarianism is a uniting thread of the work. By the use of literary and artistic images as well as quotations from the major philosophers of the period of transformation, 1500-1700, Merchant connects the loss of the image of nature as a nurturing mother with the loss of normative constraints to technological manipulation and the emergent idea of human power over nature; shows the ecological consequences of such social-political events as the enclosure movement, and the social-political consequences of the drainage of fens; connects Bacon's ideas of natural manipulation with his classism and sexism; links witch-burning and the view of nature as disorder; links the subordination of women and the scientific views of biological generation; and traces the roots of ecology and improved social status for women to organicism. In an epilogue, Merchant connects ecology with such modern instances of the leveling of hierarchies as the Civil Rights movement and the Endangered Species Act. Though her analysis takes place within the mainstream of Western Christian culture, Christianity is noticeable in this work by its near-absence.

014 Moncrief, Lewis W. "The Cultural Basis of Our Environmental Crisis." *Science* 170 (30 October 1970): 508-12.

In this counterproposal to Lynn White Jr.'s argument (026) that the Judeo-Christian tradition is the cause of the environmental crisis, Moncrief argues that religion's role has at best been indirect. He maintains that the democratic and technological revolutions in Europe led to increasing and more equally distributed wealth and to urbanization, which led to increased pollution. In America, widespread individual resource ownership and the frontier experience contributed to the environmental crisis. According to Moncrief, three characteristics of the present American scene impede solutions to the crisis: the absence of personal moral direction, the inadequacy of existing institutions, and an abiding faith in technology. Reprinted in Barbour, ed. (259), pp. 31-42. For a critique, see Coleman (003).

015 Mugambi, J. N. K. *God, Humanity, and Nature in Relation to Justice and Peace.* Church and Society Documents, Sept. 1987, no. 2. Geneva: World Council of Churches, 1987.

Seven loosely connected chapters consider the ecumenical movement, religious experience, land economics, science, and religion from an East African perspective; three are of particular interest for eco-justice. Chapter 2 argues that justice, peace, and the integrity of creation are closely interrelated in the Bible and must be dealt by the World Council of Churches as a whole and globally. Chapter 4 contrasts the ways that traditional African and post-colonial understandings of matter, duration, and space affect land values and suggests the need for a new system of valuation more appropriate to African traditions of exchange through barter and of ownership through holding land in trust. The final chapter claims that the reorientation of science and technology from supports of social and environmental degradation to supports of reconstruction and reconciliation requires insights from "marginal" religious and cultural traditions.

016 Redekop, Calvin, and Wilmar Stahl. "The Impact on the Environment of the Evangelization of the Native Tribes of the Paraguayan Chaco." *Evangelical Review of Theology* 17 (April 1993): 269-83.

Redekop and Stahl provide a useful case study of the ambiguous consequences of the economic development that often accompanies mission work. When the Mennonite settlers in the Paraguayan Chaco undertook to evangelize the nomadic, hunter-gatherer Indians, they also introduced a more settled, technological way of life and precipitated a population explosion. Environmental pollution, habitat destruction, and species extinctions have resulted—problems that are just beginning to be addressed.

017 Santmire, H. Paul. "Historical Dimensions of the American Crisis." In *Western Man and Environmental Ethics: Attitudes Toward Nature and Technology,* edited by Ian Barbour, 66-92. Reading, MA: Addison-Wesley Publishing Co., 1973.

Santmire adapts his discussion (in *Brother Earth*) (144) of American attitudes toward nature and civilization, adding a Marxist analysis of their economic functions to his biblical-existential interpretation of their roots in the anxiety of historical existence. This article first appeared in *Dialog* 9 (Summer 1970): 175-92.

018 Santmire, H. Paul. "Reflections on the Alleged Ecological Bankruptcy of Western Theology." *Anglican Theological Review* 57 (April 1975): 131-52.

Santmire critiques the "conventional ecological wisdom" that blames the ecological crisis on the classical Western theological tradition. He argues that the "*in*clusive the-anthropology" of the Reformers became the "*ex*clusive the-anthropology" of most modern Protestant theology (including liberation and political, but not feminist, theology) through the influence of natural science, Kantian philosophy, and modern industrialism. He charges that by blaming the biblical tradition, environmentalists avoid social analysis and criticism and ignore important resources of that tradition, including its emphasis on social justice.

019 Sindima, Harvey. "Community of Life." *Ecumenical Review* 41 (October 1989): 537-51.

Sindima, a theologian from Malawi, describes how the imposition of Western cultural views destroyed the ability of African peoples to understand their world and organize their society through their traditional cosmology which had focused on life as creative and self-transcending and as embracing divinity, humans, and the rest of creation. He maintains that the connectedness of life is the foundation for an understanding of community and justice which encompasses people and nature, and he proposes that the church's mission is to proclaim these ecological concepts as God's vision for creation, actualized and declared by Jesus, a model for the transformation of society. Reprinted in (066), pp. 137-47.

020 Sittler, Joseph. "An Aspect of American Religious Experience." In *Proceedings of the Twenty-Sixth Annual Convention of the Catholic Theological Society of America*, vol. 26, 1-17, 1971.

Sittler explores the "structure of spirit" that prevents Americans from dealing effectively with issues of environment and social justice. American religious experience, he claims, has been shaped by the experience of seemingly unlimited space; even now, technology provides Americans with a prolongation of that frontier experience. The mentality and spirit thus nurtured is inadequate for dealing with the problems that arise in the "closely-woven, ecologically integrated, and delicate structure" of contemporary life. Humanity needs instead an eschatological consciousness of the limits of life in time and a "theology of grace and order" that comes to terms with life "where one is and must remain."

021 Stewart, Claude Y., Jr. "Factors Conditioning the Christian Creation Consciousness." In *Cry of the Environment: Rebuilding the Christian Creation Tradition*, edited by Philip N. Joranson and Ken Butigan, 107-31. Santa Fe, NM: Bear and Co., 1984.

Stewart identifies a few of the representative, complex, and interrelated factors causing the "dis-gracing" of nature in modern Christian consciousness. "Trajectories" within Christianity itself include: the priority of the personal, humans as agents of change, otherworldly aspirations, concern for social justice, and God as unchanging. Factors within Western culture include: atomism, dualism, a "cash value" syndrome, suppression of women, and secularization. Christian reenvisionment of nature requires preserving the salutary aspects of this heritage while transcending the deleterious, and finding "metaphors of glory" to replace current "metaphors of degradation."

022 Testerman, Dennis E. "Missionary Earthkeeping: Glimpses of the Past, Visions of the Future." In *Missionary Earthkeeping*, edited by Calvin B. DeWitt and Ghillean T. Prance, 11-44. Macon, GA: Mercer University Press, 1992.

The author reviews the history of the constructive and destructive impacts that Christian missions from the Roman Empire through the Middle Ages (especially as carried out by Benedictine monks) and into modern times (usually in cooperation with European colonialism) have had on the land and those who live from it. He concludes that the theological and university education of missionaries needs to sensitize them to the environmental dimension of their work.

023 Tinker, George E. "The Integrity of Creation: Restoring Trinitarian Balance." *Ecumenical Review* 41 (October 1989): 527-36.

Tinker, an Osage-Cherokee, asserts that awareness of the sacredness and interdependence of all creation is one of the gifts that Native Americans bring to Christianity. He argues that an adequate theology of creation is the indispensable foundation for the pursuit of justice and peace. Giving creation priority in theology is also necessary for maintaining the trinitarian balance of the ecumenical creeds as opposed to the Fall-redemption Christomonism of most mainline denominations in the United States, a stance he believes has contributed to the oppression of native peoples.

024 Tinker, George E. "Native Americans and the Land: The End of Living, and the Beginning of Survival." In *Lift Every Voice: Constructing Christian Theologies from the Underside,* edited by Susan Brooks Thistlethwaite and Mary Potter Engel, 141-51. New York: Harper Collins Publishers, 1990.

A Native American of "mixed blood" who is also a Christian, Tinker is heartened by the fact that tribal spirituality is finding a place in Native American churches. He views his essay contrasting the worldview of White Americans (which he describes as being based on time) to that of Native Americans (whose worldview is based on the sacrality of space) as "a first step in this process of indigenous theology." The goal of native religion is to live within the context of a particular community and that community's geography rather than to achieve personal transformation.

025 Weigand, Paul. "Escape from the Birdbath: A Reinterpretation of St. Francis as a Model for the Ecological Movement." In *Cry of the Environment: Rebuilding the Christian Creation Tradition*, edited by Philip N. Joranson and Ken Butigan, 148-57. Santa Fe, NM: Bear and Co., 1984.

Maintaining that Francis of Assisi's "Canticle of Brother Sun" resulted from its author having followed the poor and broken Jesus Christ, Weigand criticizes Lynn White Jr.'s (026) and René Dubos's interpretations of Francis as a pantheist or naive preservationist. Francis, Weigand believes, upset the dominant "marketized" spirituality which excluded the propertyless, enabling the laity to approach God through work and nature apart from the monastic system. Weigand regards Francis's ethic of reverence for life, radical simplicity, and generosity as perfectly suited to effect the ecological recovery of a world scarred by insatiable wants.

026   White, Lynn, Jr.   "The Historical Roots of Our Ecologic Crisis." *Science* 155 (10 March 1967): 1203-7.

One of the most frequently referred-to articles in the literature dealing with the combined subject of theology and ecology, White's essay touched off a continuing debate on the responsibility of Christianity for the degradation of the environment. White suggests that the ecologic crisis, which is, he says, "the product of an emerging, entirely novel, democratic culture," calls for an examination of the presuppositions that underlie modern technology and science. He finds that the scientific leadership of the West goes back beyond both the Scientific and Industrial Revolutions to the Middle Ages during which time a new attitude of human mastery over nature was manifested in agricultural techniques and calender depictions. This attitude was conditioned by religious beliefs, specifically by the story of creation inherited by Christianity from Judaism, which "not only established a dualism of man and nature but also insisted that it is God's will that man exploit nature for his proper ends." Because of its Christian foundation and because "Christianity is the most anthropocentric religion the world has seen," the present day relationship of humans to nature is characterized by human assumption of superiority. "We must find a new religion, or rethink our old one," White declares. He suggests that the way of St. Francis of Assisi who tried to substitute "a democracy of all God's creatures" for human "monarchy over creation" provides a direction through which a religious remedy for our ecologic crisis may come. The article is reprinted in several sources including *Western Man and Environmental Ethics* (259) pp. 18-30, a collection which also contains "Continuing the Conversation," pp. 55-64, a reply by White to his critics. See Moncrief (014) and Coleman (003).

In addition to the works annotated in this chapter, readers interested in historical and cultural studies may wish to consult the following entries located elsewhere in the bibliography: 059, 077, 080, 155, 156, 227, 240, 246, 248, 249, 250, 252, 361, 377, 387, 462, 464.

2

Biblical Interpretation

Studies of the Hebrew and Christian scriptures contribute to the historical and cultural analyses of the previous section, and are basic resources for much of the constructive and critical eco-justice theology and ethics in the following sections. These entries are scholarly studies of biblical themes and texts that bear on eco-justice issues. Recurring topics are scriptural views of the relations between God, humanity, and nature; the ordering of creation and society; salvation history and eschatology; justice for the poor and the land; and covenant.

027 Anderson, Bernhard W. "Exodus Typology in Second Isaiah." In *Israel's Prophetic Heritage*, edited by Bernhard W. Anderson and Walter Harrelson, 177-95. New York: Harper and Row, 1962.

> Although this article does not address contemporary eco-justice issues specifically, Anderson's scholarship provides biblical grounds for the connection of creation and liberation. Anderson argues the close intertwining of creation and redemption in Second Isaiah: "Yahweh's creative acts belong to the history of salvation. . . . His redemptive acts are acts of creation; and his creative acts are acts of history." He says that the prophet of Second Isaiah drew the primeval, mythological traditions of creation into the eschatological, historical tradition of Exodus and its typological mode of thought and made the prophecy of a "new exodus" the counterpart of the first exodus simultaneously portrayed in the mythopoeic colors of creation. For a related argument see Landes (049).

028 Anderson, Bernhard W. *From Creation to New Creation: Old Testament Perspectives*, edited with a foreword by Walter Brueggemann. Minneapolis: Augsburg Fortress Publishers, 1994.

> This collection of fourteen essays by Anderson covers work published between 1955 and 1993. In his foreword Walter Brueggemann credits Anderson for having "spent his long and distinguished career reflecting upon the creation texts, keeping alive the potential of creation theology in the long period of scholarship when creation was neglected." Consistent throughout the essays is Anderson's concern for the way biblical language should be understood and how it differs from science. He is also concerned that the doctrine of creation be viewed as part of the larger narrative context of the Old and New Testaments and he stresses that it is best interpreted within a context of worship. Anderson's discussion of human dominion over nature (chapter 7) stresses the democratization of

the *imago Dei* in the Priestly creation story and the call to be responsible for nature which is entailed by a humankind made in the image of God. His discussion of the flood narrative (chapter 9) emphasizes that the Noachic covenant is fundamentally an ecological covenant (Earth is created for a variety of living beings; it is meant to be a habitat for human and nonhuman creatures equally) which endorses the same call to human responsibility inherent in the creation story. See also (029).

029   Anderson, Bernhard W.   "Introduction: Mythopoeic and Theological Dimensions of Biblical Creation Faith." In *Creation in the Old Testament*, edited by Bernhard W. Anderson, 1-24. Philadelphia: Fortress Press; London: SPCK, 1984.

After first establishing that poetic form and literary function must guide biblical interpretation, Anderson discusses the role of creation theology in the various strains of Old Testament tradition. He argues that in Israel's earliest poetry "creation and redemption belong together, as the obverse and reverse of the same theological coin." In a thesis relevant to eco-justice concerns, Anderson argues against the view of Gerhard von Rad that there is a sharp separation of creation from soteriology, maintaining instead that in Davidic royal covenant theology, the security, health, and peace of society depend upon the cosmic created order. He discusses Psalm 104 which he says shows creation as a continuing sustaining activity of God. Also, in the priestly creation story of Genesis the cosmos is sustained in being by the Creator. Reprinted in (028), pp. 75-96.

030   Austin, Richard Cartwright.   *Hope for the Land: Nature in the Bible.* Vol. 3 of *Environmental Theology.* Atlanta: John Knox Press, 1988.

By tracing five biblical themes, Austin shows the Hebrew and Christian scriptures expressing a "biblical ecology" of moral relationships among God, humanity, and the earth: God's *liberation* of and identification with the oppressed includes oppressed land; God's *creativity* is shared with all creatures, which are called to creative moral response; the *sabbath ecology* of the sabbatical and jubilee laws institutionalizes and gives land and living things rights as members of the covenant community; stories of temptation and the *Fall* illustrate the connection between sin and environmental degradation; and biblical *judgment and hope* embrace nature and envision the rebuilding of moral ecology in history. Austin creatively connects Old and New Testament stories (including those of David, Solomon, and Jesus), morality and aesthetics, and themes of social justice, environment, and sexuality.

031   Austin, Richard Cartwright.   "Rights for Life: Rebuilding Human Relationships with the Land." In *Theology of the Land*, edited by Bernard F. Evans and Gregory D. Cusack, 103-26. Collegeville, MN: Liturgical Press, 1987.

Austin describes the "moral ecology" of the Bible by focusing on the Sabbath tradition as encompassing both social justice and the welfare of all creatures and as the key for interpreting God's creation of the world. Applying this biblical ecology to America today, Austin proposes a human right of access to nature; re-opening the frontier to homesteading; and constitutional protection for all species, major life systems, and singular natural features.

032 Bahr, Ann Marie B. "God's Family and Flocks: Remarks on Ownership in the Fourth Gospel." In *Covenant for a New Creation: Ethics, Religion, and Public Policy*, edited by Carol S. Robb and Carl J. Casebolt, 91-106. Maryknoll, NY: Orbis Books, 1991.

Bahr uncovers differences in the meaning of "ownership" in the gospel of John and in contemporary culture. Ownership in contemporary culture implies private rights, self-interest, and control; in the Fourth Gospel ownership entails responsibility to the wider community, caring, and a familial relationship with the earth and its creatures. Bahr stresses the ecological benefits of a recovery of the older meaning rather than its justice connections, although the latter are implied in the argument.

033 Berry, Wendell. "The Gift of Good Land." In his *The Gift of Good Land: Further Essays Cultural and Agricultural*, 267-81. San Francisco: North Point Press, 1981.

Using the biblical story of the promised land and quoting from Milton's *Paradise Lost*, Berry argues that "the gift of good land" requires us to be good stewards—to pursue right livelihood, doing our everyday work skillfully and responsibly. The antithesis of such stewardship is "industrial heroism" which is guilty of abstraction and hubris, and which leads to our exile from the "great neighborhood of creation" and allies us with the principle of destruction.

034 Birch, Bruce C., and Larry L. Rasmussen. *The Predicament of the Prosperous.* Philadelphia: Westminster Press, 1978.

In a most thorough and discriminating survey of biblical resources for an eco-justice ethic, the authors argue that the American church has departed from biblical imperatives and has sanctioned the dichotomies of rich/poor and humanity/nature that make modern society socially and ecologically "unaffordable." The transition to a society that overcomes these dichotomies will be costly and painful, and will require changes in basic perceptions as well as institutional change. Certain biblical themes provide resources for the needed new perception, although *deliverance* (salvation history) becomes distorted and dangerous when appropriated by the powerful. The themes of *wisdom* (responsible freedom), *creation* (including a relational theology of nature), *prophetic judgment*, and *hope* are more appropriate. The tensions between these images are resolved in the idea of *shalom* (peace as wholeness in all creation) and its embodiment in Christ. Facing the future requires the privileged to view history "from below" and to accept guilt both for complicity in present evil and for the consequences of the risks involved in change. Our "neighbor" is past and future as well as present, nonhuman as well as human. The American church must become an experimental "anticipatory community" of prayer and doing justice.

035 Brueggemann, Walter. "Land: Fertility and Justice." In *Theology of the Land*, edited by Bernard F. Evans and Gregory D. Cusack, 41-68. Collegeville, MN: Liturgical Press, 1987.

Brueggemann reviews three land practices that are condemned in the Bible as unjust and as causing the land to lose its fertility: the altering of boundary lines to give land surpluses to the rich and deprive the poor of land; land monopolization;

and defilement of land by wrongful use. He presents the Bible's alternative form of land management which is based on land as inalienable patrimony, land redistribution, and freeing the land from contamination.

036 Brueggemann, Walter. *The Land: Place as Gift, Promise, and Challenge in Biblical Faith.* Philadelphia: Fortress Press, 1977.

Brueggemann argues that, contrary to interpretations that split history from nature and time from space, land is a central category in the Bible. The Bible is concerned with the issue of being displaced and yearning for roots in a place of security, wholeness, joy, and prosperity; it always speaks of God, people, and land together. Brueggemann organizes the biblical narrative into three histories: promise into the land; management into exile; and new promise in exile that culminates in kingdom. In each, land, which has its own claim, history, and voice, is given by God to the landless as a gift and as a part of the covenant of justice and freedom. When land is abused and treated as an object of utility and management and the covenant is forgotten, the land is lost. In the New Testament, the crucifixion and resurrection change the dialectic of land loss and the gift of land into a new theological and ethical key. Although Brueggemann does not develop the explicitly ecological dimension of his thesis, this is an excellent and provocative introduction to the extensive literature on the ethics, sociology, and theology of land in the Bible.

037 Brueggemann, Walter. "On Land-Losing and Land-Receiving." *Dialog* (St. Paul, MN) 19 (Summer 1980): 166-73.

Recapitulating his argument (036) that land in the Bible is at once a gift, the continued possession of which depends on keeping God's law, and a possession which tempts Israel to disobedience that results in exile, Brueggemann adds the contrast of the Biblical sense of land as the guaranteed cosmic order of creation and as the precarious, concrete territory that demands obedience. He also shows the various ways these two senses interact in biblical texts. Brueggemann hints at the eco-justice implications of this distinction, noting the relevance of "cosmic order" to ecological concerns, on the one hand, and the link between injustice and land loss, on the other.

038 Brueggemann, Walter. "Theses on Land in the Bible." In *Erets: Land: The Church and Appalachian Land Issues*, edited by Davis Yeuell, 4-13. Amesville, OH: Coalition for Appalachian Ministry, 1984.

In this address presented at a 1983 Coalition for Appalachian Ministry seminar, Brueggemann contrasts two ways of translating the Hebrew word *erets*—as 'earth' or as 'land'. Translated 'earth' the word implies something ultimate, pure, and belonging to God alone. Translated 'land' it refers to something owned and conflicted that participates in the ambiguities and injustices of political and economic power. He sees as "the trickiest question of Biblical interpretation in the ball-park" holding together the two translations so that neither is permitted to nullify the other. A lack of the concept of *erets* as earth leads to unbridled self-seeking, violence, and totalitarianism, while a lack of the concept of *erets* as land leads to the legitimation of present land distribution, withdrawal from the political process, and a siphoning off of the rage of the dispossessed. Brueggemann, who maintains that the American church "most needs" to learn to read the Bible as a conflict document about land, characterizes the community of Israel as an attempt to organize life outside of a prevailing land monopoly by a group with an alternative notion of land tenure, and he sees the New Testament as the promise of a new land management.

039 Brueggemann, Walter. *Using God's Resources Wisely: Isaiah and Urban Possibility.* Louisville, KY: Westminster/John Knox Press, 1993.

Calling the book of Isaiah "the great urban document of the Bible," a "public theology" addressed to an entire population rather than a religious elite, Brueggemann applies its meaning to the urban cities of today. He sees the book as being about resource management and as pointing to the full sharing of resources with one's neighbors as well as to the full sharing of political power with the powerless. The Sabbath requirement he interprets as a rejection of commodity success based on utilitarian value in favor of neighborliness. Importantly for eco-justice concerns, Brueggemann sees Isaiah as positing a linkage between social transformation and the reordering of nature, and he cites Amazon forests being cleared and United States' agricultural land being converted from crop to beef production as modern examples of this connection.

040 Cunanan, Jose Pepz M. "The Prophet of Environment and Development." In *Ecotheology: Voices from South and North*, edited by David G. Hallman, 13-27. Geneva: WCC Publications; Maryknoll, NY: Orbis Books, 1994.

This study of the book of Joel by a United Methodist minister from the Philippines finds the prophet outlining a seven-point program of environmental-development awareness and action which includes awareness of crisis, repentance, organization, warning of impending judgment and destruction, restoration and renewal, participation in transforming society, and political, economic, and social components of the ecological and development agenda. Cunanan emphasizes that the "prophets of environment" must struggle on behalf of basic human needs against those who control resources and technology. This article appeared previously in *Tugon* 12 (1992): 295-314.

041 Duchrow, Ulrich, and Gerhard Liedke. *Shalom: Biblical Perspectives on Creation, Justice, and Peace.* Geneva: WCC Publications, 1989.

This view of the conciliar process of Justice, Peace, and the Integrity of Creation (JPIC) from a European perspective is informed by liberationist readings of the Bible. The authors survey the church in the global context of "a destroyed creation, injustice, and no peace," providing biblical perspectives on each of these problem areas and quick surveys of how later church teaching and practice have dealt with each. They emphasize that understanding must begin with the fact of suffering and violence rather than with the "good creation," that God suffers with nature and human beings, and that the human task is "reducing violence—advancing life." Creation, justice, and peace find their ultimate unity in the biblical concept of *shalom*, meaning 'peace' or 'wholeness'. In an effort to discern how the churches can become more committed to restoring *shalom*, the authors examine different historical ways of being "the church"—the Jesus-style peace church, the liturgical-eucharistic-contemplative church, and the liberation church. Appendices give examples of the "Shalom Process" as it has functioned in actual churches.

042 Dyrness, William. "Stewardship of the Earth in the Old Testament." In *Tending the Garden: Essays on the Gospel and the Earth*, edited by Wesley Granberg-Michaelson, 50-65. Grand Rapids, MI: William B. Eerdmans Publishing Co., 1987.

The author explains that covenant in the Old Testament is based upon the recognition that when human beings respect God's moral order the earth is fruitful and the poor are cared for; when they fail to respect it, both persons and land suffer ecological disaster and social oppression.

043   Falcke, Heino.   "Biblical Aspects of the Process of Mutual Commitment." *Ecumenical Review* 38 (1986): 257-64.

Falcke describes the ancient Hebrew "renewal of the covenant" ceremony as a basis for understanding covenanting for justice, peace, and the integrity of creation.   The divine covenant with God's people does not itself need renewal; what the ceremony can renew is our grasp of what the covenant means for us today. The ceremony includes: remembering God's acts, proclaiming God's will (here Falcke notes the connections made by the covenant tradition between justice, peace, and the integrity of creation), rejecting idols, celebrating, and opening up the covenant to those outside the covenanting community.

044   Fretheim, Terence E.   "The Plagues as Ecological Signs of Historical Disaster." *Journal of Biblical Literature* 110 (1991): 385-96.

Though not explicitly connected to contemporary eco-justice issues, this article, by means of a close analysis of the Exodus narrative, examines the relation of the just ordering of society to the creation of the world in biblical thought.   Fretheim argues that Pharaoh's oppression of Israel is "antilife and anticreation," for Israel is the point at which God has begun to actualize the promise of creation.   Thus the plagues, as disorders in nonhuman spheres of creation, are the effect of Pharaoh's disruption of the moral order and an expression of God's consequent judgment.

045   Fretheim, Terence E.   "The Reclamation of Creation: Redemption and Law in Exodus." *Interpretation* 45 (1991): 354-65.

Fretheim contends that the usual approach of interpreting Genesis in the light of Exodus minimizes creation and distorts redemption.   Reversing that order shows that redemption serves, fulfills, and reclaims creation; that creation is dynamic; and that the law at Sinai is a re-presentation and specification for Israel of the law already in creation.   Eco-justice implications are suggested by Fretheim's argument that the Exodus was the triumph of God's creative power over anti-creational forces; that cosmic and social orders are symbiotically linked; and that a proper creation theology challenges, rather than supports, the status quo.

046   Gebara, Ivone.   "The Face of Transcendence as a Challenge to the Reading of the Bible in Latin America."   In *Searching the Scriptures*, edited by Elizabeth Schüssler Fiorenza, Vol. 1, *A Feminist Introduction*, 172-86.   New York: Crossroad Publishing Co., 1993.

Gebara believes that attempts to present God as liberator of the poor have been unsuccessful in practice, since women remain the victims of men's war games, and that, in spite of feminist readings of the Bible, a patriarchal image of God as a self-contained being continues to oppress women and the poor.   She suggests, however, that the Bible can be read so as to make it an "ally" of Latin American women in their struggle for right relations with other humans and the earth.   She foregrounds experience of love toward those who are different and in difficult straits, the experience of which motivated the prophets and early participants in the Jesus movement.   For Gebara, resurrection understood as "a transcendence of situations in which death, murder, injustice, or destruction of a people, a group, or a person has been present" is the key to understanding Christianity.

047 Gottwald, Norman K. "The Biblical Mandate for Eco-Justice Action." In *For Creation's Sake: Preaching, Ecology, and Justice*, edited by Dieter T. Hessel, 32-44. Philadelphia: Geneva Press, 1985.

On the basis of an interpretation of the religion of early Israel as an ideology that supported an agrarian social revolution committed to a society of equals living in mutual respect and just order, Gottwald concludes that there is a biblical mandate for eco-justice.

048 Kehm, George H. "The New Story: Redemption as Fulfillment of Creation." In *After Nature's Revolt: Eco-Justice and Theology*, edited by Dieter T. Hessel, 89-106. Minneapolis: Augsburg Fortress Publishers, 1992.

Noting along the way the social-justice dimensions of covenant and eschatology, Kehm surveys biblical texts dealing with the Noachic covenant; Israel and the land; and the eschatological teachings of the prophets, Jesus, the Pauline and deutero-Pauline epistles, and the book of Revelation. He argues that the ultimate salvation of the whole creation is essential to the Christian story, and that cosmic redemption is theologically necessary to secure the intrinsic value of creation and its eternal value for God.

049 Landes, George. "Creation and Liberation." In *Creation in the Old Testament*, edited by Bernhard W. Anderson, 135-51. Philadelphia: Fortress Press; London: SPCK, 1984.

In this article originally published in *Union Seminary Quarterly Review* 33 (Winter 1978): 78-99, Landes discusses the relationship of creation faith to liberation faith in the Old Testament, maintaining that cosmic creation is the crucial supposition of God's liberating work in history. Recent theology, which tends to ignore creation and its connection with liberation, tends also to lose a sense of the transcendent power of God to deal with evil, of the liberating work of God through the forces of creation, and of the scope of God's liberating work for both the oppressed and the oppressors. Important features of biblical creation faith for liberation thought and action include a clear demarcation between human and divine activity and an understanding that God's work sets the tone and limits for liberation work. See Soelle (318), pp. 9-10 for a negative evaluation of Landes' contribution. For a related argument see Anderson (027).

050 Liedke, Gerhard. "Solidarity in Conflict." In *Faith and Science in an Unjust World: Report of the World Council of Churches' Conference on Faith, Science and the Future*, Vol. 1, *Plenary Presentations,* edited by Roger L. Shinn, 73-80. Geneva: World Council of Churches, 1980.

Liedke distinguishes between specifically Christian and generally human responses to the "rupture" of humans from nature, and he applies social conflict theory to human/nature relations. On the basis of Romans 8, Liedke claims that Christians make visible the hope of the rest of creation by reducing suffering through realizing the sustainable society. The more general human situation is described in Genesis 1 and 9, where the intended harmony between humans and land animals is broken by violence, and human dominion must be exercised under conditions of social and ecological conflict in such a way that nature is protected.

051   Mihoc, Vasile.   "Aspects of the Biblical Theology of Creation."   In *Justice, Peace, and the Integrity of Creation: Insights from Orthodoxy*, edited by Gennadios Limouris, 94-99.   Geneva: WCC Publications, 1990.

Mihoc, an Orthodox theologian, explains that Genesis describes humans as being in full solidarity with creation, as well as partners with God in their own development.   It also attests to their equality and solidarity with one another.   Sin disrupted not only the harmony between humans and nature, but human solidarity.   Humans must participate in Christ's work of re-creation as peacemakers.   Jesus' messianic way of service and sacrifice shows how the power of dominion is to be exercised; this way is opposite to that of the world's leaders who rely on military strength and oppression.

052   Miller, Patrick D., Jr.   "The Gift of God: The Deuteronomic Theology of the Land."   *Interpretation* 23 (October 1969): 451-65.

Although not focused on ecological issues, this is an early statement of the Deuteronomic theology of land's relevance to contemporary societies.   In Miller's interpretation, while the human desire for land as home and a source of the means of life is proper, land ultimately is God's gift; pride of ownership is secondary; and the gift is communal as well as individual.   The land and its benefits must be shared with all who dwell in it; justice and righteousness define, and are the pragmatic conditions for, a good life in a good land.

053   Murray, Robert.   *The Cosmic Covenant: Biblical Themes of Justice, Peace, and the Integrity of Creation*.   Heythrop Monographs 7.   London: Sheed and Ward, 1992.

In a fascinating study of the biblical theme of covenant as it relates to order in cosmos, nature, and society (a theme neglected in part because of overemphasis on Deuteronomic theology, according to the author), Murray marshals biblical evidence for Israel's belief in a cosmic harmony established by God at creation but under attack by hostile supernatural powers.   Humans (particularly the king) collaborate in preserving cosmic harmony by doing justice and mercy and performing ritual actions.   He details in successive chapters the covenantal binding of the cosmic elements at creation; the breach of this covenant by rebellious divine beings; God's re-establishment of the "eternal covenant"; the effects of the breach on earthly society, agriculture, and economics; the preservation of cosmic order through ritual; relations between humans and animals in the "kingdom of peace"; and the development of these themes in Judaism and Christianity.   Murray proposes that ritual and a democratized concept of kingship can be "imaginatively transposed" to address present-day concerns for justice, peace, and environment.   The Bible teaches that "you are brothers and sisters of every other human being, and fellow-creatures of everything else in the cosmos; you have no *right* to exploit or destroy, but you have *duties* to all, under God to whom you are responsible."

054   Pobee, John S.   "Creation Faith and Responsibility for the World."   *Journal of Theology for Southern Africa* 50 (March 1985): 16-26.

Pobee, a teacher of New Testament at the University of Ghana, draws out the implications of biblical affirmations about creation and *imago Dei* for issues of environment and social justice (including population growth and authentic development).   In addition to arguing that human dominion must be responsible to God's purposes for creation, and that humanity's relation to nature should be like that of a gardener and artist, Pobee emphasizes the communitarian aspect of *imago Dei* over the cult of individualism, the ethic of economic growth, and the neglect of the human dignity of the poor and marginalized.

055 Ruether, Rosemary Radford. "The Biblical Vision of the Ecological Crisis." *Christian Century* 95 (22 November 1978): 1129-32.

Ruether dismisses the Western models proposed as religious solutions to the ecological crisis—the neoanimistic model represented by Theodore Roszak and the Protestant stewardship model—because both fail to address the underlying economic injustice at the root of the crisis, seeing the problem as one of enmity between "man" and "nature" rather than the consequence of an exploitative relationship between classes, races, and nations in natural resource use. She suggests that the foundation for a theology of eco-justice lies in the vision of the Hebrew prophets for whom the despoilation of nature and the exploitation of persons in society are part of one reality and one covenant.

056 Santmire, H. Paul. "Genesis Creation Narratives Revisited: Themes for a Global Age." *Interpretation* 45 (1991): 366-79.

Santmire's interpretation of Genesis within a cosmic eschatological context suggests some implications of his analysis of metaphors and motifs in *The Travail of Nature: The Ambiguous Ecological Promise of Christian Theology* (Philadelphia: Fortress Press, 1985) for justice concerns, although they are relatively undeveloped. His universalizing hermeneutic of "the Future and the Fullness Thereof" is based on the complementary Old Testament theologies of blessing manifest in the fullness of the cosmos and deliverance to a land of fecundity and justice. Read through this hermeneutic, Santmire argues, Genesis 1 and 2 present a framework for the church's thinking about global issues of justice and environment that is nonanthropocentric and oriented toward *shalom*.

057 Schillebeeckx, Edward. "Kingdom of God: Creation and Salvation." In his *Interim Report on the Books "Jesus" and "Christ,"* 105-24. New York: Crossroad Publishing Co., 1981.

The author describes Jesus Christ as confirming and fulfilling the Old Testament Yahwist interpretation of Adam in which God's trust in creation is conceived as trust in humankind. As the perfect human response to God's unconditional trust in humankind, Jesus warrants continued belief in God as Creator in face of human apostasy. Mystical liberation, political liberation, and "collective asceticism" in the face of the environmental crisis all belong to human salvation revealed in Christ.

058 Swartley, Willard M. "Biblical Sources of Stewardship." In *The Earth is the Lord's: Essays on Stewardship*, edited by Mary Evelyn Jegen and Bruno V. Manno, 22-43. New York: Paulist Press, 1978.

This article reviews the theme of stewardship in the Bible and the church fathers. In the Old Testament, the earth belongs to the Creator, who has entrusted it to humanity to care for. When fallen humans seek independent dominion, ecological crisis and injustice result. Israel's stewardship is set in a covenant relationship with God in which God's ownership of the land and concern for justice is expressed in the laws of the Sabbath day and the sabbatical and jubilee years. Jesus' deeds fulfill these laws and embody the meaning of exercising stewardship as God's image. The teachings of Paul and the later church stress sharing with others, especially the poor.

059   Wink, Walter.   "Ecobible: The Bible and Eco-justice."   *Theology Today* 49
(January 1993): 465-77.

> In this gospel-based rationale of eco-justice, Wink draws on Riane Eisler's *The
> Chalice and the Blade* (San Francisco: Harper and Row, 1987) as well as his own
> and others' work to establish the message of Jesus as a critique of the "Domina-
> tion System" in which all dominations are linked—class and environmental, race
> and waste, women and nature.   The gospel "is a single message directed against
> domination in all its forms.   Hence the inspired coining of the term 'eco-justice':
> here in a single word the connection is made between social justice and justice to
> life in all its forms.   All justice is now ecological."

060   Wright, Chris.   "Biblical Reflections on Land."   *Evangelical Review of Theology*
17 (April 1993): 153-67.

> Wright organizes his reflections under the headings: "God's Earth: Reflections
> from Creation," "Israel's Land: Reflections from Redemption," and "New Crea-
> tion and Reflections from Eschatology."   Among the eco-justice themes he
> highlights are the priority of human needs over those of other creatures when
> both cannot be met; economic justice as part of stewardship; the paradigmatic
> nature of Israel's political, economic, and social structures with their emphasis on
> justice; and the ecological aspects of the covenant.

---

*In addition to the works annotated in this chapter, readers interested in biblical inter-
pretation may wish to consult the following entries located elsewhere in the bibliography:* 155, 345, 361, 377, 434, 454.

3

Theological and Philosophical Perspectives

The eco-justice literature as a whole tends to assume that religious beliefs are crucial for our treatment of the biosphere and its human and other inhabitants. Judgments as to which beliefs are most crucial, and which retrievals or alterations will be most help-ful, vary greatly. A wide range of theological viewpoints (evangelical, Roman Catholic, Orthodox, liberal Protestant, process, political and liberationist, etc.) on a great many theological topics (the doctrine of God, Christology, sin, eschatology, etc.) are represented here. Many philosophical fields (e.g., epistemology, ontology, anthropology) and concepts (e.g., dualism, organicism, atomism, anthropocentrism, hierarchies of being and value) are attended to in the course of the theological critiques and (re)constructions surveyed here.

061 [Abrecht, Paul]. "Humanity, Nature, and God." In *Faith and Science in an Unjust World: Report of the World Council of Churches' Conference on Faith, Science and the Future,* Vol. 2, *Reports of Sections,* edited by Paul Abrecht, 28-38. Geneva: World Council of Churches, 1980.

> This section 2 report from the 1979 conference held at the Massachusetts Institute of Technology summarizes the Christian understanding of humanity, nature, and God in relation to modern Western thought, the Bible, and other faiths. It stresses repeatedly the indivisibility of justice, sustainability, and participation, and concludes with recommendations for further dialogue and theological exploration.

062 Ayers, Robert H. "Christian Realism and Environmental Ethics." In *Religion and Environmental Crisis*, edited by Eugene C. Hargrove, 154-71. Athens: University of Georgia Press, 1986.

> Ayers maintains that Reinhold Niebuhr's dialectical theological perspective, which sees the human being as "the creature of necessity and the child of free-dom," does more justice to the biblical understanding of the relationship of humanity and nature and is truer to the facts of human experience than the view-point expressed by Lynn White Jr. in "The Historical Roots of Our Ecologic Crisis" (026). The latter viewpoint is characterized by Ayers as romantic and idealistic, emphasizing humanity's oneness with nature at the expense of its trans-cendence. Niebuhr's perspective locates the root cause of the ecological crisis in the same kind of sinful escape from the anxiety of finitude/freedom, in the same sinful egoism, that marks humankind's immoral social relations. Thus, for Niebuhr, effective strategies for social action involve both persuasion and coer-

cion. Yet Niebuhr's viewpoint is not pessimistic because humankind possesses possibilities for good as well as evil. The "ultimate norm of acting in the world for the harmony of the whole and the good of all creatures is the self-giving love or *agape* of God as disclosed in Jesus Christ."

063 Barnes, Michael, ed. *An Ecology of the Spirit: Religious Reflection and Environmental Consciousness.* The Annual Publication of the College Theology Society, 1990, vol. 36. Lanham, MD.: University Press of America, 1994.

This collection of seventeen essays by prominent theologians and scholars, including Paul Santmire, Rosemary Radford Ruether, and Michael Fox, addresses critical issues of environmental concern. They were originally presented at the 1990 Annual Meeting of the College Theology Society at Loyola University of New Orleans entitled "Theology in an Ecological Perspective." The essays are placed into divisions covering Christianity, ecofeminism, spirituality, ethics, Eastern religions, and symbols, myths and metaphors. See Donahue (175), French (182), McDaniel (241), Ruether (246), and Santmire (147).

064 Berry, Thomas F., and Thomas Clarke. *Befriending the Earth: A Theology of Reconciliation Between Humans and the Earth*, edited by Stephen Dunn and Anne Lonergan. Mystic, CT: Twenty-Third Publications, 1991.

Formatted as an exchange between Thomas Berry and Thomas Clarke, both Catholic theologians, each chapter of this work is introduced by the editors, followed by Berry's address on the topic, Clarke's response, and ending with a list of questions for reflection and discussion. Berry and Clarke explore many themes found in traditional Roman Catholic theology—the concept of God, the Trinity, Christology, creation, the Fall, redemption, evil, grace, sacraments, ritual and spiritual discipline—with particular emphasis on the changes they perceive as necessary for the transition to what Berry terms the Ecozoic Age, an age characterized by a changed relationship with the earth and all of nature, guided by the female archetype, and holding a dream for the future built upon poetry, music, dance, and story.

065 Birch, Charles, and John B. Cobb, Jr. *The Liberation of Life: From the Cell to the Community.* Cambridge: Cambridge University Press, 1981.

In this major statement on the implication of process thought for environmental ethics, Birch and Cobb argue that the paradigm of the living organism as a machine is responsible for the oppression of both humans and animals. Process metaphysics provides an alternative ecological model and a "religion of Life" that makes each existent entity a subject of experience, and makes "richness of experience" the telos of evolution and the good to be enhanced by ethical choice. The principle that every entity is to be respected for its intrinsic value as well as its instrumental value to others is applied to plants, animals, and humans to yield a hierarchy of moral value determined by the relative degree of intrinsic to instrumental value. The authors argue that such a hierarchy provides a basis for rights claims and for moral choice. The vision of future good is based on maximizing the quality of human life while minimally impacting non-human life. This principle prescribes a large human population learning to live comfortably and frugally, and forms of development that are just (promote personal freedom, equality of opportunity, and participation) and sustainable. The ecological model itself suggests ways to achieve such a transcending global community of communities.

066 Birch, Charles, William Eakin, and Jay B. McDaniel, eds. *Liberating Life: Contemporary Approaches to Ecological Theology*. Maryknoll, NY: Orbis Books, 1990.

The editors categorize these essays as articulations, from different points of view, of non-anthropocentric theologies and ethics that extend liberation to include other living creatures, and that show the linkage of ecological sustainability and justice for the oppressed. Several essays originated as papers delivered in 1988 to a World Council of Churches consultation on ecological theology. See the Annecy Report (196), Cobb (434), Noh (303), and Sindima (019).

067 Bloomquist, Karen. "Creation, Domination, and the Environment." *Lutheran Theological Seminary Bulletin* 69, no. 3 (1989): 27-31.

The author points out that, although Christianity embraces theological affirmations for addressing the environmental crisis, it has helped to legitimate the conquest of people and nature, and has lent a meaning to stewardship of "control over." She stresses that creation must be regarded as a matrix of interrelationships within God's household, and stewardship must mean sufficiency for all. Bloomquist regards as ecologically sound theology Sallie McFague's models of God as mother, lover, and friend (125).

068 Boff, Leonardo. *Ecology and Liberation: A New Paradigm*. Translated by John Cumming. Maryknoll, NY: Orbis Books, 1995.

A leading liberation theologian combines liberationist, ecological, and mystical themes in this collection of loosely connected essays (originally published in Portuguese in 1993). In part 1, "Ecology: A New Paradigm," Boff acknowledges that the environmental crisis is a global concern and defines ecology as the view that all creatures exist in relationships and that each has intrinsic value. The exploitation of nature and people to serve the interests of a minority calls for a fundamental transformation in our technological (economic), political, social, ethical, intellectual, and spiritual projects in accordance with the ecological paradigm. An "ecological-social democracy" embraces nonhuman beings as co-citizens and extends the "option for the poor" to all threatened beings. Boff notes that a minimum of social justice is necessary for the realization of ecological justice (respect for the rights of nature), and that social and ecological injustice go hand in hand. His theology affirms that humans are part of, but uniquely responsible for, the earth and that God is sacramentally present in the cosmos and the human self. In part 2, "From Ecology to Globalization," Boff maintains that liberation theology's socialist vision and its critique of capitalism remain valid. He articulates a democratic ideal that includes meeting basic needs, participation, equality, solidarity, diversity, cultural reciprocity, communion, and human and ecological welfare. Part 3, "From World Consciousness to Mysticism," describes mysticism as supporting commitment and struggle on behalf of a utopian social vision and as rooted, with sexuality, in the energy of the Holy Spirit that permeates human beings and the cosmos.

069 Brun, Tony. "Social Ecology: A Timely Paradigm for Reflection and Praxis for Life in Latin America." In *Ecotheology: Voices from South and North*, edited by David G. Hallman, 79-91. Geneva: WCC Publications; Maryknoll, NY: Orbis Books, 1994.

Brun, teacher of pastoral theology and social issues in Costa Rica, proposes social ecology, the study of human systems in interaction with their environmental systems, as a needed paradigm for the reorganization of society from a human and ecological perspective, starting with the interests of the impoverished majorities in Latin America. Social ecology corrects the dualism between the social and natural sciences that has obscured the ecological consequences of the social crisis and the social component of environmental problems. A unique contribution of this essay is its discussion of humor as a tool for teaching the socio-ecological perspective in the church. Humor, Brun says, is a way of speaking about God and about humanity; it is liberating, promotes communion, inspires the utopian disposition, and has a questioning and self-critical character. The essay concludes with two "observe, interpret, apply" exercises, each incorporating reflections on a comic strip and a biblical text.

070   Caldecott, Stratford. "Cosmology, Eschatology, Ecology: Some Reflections on *Sollicitudo rei socialis.*" *Communio* 15 (Fall 1988): 305-18.

This article develops several themes from recent papal teachings in ways that show Orthodox influence: the role of human dominion and Christ's incarnation in leading the cosmos to its destined fulfillment; respect for the feminine cosmos and the female body as entailing the rejection of artificial contraception; and the source of the ecological crisis in the loss of a sense of objective moral value.

071   Cauthen, Kenneth. *Christian Biopolitics: A Credo and Strategy for the Future.* Nashville: Abingdon Press, 1971.

In one of the earliest full-length treatments of ecojustice, a work addressed to "the disenchanted minority who also belong to churches" the author defines the unique challenge of our age as one of creating a just planetary society within the boundaries of ecological limits while seeking to make possible "the optimum enjoyment of existence" for all creatures. Among the profound changes in ideas, values, and power coalitions required to realize this goal is a utopian vision based on process-philosophy metaphysics and a religio-ethical perspective centered on the quest for enjoyment in a technological age. The Christian community may contribute by nourishing a consciousness of a desirable human future arising from the inspiration of the Christian past and of God's power to create a reign of justice and joy. Aware of the human capacity for evil and the trauma associated with rapid change, Cauthen nevertheless believes that "salvation is the enjoyment of existence, despite its ambiguity."

072   Cauthen, Kenneth.   "Imagining the Future: New Visions and New Responsibilities." *Zygon* 20 (September 1985): 321-39.

Cauthen detects an emerging paradigm characterized by holism, synthesis, and interdependence at the global, national, organizational, and individual levels. Included in this paradigm are ideas of biological and resource limits to human technology and industry, and of justice as "healthy functioning" that promotes the goals of the whole system while meeting the needs of individuals. Theology participates in the new paradigm through the conversation between liberation and establishment theologies, interreligious dialogue, and the growing influence of process theology.

073   Christiansen, Drew. "Moral Theology, Ecology, Justice, and Development." In *Covenant for a New Creation: Ethics, Religion, and Public Policy,* edited by Carol S. Robb and Carl J. Casebolt, 251-71. Maryknoll, NY: Orbis Books, 1991.

Christiansen addresses the relationship of God, humanity, and nature. He finds values in the principles of deep ecology, but asserts that, since nature cannot be seen as a reality apart from humanity, humans need to combine reverence for nature with intelligent action. Humanity also needs to see itself as embedded in nature. For Christiansen, traditional Christian concepts such as sin and conversion deal better with moral failure and renewal than do notions of Earth wisdom.

074 Chung Hyun Kyung. "Come Holy Spirit, Renew the Whole Creation." *The Woman's Pulpit* (July/September 1991): 4-7.

The subject of controversy when it was delivered at the World Council of Churches' Assembly in Canberra in 1990, this paper begins with an invocation to victimized spirits, human and nonhuman, throughout the ages. Its author fears that the Assembly theme, "Come Holy Spirit, Renew the Whole Creation!" is an excuse not to struggle in solidarity with all forms of life. She suggests use of the traditional Korean concept of *Han* (anger and the raw energy to struggle for liberation) to avoid passivity. She brings a message from Christian grassroots activists in her community: repentance for our exploitative lifestyles is the beginning of change and includes practicing voluntary poverty in every area of life. She suggests a change from anthropocentrism to the perspective of all creatures including the most wretched; from dualism to interconnection so that the life energy of *Ki* can freely circulate; and from the violence of war to compassion. The Holy Spirit may be likened to *Kwan In*, a female *bodhisattva*, who refuses to go into Nirvana alone but waits until the whole universe—including its creatures, air, and water—also gain enlightenment.

075 Cobb, John B., Jr. *Is It Too Late? A Theology of Ecology.* Beverly Hills, CA: Bruce, 1972.

Written as a contribution to the adult religious-education *Faith and Life* series edited by Francis Buckley and Cyr N. Miller, this work treats theological and moral issues with candidness and clarity, while stressing "the importance of the vision within which one operates." Responding to criticism of the environmental movement in the face of mounting social problems, Cobb suggests that the relation of ecology issues to justice ones is analogous to the situation on board a ship that has sprung a leak while its passengers struggle over inequitable accommodations. He asks, can the sides stop their warring and work on a solution to the larger, more immediate, life-threatening problem? Agreeing that aspects of Christian belief have provided the context for a technological approach to nonhumans, he finds other world views, including primitivism, Taoism, and paganism, equally lacking. "New Christianity" must substitute the biotic pyramid for the absoluteness of humanity; its commitment should be to the inclusive Creative Process, which is also the grounds for believing it is not too late to save life. Cobb discusses the economic choices that will be needed to make ecological gains, and the choices, including abortion, that might stem population increase.

076 Cobb, John B., Jr. "Points of Contact Between Process Theology and Liberation Theology in Matters of Faith and Justice." *Process Studies* 14 (Summer 1985): 124-41.

Of particular interest for eco-justice concerns in this paper organized around the tensions between process and liberation theology is the fifth section, "The Poor and Non-Human World." Cobb notes that while process theologians and liberation theologians both oppose the dominant pattern of development economics, process theologians are more likely to make the point that development economics treats nature as if it were an inexhaustible resource for human beings whereas, in reality, the earth is not inexhaustible, liberation of the poor belongs with improving the land on which the poor depend, and nature is not simply a resource for human beings. This latter point liberation theologians have attacked on the grounds that it expresses the interests of the affluent and works against the interests of the poor. Cobb defends it on the grounds that all living things are of worth to themselves and to God regardless of their worth to human beings. He believes that the anthropocentrism of the opposite view is, in fact, associated with Western imperialism. Though admitting they may in some instances work against the interests of the poor, Cobb gives examples to show that those who have been most sensitive to the values of other creatures have also been foremost in urging policies for the sustaining of human society.

077   Cobb, John B., Jr. "Postmodern Christianity in Quest of Eco-Justice." In *After Nature's Revolt: Eco-Justice and Theology*, edited by Dieter T. Hessel, 21-39. Minneapolis: Augsburg Fortress Publishers, 1992.

Cobb argues that theology must overcome modernity's extreme anthropocentrism, individualism, and dualism as well as its literalistic, objectifying, and foundationalist approach to knowledge. While postmodernity is more compatible with biblical thinking, the church has resisted shedding its modernist commitments—including its history/nature dualism that pits social justice against environmental concerns. A postmodern biblical theology must face new ethical questions and critique other disciplines in light of its understanding of the world. Cobb summarizes his own view of our obligations to animals and his proposal for an economics that serves the human community and the wider community of life.

078   Cobb, John B., Jr. "Sociological Theology or Ecological Theology." In his *Process Theology as Political Theology*, 111-34. Philadelphia: Westminster Press; Manchester: Manchester University Press, 1982.

Cobb maintains that Johann Baptist Metz's "sociological" theology, which is influenced by Kantian philosophy, can deal with nature only insofar as nature is part of human history. Ecological theology needs sociological theology to deal realistically with political and economic power, but sociological theology should express the realization that sustainability and justice require each other. To the extent that sociological theology remains Kantian it cannot acknowledge the demand of justice to the nonhuman creation that is part of the biblical vision.

079   Cooey, Paula M. "Resurrection of the Body: Finding a Misplaced Future." *Buddhist-Christian Studies* 12 (1992): 167-73.

Because it dissociates Jesus from the rest of sentient existence, the author maintains that the doctrine of the incarnation as presently interpreted is an obstacle to a just future for natural and human environments. In contrast, the ancient insistence upon Jesus' full humanity makes Jesus "the epistemological linchpin" by which Christians recognize the requirement to participate in the betterment of the world. So too, Jesus' resurrection as presently interpreted undermines the value of the physical environment. But when resurrection refers to a future on Earth, as in the view long held within Christian traditions that the community of followers incorporates the mystical body of Christ, there is hope for ecological reform with social justice.

080   Deloria, Vine, Jr. *God Is Red.* New York: Grosset and Dunlap, 1973.

This wide-ranging critique of Christianity by a Native American concludes that the Christian religion has been wrong from its inception and needs to be thoroughly reconceptualized. Its most essential need is for an understanding of the world in terms of space and place rather than of time and history.

Christianity "appears to be incapable of providing any reality to the life in which we are here and now presently engaged—space and the planet Earth." As a result, Christian churches are more helpless in the area of ecology than in any other field. Deloria finds serious shortcomings in the Christian doctrine of creation which sees creation as a specific event rather than, as in tribal religion, an ecosystem present in a definable place; places nature and humans in polarity; and tinges nature with evil. He uses Velikovsky's theories and the links between creation stories and particular lands to critique Christian claims to a universally valid history of creation. Christianity also needs to reform its social and political ideas around communal rather than individual considerations. Its failure to determine, rather than be determined by, cultural influences is contrasted with the communal character of tribal religion. He suggests that the various denominations do not serve to integrate cities, suburbs, or neighborhoods; that the events of the Christian era do not justify the notion that Christianity is capable of bringing peace on Earth, or that the Christian God is working in the events of humankind. He calls for White America to become aware of contemporary American Indian reality and for Christians to explore rejected areas of religious belief, including many tribal religious practices.

081 Dumas, André. "The Ecological Crisis and the Doctrine of Creation." *Ecumenical Review* 27 (January 1975): 24-35.

Dumas reviews the new "preoccupations" arising from the ecological crisis and recounts the history of the doctrine of creation in terms of the preoccupations of different periods. Today, the doctrine of creation is a confession that human beings are created for common survival and are not to be dismembered into rival tribes. He reminds us that, paradoxically, global sustainability also requires regional autonomy.

082 Elder, Frederick. *Crisis in Eden: A Religious Study of Man and Environment.* Nashville: Abingdon Press, 1970.

In one of the first books on environmental theology, Elder anticipates some of the conflicts that would soon erupt between environmentalists and social justice advocates. He contrasts "inclusionists" (Loren Eiseley, various ecologists, and other scientists) and "exclusionists" (Teilhard de Chardin, Harvey Cox, and Herbert Richardson), classified by whether their definition of nature includes or excludes human beings. Cox, for example, in celebrating the desacralization of nature and the pragmatic human dominion that he believes is needed to solve such problems as racism and poverty separates the "secular city" from the natural world. Support for the inclusionists is found in scripture, in theologians such as Calvin and H. R. Niebuhr, and in the environmental crisis which shows the reality of environmental limits on human action. Transforming society in a more inclusionist direction can make use of current social values such as individualism, but also requires rethinking the meaning of freedom. The church by broadening its view of "relevance" beyond such (admittedly urgent) issues of peace and social justice can play a role in bringing about an environmental ethic.

083 Elsdon, Ron. *Bent World: A Christian Response to the Environmental Crisis.* Downers Grove, IL: InterVarsity Press, 1981.

In an evangelical Anglican treatise representative of the significant eco-justice literature generated in recent years among conservative Christians in England, Ireland, and Scotland, Elsdon argues that environmental and social problems are due to the Fall and therefore require for their solution insights from Christian revelation. The root of contemporary problems, which ultimately stems from estrangement from God, is industrial society's selfish quest for ever higher standards of living. Loss of right relationship perverts the human capacity to exercise proper dominion over creation and to do justice to one's neighbor. Although persons of "evangelical persuasion" often fail to realize their social responsibilities, salvation through Jesus Christ releases individuals from slavery to sin and generates a new moral influence in society and the possibility of persuasive new sustainable lifestyles.

084 Falcke, Heino. "Deliverance and Renewal: The Integrity of Creation." *One World*, no. 124 (April 1987): 15-18.

Falcke provides a good summary of the ecumenical discussion revolving around the issue of the integrity of creation. He identifies emerging points of consensus regarding creation and salvation, the meaning of the integrity of creation, faith and science dialogue, the relational understanding of reality, intrinsic value in nature, human transcendence and responsibility for fellow creatures, and openness to God versus trying to control the future. He finds that some eschatological problems remain unresolved.

085 Fernandez, Eleazar S. "People's Cry, Creation's Cry: A Theologico-Ethical Reflection on Ecology from the Perspective of the Struggling Poor." *Tugon* 12 (1992): 277-94.

The author, former coordinator of the Socio-Pastoral Institute at Cebu City, Philippines, and at the time of writing, a doctoral student at Vanderbilt University, affirms the need to keep justice and ecology together but is strongly critical of the eco-theology of "leisured-class-liberal-existentialist-whiteWestern-male-theologians," represented by Arthur Peacocke and Holmes Rolston, for remaining at a general and ontological level and thus ignoring the question of social justice. Fernandez proposes that the issue of ecology be viewed "from the perspective of the struggling poor," and that eco-justice have as its point of departure justice rather than ecology, because the struggling poor, including North American native peoples and the Igorots of the Philippines "live daily in constant awareness of their dependence on nature" and thus can best illustrate the links between justice and ecology.

086 Finger, Thomas. "Modern Alienation and Trinitarian Creation." *Evangelical Review of Theology* 17 (April 1993): 190-208.

Finger examines two understandings of contemporary psychological and ecological alienation. Newtonian (Freudian/Darwinian) approaches stress conflict while organismic psychologies and the Gaia hypothesis argue that wholeness is primary. Christians tend toward the latter, especially panentheists for whom the world is God's "body." Finger prefers a trinitarian perspective that preserves the distinctive identities of, and intimate relations among, God and creatures and that looks forward to a harmony brought about by God's uniting love. Finger notes, but does not explore, the applicability of such an analysis to the social level.

087 Fox, Matthew. *The Coming of the Cosmic Christ: The Healing of Mother Earth and the Birth of a Global Renaissance*. San Francisco: Harper and Row, 1988.

The heart of this work by a former Dominican and founder of the creation spirituality movement is a conflation of the paschal mystery with Earth's destruction and restoration—the "life, death, and resurrection of Mother Earth." Earth is viewed as Mother, and as "the ultimate *anawin*" or oppressed victim of social injustice; Earth's environmental destruction is viewed as a matricide that is also deicide at the hands of a patriarchial culture. Fox believes that the present way of conceiving of Jesus is overly anthropocentric, and he urges the general adoption of the Cosmic Christ (or, in the interests of greater ecumenism, of Cosmic Wisdom) as a means of restoring an environmentally damaged Earth. He calls for an end to the denial of the mystic in religion, the test for authentic mysticism being justice-making and compassion. Justice is defined as homeostasis; compassion as both mother-love and the unitive experience of panentheism.

088 Fox, Matthew. *Original Blessing: A Primer in Creation Spirituality Presented in Four Paths, Twenty-Six Themes, and Two Questions.* Santa Fe, NM: Bear and Co., 1983.

Given the plight of Earth and its people, Fox finds it imperative to let go of the dominant Fall/redemption model of spirituality and recover the authentic "creation-centered" Christian tradition. The Fall/redemption model perpetuated by Augustine is dualistic, patriarchal, and private and fails to teach justice-making and care of the earth. The creation-centered tradition, found in the biblical writings of the Yahwistic (J) author, the prophets, wisdom, the parables of Jesus, the writings of Paul, many neglected Christian theologians and mystics (Irenaeus, Hildegard, Eckhart), artists, philosophers, and scientists, begins with Dabhar, the "creative word" of God, and defines sin and salvation in the light of the original blessing of creation; it envisions human beings as co-creators of the cosmos as a divine work of art; reflects Eastern, mystical, feminist, and liberation theology motifs; and is open to correlations with post-Einsteinian physics. The creation-centered tradition is an eco-justice spirituality because it rejects the distinction between creation and salvation and instead sees redemption as the fulfillment of God's intention for all creation; views justice as inherent in the harmony of cosmic creation, and human injustice as jeopardizing the cosmos itself; is the spirituality of the oppressed of Western history; witnesses to the prophethood of all persons as co-artists and to the prophetic word which breaks out when the creative energy of Dabhar is dammed by greed and corruption; and is uniquely concerned for "erotic justice" or feeling in right relationship with Earth and people.

089 French, William C. "Beast-Machines and the Technocratic Reduction of Life: A Creation-Centered Perspective." In *Good News for Animals? Christian Approaches to Animal Well-Being*, edited by Charles Pinches and Jay B. McDaniel, 24-43. Maryknoll, NY: Orbis Books, 1993.

French maintains that the views of medieval Catholic thinkers can serve as a foundation for moral responsibility toward creation, providing interpretations consistent with the reemergence of categories of purpose and telos in current notions of a biosphere. He says that while Francis of Assisi's view of the natural world as an interdependent community is rightly considered a model of ecological sensitivity, Thomas Aquinas's views are not so typically well-regarded because of his stress on a hierarchical model where lower creatures serve as means for higher ones. But Thomas also affirmed that each creature exists for the perfection of the universe, and that the "good order of the universe" is a higher good than that of the human community alone.

090 Fritsch, Albert J. *Renew the Face of the Earth.* Chicago: Loyola University Press, 1987.

Fritsch supplies a carefully crafted synthesis based on the vision of Teilhard de Chardin. The major themes of the liturgical year, each associated with a different season in the natural rhythm of the northern temperate zone, provide opportunities for meditations on the renewal of the earth and its people—incarnation and suffering servant (winter), resurrection and creation (spring), Pentecost and liberation (summer), and Thanksgiving and Advent (autumn). Fritsch argues that regeneration of the earth will come only with the regeneration of the poor and powerless at grassroots levels and will most likely depend upon their active leadership in global processes. The ultimate aim of all human action, most perfectly symbolized in the Eucharist, is the growth of the incarnate Christ through creative collaboration with processes active in nature and society. He makes a variety of recommendations regarding a unified Christian approach to environmental and social action, with illuminating insights into the meaning of contemporary environmental ecumenism. Fritsch has been active in the North American Conference on Christianity and Ecology. This work is a further development of his *A Theology of the Earth* (Washington, DC: CLB Publishers, 1972.)

091　Gilkey, Langdon. *Reaping the Whirlwind: A Christian Interpretation of History.* Harper San Francisco, 1984.

In this work, first published in 1976 (New York: Seabury Press), Gilkey develops his ideas of history in relation to alternative scientific, philosophical, and theological ideas. He draws primarily on the thought of Paul Tillich, Reinhold Niebuhr, and Alfred North Whitehead. He discusses Robert Heilbroner as well as Herman Kahn and A. J. Weiner's optimistic *The Year 2000.* His analysis of historical experience and its contemporary interpretations is useful for understanding the importance of the theology and philosophy of history for projections about the future—and thus for thinking about eco-justice.

092　Gilkey, Langdon. "The Theological Understanding of Humanity and Nature in a Technological Era." *Anticipation* 19 (November 1974): 33-35.

This brief exposition of the meaning of Christian hope in the face of a threatening future is from the report of a 1974 World Conference of Churches' Bucharest Conference. Gilkey affirms that history is purposive and the future remains open, and that God has conquered death and suffering in the incarnation and lures history toward an eschatological goal which is never perfectly fulfilled. Thus we can hope not for material abundance or a perfect society, but that "through our freedom, grace may remake both us and our world" by new styles of life, new social structures, and technologies that respect nature and promote community. Reprinted in (091) pp. 319-22.

093　Gosling, David. "Towards a Credible Ecumenical Theology of Nature." *Ecumenical Review* 38 (July 1986): 322-31.

Explaining that "Justice, Peace, and the Integrity of Creation" has replaced "The Just, Participatory, and Sustainable Society" following the Sixth Assembly of the World Council of Churches (WCC) held in Vancouver in 1983, Gosling cautions that the new theme must be expressed from within a variety of cultural contexts and be related to the daily struggles of peoples, especially those of developing countries. It must incorporate data about ecology, physics, biology, and limited resources into an ethic which recognizes the intrinsic value of all creation. Such a theology must be panentheistic (God immanent in, but not identified with, nature), recognize the difference between scientific and doctrinal language, and develop an expanded ecumenical Christology within a more balanced trinitarian theology. Although rather loosely organized, this essay indicates the framework in which eco-justice issues have been discussed in the WCC. Gosling directed the WCC's sub-unit on Church and Society.

094 Granberg-Michaelson, Wesley. "Redeeming the Earth: A Theology for This World." *Covenant Quarterly* 42 (1984): 17-29.

Among Granberg-Michaelson's tenets for a theology that includes all creation is the belief that the foundation for justice is creation as God's gift. This makes inseparable the calls for wilderness preservation and ghetto relief. Granberg-Michaelson says that injustice is rooted in seizing and controlling creation for selfish ends—but since creation belongs to God, no one can hoard its bounty without sin.

095 Granberg-Michaelson, Wesley. *A Worldly Spirituality: The Call to Redeem Life on Earth*. San Francisco: Harper and Row, 1984.

According to the author, our modern sentimental and dominating attitudes toward nature run counter to both the Old and New Testaments. In the Old Testament a triadic covenantal relationship exists between God, human beings, and the land. Interpersonal violence affects humanity's relationship to God and creation; injustice, because it involves seizing God's creation for selfish use, is a disruption of the divine intention that creation confer the gift of life on all creatures; humanity's destruction of creation destroys its relationships to God and other human beings. The New Testament, often misunderstood as being solely about personal salvation, discloses that through Jesus Christ, God's redemptive work reaches out to all of creation. It follows that ecology is not another issue to be addressed alongside racism, sexism, and militarism, but is the basic framework for perceiving the church's life and internal relationships to creation. The global mission of the church is to build an ecumenical ecological economy within the church as well as a "development theology" outside it, one that recognizes patterns of exploitation between persons and toward creation.

096 Granberg-Michaelson, Wesley, ed. *Tending the Garden: Essays on the Gospel and the Earth*. Grand Rapids, MI: William B. Eerdmans Publishing Co., 1987.

The majority of essays in this collection are from papers presented at an AuSable Institute forum. Granberg-Michaelson notes the growing rediscovery among Christians of the biblical message that God's intention is to save and restore the whole creation. See Dyrness (048), Gregorios (098), and Rasmussen (210).

097 Gregorios, Paulos Mar. *The Human Presence: An Orthodox View of Nature*. Geneva: World Council of Churches, 1978.

The author, a leader in the Indian Orthodox Church and the World Council of Churches, proposes an Eastern-Orthodox solution to ecological and social problems caused by the Western European age of expansion, its industrial/technological/capitalist system, and its false view that reality is divided between individual subjects and objects. He locates the wisdom necessary for human survival in classical Christianity as presented by the Eastern tradition, especially by Gregory of Nyssa and Maximus the Confessor. In this patristic world picture, God is the fundamental reality, the world is the second reality, and humanity is the mediating third reality participating in both God and world. God entered the fallen universe through the incarnation of Jesus Christ whose purpose is to restore the harmony of the universe by restoring human nature. Social and ecological justice will be done as humanity is redeemed and the cosmos with it. The new civilization cannot be built on the individualistic perspective of Western ethics but must arise from new corporate inter-faith understandings and ways of life.

098   Gregorios, Paulos Mar.   "New Testament Foundations for Understanding the Creation."   In *Tending the Garden: Essays on the Gospel and the Earth*, edited by Wesley Granberg-Michaelson, 83-92.   Grand Rapids, MI: William B. Eerdmans Publishing Co., 1987.

In contrast to three Hindu principles articulated by Sunderlal Bahuguna as the basis for the Chipko movement in India, Gregorios frames what he considers as the Christian foundation for environmental social action: (1) all creation participates in the liberation of humanity from bondage to sin and death—eco-justice is therefore inherent in the nature of justice as such; (2) Jesus Christ is incarnate in the church, the human race, and the cosmos—all parts of creation are now reconciled in Christ; and (3) Christ and the Holy Spirit are active in the creation, redemption, and consummation of the whole created order—it is therefore a redeemed cosmos as well as a redeemed humanity that we meet in our environment and as such they are both worthy of respect.

099   Hadsell, Heidi.   "Eco-Justice and Liberation Theology: The Priority of Human Well-Being."   In *After Nature's Revolt: Eco-Justice and Theology*, edited by Dieter T. Hessel, 79-88. Minneapolis: Augsburg Fortress Publishers, 1992.

Hadsell argues that Latin American liberation theology, because of its anthropocentric focus on justice within human society and its critique of capitalism and of scientific neutrality, provides essential resources for eco-justice. She says that liberation theologians, while they are critical of talk of nature's "rights," do maintain that both human labor and the natural world are exploited and degraded by the search for profit.

100   Hall, Douglas John.   *Imaging God: Dominion as Stewardship*.   Grand Rapids, MI: William B. Eerdmans Publishing Co.; New York: Friendship Press, 1986.

Hall's interpretation of *imago Dei* within an "ontology of communion" provides a basis for an eco-justice ethic in which God/human, interhuman, and human/nature relations are seen as dimensions of human relatedness, rather than distinct relationships. Hall begins by reviewing historical Christianity's contribution to the environmental problem, including its image of the human as "above" nature. He argues that despite past distortions, the symbol of *imago Dei* can still help us discover the truth, and contrasts two historical conceptions of the *imago*. Substantialist interpretations identify it with a human trait (such as reason), thus denigrating nonhumans and such humans as are believed to be lacking in that trait. In a relational view of the Bible and the Reformers, however, bearing God's image depends on turning toward God (like a mirror) in faith and love, and presupposes an ontology in which being is "being-with." Being-with-God expresses itself in engagement with God's world. Being-with-human-neighbor involves equality, mutual service, solidarity, and individuality. Being-with-nature means that humans are part of nature but have a special vocation of reflecting God's faithfulness and articulating creation's praise of its Creator through a Christlike "dominion" of sacrificial, self-giving love and service to the nonhuman creation. This is one of three studies on stewardship; the other two are *The Steward: A Biblical Symbol Come of Age* (190), and *Christian Mission: The Stewardship of Life in the Kingdom of Death* (New York: Friendship Press, 1985).

101   Hall, Douglas John.   *Professing the Faith: Christian Theology in a North American Context*. Minneapolis: Augsburg Fortress Publishers, 1993.

Hall continues his project that began with *Thinking the Faith* (102). "Professing the faith" means articulating the intellectual and spiritual foundations for confessing the faith, as well as actively engaging the threats to life (the subject of the final volume). God, creaturely being, and Christ are viewed from three perspectives: historical, critical, and constructive. Hall argues that traditional views of "almighty" God have eclipsed the realities of doubt, failure, and incompleteness and cannot speak to the suppressed yet growing despair of North American society. He presents, instead, an understanding of a mysterious, suffering God who wills to be with and for creation. Similarly, the anthropology of the tradition lacks credibility for a culture that is fundamentally passive and fatalistic in spite of its clinging to an outworn Promethean rhetoric. Hall's proposal (which references the World Council of Churches' Justice, Peace and the Integrity of Creation program, including its justice versus the environment disputes) includes an "ontology of communion" (being as "being-with"), affirming the world while resisting evil, grateful acceptance of human creaturehood and vocation among other creatures, and the destined consummation of creation. He reviews traditional Christologies and their problems, and finds a "representational" Christology the best expression of Christ's solidarity with the world for the life of the world.

102 Hall, Douglas John. *Thinking the Faith: Christian Theology in a North American Context*. Minneapolis: Augsburg Fortress Publishers, 1989.

In this first volume of a projected three-volume work, Hall argues that theology must be contextual, that is, a reflection on the faith of the "discipleship community" in its engagement with its particular time and place. As a Canadian living on the "edge of the American Empire" he asks: "How shall we think the Christian faith in the present North American context?" He defines the context as one of a dominant culture increasingly disillusioned with modernity and its dreams of progress, mastery, and success, yet without a vantage from which to understand its failure. For Hall, North American theology must take the unaccustomed way of the cross, entering the darkness rather than trying to sustain false hopes. Among several components of the context that are symptomatic of the root problem are the revolution of the oppressed, the rebellion of nature, and the nuclear crisis, all of which raise the question whether the fate of this world—a fate that matters supremely to God, as the cross shows—is of ultimate concern to Christians. Hall examines the nature of the discipline of theology, of theological method, and of the relationship between reason and revelation, insisting that all are conditioned by contextual factors and must be understood accordingly.

103 Hallman, David G., ed. *Ecotheology: Voices from South and North*. Geneva: WCC Publications; Maryknoll, NY: Orbis Books, 1994.

This volume collects essays on ecological theology and ethics from around the world—Africa, Asia, North and South America, and Europe—under the headings of "The Biblical Witness," "Theological Challenges," "Insights from Eco-Feminism," "Insights from Indigenous Peoples," and "Ethical Implications." Hallman's introduction notes that the central issues in North-South dialogue on environment revolve around the relation between protecting nature and meeting the basic needs of the poor and the post-UNCED consensus that environment and development are inextricably linked. He identifies the potential contributions of liberation theology, feminists, indigenous peoples, and scripture to "ecotheology" and describes the nature, role, and sources of hope. See Abraham (161), Boff (280), Brun (069), Chung Hyun Kyung (231), Cooper (004), Cunanan (040), Daneel (435), Gnanadason (232), Granberg-Michaelson (480), Hallman (354), Hessel (268), Keller (292), Kwok Pui-Lan (113), McKay (012), Primavesi (244), Rasmussen (138), Rayan (140), Ruether (247), Sowunmi (272), and Tinker (156).

104   Hallman, David G. *A Place in Creation: Ecological Visions in Science, Religion, and Economics.* Toronto: United Church Publishing House, 1992.

This informed and informing work presents clearly the arguments for an eco-justice approach. It also, after reviewing current thought on the linkages of science, religion, and economics to humanity's imbalance with the rest of nature, introduces new positive directions in each of these disciplines—in science: recent insights into the origin and future of the universe, the holistic approach of ecology, the Gaia hypothesis, and chaos theory (each of which is explained adequately for the non-scientist to understand)—in religion: new theological approaches that affirm the value of all creation (rather than that of humans alone) including process thought, new models of God, an ecological liberation theology that understands Jesus Christ as liberator of all creation, a renewed emphasis on spirit operating in nature, and contributions of feminist theology, (but not including stewardship, which Hallman views as too much of a management model, inadequate to help humans learn to live *with* creation)—in economics: the concept of sustainable development (explained in detail). A chapter on political challenges defines strategies for pursuing justice and sustainability. Hallman is active in international environmental and eco-justice movements, a fact reflected in notes and examples, as well as in the included annotated bibliography.

105   Hefner, Philip J.   "The Politics and Ontology of Nature and Grace." *Journal of Religion* 54 (April 1974): 138-53.

Hefner interprets, using Jürgen Habermas's theory of "knowledge-constitutive interests," Joseph Sittler's nature/grace program as a call to emancipation from technical-cognitive interests which lead us to perceive the world as an object for human manipulation and which have distorted our interpretation of traditional doctrines. Such cognitive emancipation also requires social and political emancipation.   The theologies of Sittler and Teilhard de Chardin are seen as complementary correctives to the critical theologies of Johannes Metz, Gustavo Gutierrez, and the like; they provide the ontological-theological substance for the latter's critiques and point to their utopian defects. Both perspectives suggest the need for a full doctrine of the Holy Spirit which attends to the transformation of the anti-transcendent order of nature by ecstatic self-transcendence.

106   Hessel, Dieter T., ed. *After Nature's Revolt: Eco-Justice and Theology.* Minneapolis: Augsburg Fortress Publishers, 1992.

This important eco-justice resource is the outcome of a 1990 theology and ethics symposium cosponsored by the Commission for Church in Society of the Evangelical Lutheran Church in America and the Committee on Social Witness Policy of the Presbyterian Church (USA). Its focus, described by Hessel, who is both editor of the collection and a major organizer of the conference, is the response of Christian faith to the dual crisis of the degradation of the natural environment and the impoverishment of low-power people. Hessel argues that, although the church has tended not to keep ecology and justice together, biblical resources for a theology and ethic of eco-justice exist. Among the tasks for the church are overcoming rationales for ecological and social oppression, and facing up to the structures of economic and political power. See Cobb (007), Gibson (398), Hadsell (099), Johnston (356), Kehm (048), Rasmussen (137), Rolston (424), Santmire (146), and Tinker (155).

107 Himes, Michael J., and Kenneth R. Himes. "The Sacrament of Creation: Toward an Environmental Theology." *Commonweal* 117 (26 January 1990) 42-49.

Himes asserts that an ethic of companionship must replace the ethic of individualism as a precondition to solving the ecological crisis. While stewardship tends to put humans as caretakers in the place of an absent God, companionship evokes an attitude toward creation that encourages the development of an environmental ethic oriented toward more than the good of the individual self, that does not treat creation only as an instrumental good for humanity but is grounded in an expanded notion of the common good that includes non-human creation. This notion requires justice in economic development, economic growth premised on sustainable efficiency, and a heightened role for the environment.

108 John Paul II. "Peace with All Creation." World Day of Peace Message, 1 January 1990. *Origins, CNS Documentary Service* 19 (14 December 1989): 465-68.

This message states that humanity's rebellion against God's call to share in the unfolding plan of creation by wise and loving dominion is the cause of the ecological crisis. A solution requires respect for the dignity and rights of the human person and for the order of creation; international cooperation and solidarity, especially between developing and highly industrialized nations; addressing war and structural forms of poverty; a lifestyle of discipline and sacrifice; and attention to aesthetic values.

109 Kaufman, Gordon D. "A Problem for Theology: The Concept of Nature." *Harvard Theological Review* 65 (1972), 337-66.

Frequently referred to, this article is important because it questions the grounds on which an ecological theology, and especially (because of its focus on morality) an eco-justice orientation, rests. Kaufman, Professor of Divinity at Harvard Divinity School, argues that 'nature' is a concept embracing both the totality of "natural process" and that which is experienced as "natural" in the sense of "distinct from human society and culture." He sees Christian faith as having developed on a framework of "God, man, and the world" wherein 'God' is preeminently a personal and moral agent; 'man' "conceived in God's image" is distinguished from 'world' by having volitional and moral capacities; and 'world' is purely contextual and nonvolitional. Thus, "the metaphysical tendencies implicit in [the concept of nature] are not obviously congruent with those of Christian faith." This "theological problem of nature" is far too serious to be solved by simple reconstructions, such as that of an emphasis on stewardship, and requires a reexamination of our notions of God and man. Nor can the problem be solved by substituting 'creation' and 'grace' for the different attributes of nature because the question remains whether personalistic and political metaphors are adequate or even appropriate. Kaufman also points out that the concept of "man" as simply a natural being within a nature conceived as ultimate reality also has problems in that it does not do justice to the personal and moral, which are the distinctively human aspects of human being. The essay ends with reflections on the possibly unifying move of seeing history as rooted in nature, and nature as having a history continuous with human history.

110 Kaufman, Gordon D. *Theology for a Nuclear Age.* Philadelphia: Westminster Press; Manchester: Manchester University Press, 1985.

Kaufman believes that the dropping of the atomic bomb on Hiroshima which opened up the possibility of a human-caused end to human life, has necessitated a reconstruction of theology, specifically of the meaning of 'God' and 'Christ', God being necessarily conceived in ways dependent on models and metaphors, and theology being essentially a matter of imaginative construction. God, as depicted in Western religious symbolism—a creator/king and director of human events—is not only inadequate to deal with our present day ecological and political crises, but represents a way of perceiving that has fostered evil. God must be reenvisioned as the cosmic evolutionary movement leading toward the possibility of life and community characterized by freedom, justice, meaning, and creativity. God's being, Kaufman suggests, is tied to human history; God's fate is ours; and nuclear disaster will be a disaster for God. Jesus as a resurrected savior who by dying restored humans to communion with God is not a helpful conception for the contemporary situation either, for "no individual person can have this sort of absolute significance and cosmic efficacy for all others, for every individual is an expression of and interdependent with the complex ecological web of life and nature which gives them all birth and sustains them all." Kaufman suggests that true salvation lies in a mode of life which Jesus exemplified, in movements toward reconciliation, healing, liberation, and overcoming oppression, alienation, and deterioration.

111   Keller, Catherine. "Talk About the Weather: The Greening of Eschatology." In *Ecofeminism and the Sacred*, edited by Carol J. Adams, 30-49. New York: Continuum Publishing Co., 1993.

In a many-sided discourse on eschatology—its various meanings and varieties in the modern world, its origins and evolution, and especially, the necessity for its reconstruction in light of the ecological crisis—the author draws on Bill McKibben's *The End of Nature* (New York: Random House, 1989), seeing it as both an apocalyptic text that Christian theology must address, and an example of the dualistic ideology of separation from nature that has contributed to the ecological problem. Keller maintains that modern views of Christian eschatology as an end of the world are a distortion of its biblical origins, serving technology, growth, and the unjust status-quo while ignoring the cause of the ecological crisis in "man's conquest of nature." Recycling eschatology means defusing the self-fulfilling prophecy of worldly doom and working toward social and ecological health on Earth.

112   Keller, Catherine. "Women Against Wasting the World: Notes on Eschatology and Ecology." In *Reweaving the World: The Emergence of Ecofeminism*, edited by Irene Diamond and Gloria Feman Orenstein, 249-63. San Francisco: Sierra Club Books, 1990.

In this reflection on the connections between the biblical myth of the Apocalypse and the wasting of Earth, Keller suggests that the prophecies of Revelation are a formative text inscribed in Western consciousness that have shaped the course of Western development and led scientific modernity in the direction of progress by exploitation. She also points out that eschatology can be a positive force, as expressed in the cry for justice by the classical prophets, responsible for a sense of the irreversibility of history and the idea that there is not endless time to repair Earth's damage; and that it can serve the cause of a socially and historically responsible ecocentrism, as in Mary's *Magnificat* of the synoptic Gospels, suggesting the possibility of a sacred community to be partially realized in the present.

113 Kwok Pui-Lan. "Ecology and the Recycling of Christianity." In *Ecotheology: Voices from South and North*, edited by David G. Hallman, 107-11. Geneva: WCC Publications; Maryknoll, NY: Orbis Books, 1994.

Hong Kong born "mother, story-teller, and theologian" Kwok Pui-Lan argues that the degradation of women and the ecological crisis challenge Christians to "recycle" their traditional beliefs, moving from a hierarchical to an ecological model, from anthropocentrism to biocentrism, from passive spirituality to passionate spirituality, and from ecclesiastical solidarity to ecological solidarity. This essay originally appeared in *Ecumenical Review* 44 (July 1992): 304-7.

114 Lazareth, William T. "Theological Dimensions of the Energy Situation." In *Energy Ethics: A Christian Response*, edited by Dieter T. Hessel, 132-36. New York: Friendship Press, 1979.

In a clear, strong, ecologically informed and oriented interpretation of classical Christian doctrines of creation, sin, idolatry, injustice, and redemption in light of the energy issue, Lazareth concludes that just as Jesus expanded the meaning of "neighbor" to include all other human beings, now "we are called to explore the ultimate physical and temporal boundaries of the community of life."

115 Limouris, Gennadios. "Orthodox Perspectives on Creation." In his *Justice, Peace, and the Integrity of Creation: Insights from Orthodoxy*, 1-15. Geneva: WCC Publications, 1990.

This report from a 1987 consultation at Sofia, Bulgaria states that creation is the context for humanity's deification and God's incarnation. Humanity, as microcosm of creation, draws the material world toward or away from God; the incarnation united humanity and creation with the Creator. Human sin brought forces of disintegration into creation—racism, economic injustice, environmental degradation, injustice to women, and the arms race. The eschatological promise of salvation for all creation through Christ's death and resurrection is made present through the Spirit in the church. Christians are thus empowered, as co-workers with God, to transfigure creation and to work for justice, peace, and the integrity of creation.

116 Limouris, Gennadios. "Orthodox Perspectives on Justice and Peace." In his *Justice, Peace and the Integrity of Creation: Insights from Orthodoxy*, 16-27. Geneva: WCC Publications, 1990.

This statement from a 1989 meeting at Minsk, USSR, lists the unjust treatment of Earth, militarism, economic and social injustice, and threats of nuclear war as issues of peace and justice. It declares that the Orthodox response is based on Jesus Christ, the divine-human standard of justice, who has overcome sin and death, which are the causes of injustice. Justice and peace can come only as men and women regain communion with God, renewal and glorification in Christ, and the illumination of the Holy Spirit. Limouris lists ways for Christians to carry out their mandate to work with God for the restoration and transfiguration of creation.

117 Limouris, Gennadios, ed. *Justice, Peace, and the Integrity of Creation: Insights from Orthodoxy*. Geneva: WCC Publications, 1990.

These statements and selected presentations are from two consultations on Justice, Peace, and the Integrity of Creation for Eastern Orthodox and Oriental Orthodox churches, one held at Sofia, Bulgaria in 1987 (115) and the other at Minsk, U.S.S.R. in 1989 (116). Limouris's introduction provides an interpretive summary. Orthodoxy holds that in spite of injustice, environmental degradation, and conflict, Christians must restore a vision of creation as filled with the energies of the Spirit and, though fallen, destined for transfiguration in Christ. Humans are priests as well as kings, co-creators with God, and mediators of creation's praise of God. Salvation has both a vertical and a horizontal dimension: Christ is the source of true peace and eternal life, but Christians are also to fight and suffer for the sake of the world.

118 Lockman, James. "Reflections on the Exploitation of the Amazon in Light of Liberation Theology." In *Covenant for a New Creation: Ethics, Religion, and Public Policy*, edited by Carol S. Robb and Carl J. Casebolt, 165-95. Maryknoll, NY: Orbis Books, 1991.

Defining the poor as "the objects of exploitation, impoverishment, and marginalization," a definition that includes both the human poor of the Brazilian rain forest and the rain forest itself, Lockman proposes a broadening of the usual anthropocentric perspective of liberation theology to include the ecosystem.

119 Lonergan, Anne, and Carol Richards, eds. *Thomas Berry and the New Cosmology*. Mystic, CT: Twenty-Third Publications, 1987.

This book is a useful starting point for evaluating Berry's thought relative to eco-justice concerns. Two essays by Berry are followed by short responses by sympathetic critics and commentators; the book closes with a final statement by Berry and a list of principles summarizing his understanding of the universe process and humanity's role in it. Lonergan's "Introduction: The Challenge of Thomas Berry" gives some biographical background, and Richards's "The New Cosmology: What It Really Means" compares Berry with post-Vatican II trends in Catholic theology (including liberation theology) and with Thomas Aquinas and Teilhard de Chardin. Social justice issues are the focus of the responses by Baum (278) and Brennan (228), but they are also touched on in other essays and in some of the discussion questions following each essay. A slightly different version of Berry's essay on economics which appears in this volume is annotated as (331).

120 McCoy, Charles S. "Covenant, Creation, and Ethics: A Federal Vision for Humanity and the Environment." In *Cry of the Environment: Rebuilding the Christian Creation Tradition*, edited by Philip N. Joranson and Ken Butigan, 355-75. Santa Fe, NM: Bear and Co., 1984.

McCoy proposes creation, creativity, and covenant as a pattern for a Christian environmental ethics. 'Covenant' is an unconditional relation based on grace which encompasses creation as a symbiotic whole moving toward a consummation given by and hidden in God. Ethical criteria are taken from the world as created and valued by God; but God, not nature or humanity, is the center of value. Creativity is important because creation is "making new," but this process does not imply inevitable progress. Implications for policy ethics are indicated.

121 McDaniel, Jay B. *Earth, Sky, Gods, and Mortals: Developing an Ecological Spirituality*. Mystic, CT: Twenty-Third Publications, 1990.

Seeking a Christianity committed to the flourishing of nonhuman as well as human life, one that "takes the fact of our connectedness with the entire range of existence, and with God, as the heart of Christian spirituality," McDaniel develops a process-oriented version of ecological spirituality "*explicitly* but not *exclusively* Christian," a "faith without absolutes" that draws on Buddhism and Hinduism and is open to gods and goddesses, Earth, other animals, the cosmos, and the world of spirits. It is also open to human mortals who are victims along with other species in the "sustained, ongoing war against the earth" in which humanity is engaged. He sees as our best hope of turning this war around and preventing an "ultimate holocaust" the establishment of a "global village" characterized by *shalom* in which the social values of justice and sustainability are realized.

122 McDaniel, Jay B. *Of God and Pelicans: A Theology of Reverence for Life.* Louisville, KY: Westminster/John Knox Press, 1989.

To answer the problem posed by the existence of violence in nature, McDaniel draws on process theology. He develops a "life-centered" theology, positing a world that is immanent within, and other than, the creating, suffering God who remembers and redeems all creatures, and a "life-centered" Christian ethic that respects the intrinsic value of individual creatures as well as ecological wholes (while maintaining that some organisms have greater intrinsic value than others). McDaniel finds disappointing the tendency of liberation theology to ignore non-human creation as it attends to peace and justice, and he judges both stewardship and the egalitarian monism of Deep Ecology inadequate for a life-centered ethic. One of his aims is to identify inward dispositions that can nourish a life-centered Christianity, and in a clear discussion of Buddhism he shows its relationship to a biocentric spirituality. Feminist theologies are said to best unite concern for Earth plus concern for people; the bibliography is rich in women writers.

123 McDaniel, Jay B. "'Where Is the Holy Spirit Anyway?' Response to a Skeptic Environmentalist." *Ecumenical Review* 42 (April 1990): 162-74.

Responding to a student who (in the face of a lack of divine intervention to prevent the harming of poor persons by environmental toxins) questioned the reality of a Holy Spirit, McDaniel blames the question itself on "secular humanism" that he characterizes as believing in and valuing only the physical world and human life and focusing only on justice at the expense of ecological sustainability. He addresses how and under what limitations the Holy Spirit operates, arguing for a "recast theology of creation" that puts humanity within creation, sees the whole creation as God-infused, takes sin seriously, and defines God as an invitational lure, not a dictating force.

124 McFague, Sallie. *The Body of God: An Ecological Theology.* Minneapolis: Augsburg Fortress Publishers, 1993.

This important work highlights ecological justice as it propounds a "theology of embodiment"—Earth and the cosmos as the visible reality of the invisible God. McFague emphasizes the need for theology to move from a temporal/historical perspective to a natural/spatial highlighting of the relationship between ecological and justice issues. "In a theology of embodiment, space is the central category, for if justice is to be done to the many different kinds of bodies that comprise the planet, they must each have the space, the habitat, they need." She sees Christianity as limited and partial, but distinctive in its focus on oppressed, vulnerable, suffering bodies; and suggests that its insistence on love that reaches out to the victim, overturning conventional dualistic hierarchies, needs now to be applied to nature, the "new poor." A new Christic paradigm stresses interdependence, learning to live appropriately, finding salvation in the satisfaction of basic needs, solidarity with the oppressed, and stewardship of Earth.

125   McFague, Sallie.   *Models of God: Theology for an Ecological, Nuclear Age.* Philadelphia: Fortress Press, 1987.

Claiming that Christian "patriarchal, imperialistic, triumphalist" metaphors for God "may work against the continuation of life on our planet," McFague experiments with new ones—the notion of the universe as God's "body," and God as mother, lover, and friend.   Each of these models is put forward tentatively, its crucial test being whether or not its adoption would enable humans to feel and act in a more ecologically responsible manner toward Earth and its creatures. Although her sources include Christian scripture, they are not limited to it, and McFague rejects much of Christian doctrine, including vicarious atonement, individual salvation, the resurrection, and a single savior.   What she highlights from Christianity is Jesus's radical identification with all, as modeled especially in his inclusive table fellowship.   Because there must be bread enough to go around as well as equitable distribution of basic necessities if all are to share in the communal feast, McFague sees both an ecological attitude and inclusive justice as necessities at the heart of Christian faith.   She extends this justice to all species and unborn generations.   McFague's models of God are not difficult to grasp by non-theologians, and her thought-provoking approach includes an illuminating discussion of metaphor and a consideration of each model's negative aspects.

126   McFague, Sallie.   "A Square in the Quilt: One Theologian's Contribution to the Planetary Agenda."   In *Spirit and Nature: Why the Environment Is a Religious Issue*, edited by Steven C. Rockefeller and John C. Elder, 39-58.   Boston: Beacon Press, 1992.

In this address delivered at the 1990 Middlebury College Spirit and Nature Symposium, McFague stresses the interrelationship of justice and ecological issues.   She offers as her "square" in a quilt composed of remedies for Earth's deterioration the "common creation story," a science-based understanding of planetary origin that links all living things at the moment of creation and in subsequent evolution, that decenters human beings who are no longer the sole meaning and purpose of creation, and recenters them as co-creators with God of their planetary home.   Another version of this address is in (225), pp. 84-98.

127   Metz, Johann Baptist, and Edward Schillebeeckx, eds.   "No Heaven Without Earth."   *Concilium* 4 (August 1991).

In this issue of *Concilium* nine authors examine the relationship of nature and social ecology to theology and ecclesiology under three headings: "God brings about Redemption through Cosmic and Historical Mediations"; "'Justice, Peace and the Integrity of Creation'" (subdivided into "'The Conciliar Process,'" and "Ecology related to Theology, Nature and Society"); and "The Significance of the Biblical Vision of a 'New Heaven and a New Earth'."   The introductory editorial affirms that "the commitment to justice, peace, and the integrity of creation extends to the foundations of the church's identity."   Of particular eco-justice relevance are the essays by Altner (163), Coste (475), and Kroh (293).

128 Moltmann, Jürgen. *Creating a Just Future: The Politics of Peace and the Ethics of Creation in a Threatened World.* London: SCM Press; Philadelphia: Trinity Press International, 1989.

Moltmann argues that the future is no longer a matter of course but must be deliberately "created" despite contemporary pessimism. Christian action anticipates God's future of peace and justice, which includes communal, inter-generational, and ecological dimensions. Moltmann discusses nuclear deterrence, its connections to justice and environment, and the theological issues it raises—political theology, apocalypticism, theodicy, hope, and the application of Jesus' message of nonviolence and love for the enemy. In a discussion of the theology and ethics of creation, he urges change from one-sided domination to reciprocal community grounded in the community and mutuality of the triune God. He elaborates his understanding of the Sabbath as the law and goal of creation, paying special attention to legal rights for all creatures and the earth system and to human bodily experience. He sees China's transition from pursuing harmony with nature to pursuing progress in world history as bringing out the basic problem of the modern world—how to mediate between those two projects. This is a shorter presentation of many ideas found in (130) and (132).

129 Moltmann, Jürgen. "Creation as an Open System." In his *The Future of Creation*, 115-27. Philadelphia: Fortress Press, 1979.

Moltmann argues that creation must not be understood as a "closed system," something finished and perfect, with man as its lord. Rather, creation should be interpreted eschatologically, as participating in the history of God's redemptive opening of systems that have become closed and isolated through sin. Humanity's true destiny is to help create new associations with nature and among individuals that realize justice, and are symbiotic, open systems, capable of survival and evolution.

130 Moltmann, Jürgen. *God in Creation: A New Theology of Creation and the Spirit of God.* San Francisco: Harper and Row, 1985.

This effort to construct a biblical theology of creation is in marked contrast to key themes in Moltmann's earlier work. Moltmann argues for a trinitarian, messianic, eschatological theology of creation oriented by the concept of the Sabbath as the goal of creation. Creation is open to God's future; it awaits its fulfillment in the "Sabbath of Creation" when God will dwell at rest within it, and the tensions within creation will all be overcome. In contrast to "monotheistic" theology, a fully trinitarian theology, because it supports relatedness, participation, and interpenetration, also emphasizes God's immanence in creation as well as the unity between human beings and the rest of nature. Moltmann calls for a turning away from anthropocentrism to a cosmological theocentrism in which the Sabbath, not humanity, is the "crown of creation." Human beings represent God's glory and rule in creation—but only as a community and only as part of nature. Much of the book is devoted to discussing God's self-definition and self-limitation prior to the act of creation itself, to the "time" and "space" of creation, and to creation as a dual world of "heaven and earth."

131 Moltmann, Jürgen. *The Spirit of Life: A Universal Affirmation.* Minneapolis: Augsburg Fortress Publishers, 1992.

In this work, part of the series on the logic of trinitarian thinking, Moltmann refers to the Holy Spirit as "the Spirit of Life" and says that the operations of the

Spirit can be recognized in everything that ministers to life and resists life's destruction. Moltmann thus opposes a trend he finds in both Protestant and Catholic theology to view the Holy Spirit solely as the Spirit of Christ or the Spirit of redemption, and not as a part of bodily life, the life of nature, and the Spirit of the Father. Moltmann emphasizes that the Spirit is not confined to the church but is discoverable in ordinary life, including nature and Earth's ecosystems; in fact, the community of creation is the fellowship of the Holy Spirit. He speaks of the Holy Spirit both as a spirit of righteousness and justice experienced when people who are unjustly treated and people who act unjustly are set right, and as that which sanctifies life with the passion of the Creator for creation. The earth, because it is God's beloved creation, must be encountered with a reverence that begins with respect for weaker and more vulnerable life. "Sanctification," an important concept for Moltmann in this work, means defending creation against all forms of destruction, including technological violence, as well as searching for harmony and integration into the web of life. Moltmann speaks in praise of peace, anti-poverty, and environmental-action groups composed of non-Christians, and says that a way of access to the community of Christ appears to be through such shared work for the Kingdom of God. Each individual church must see itself as a "church of the cosmos," and Christians must perceive social and ecological crises as having personal relevance.

132 Moltmann, Jürgen. *The Way of Jesus Christ: Christology in Messianic Dimensions*. San Francisco: HarperSanFrancisco, 1990.

After discussing the "messianic perspective" that orients his theology toward God's promised future, Moltmann briefly reviews the history of Christology and brings it into the present-day context, asking, "Who really is Christ for the poor of the Third World, for the poor and unemployed 'surplus' masses of industrialized nations, and for ourselves and nature threatened by the nuclear inferno and environmental catastrophe?" Traditional Christological topics are dealt with in each of the book's sections—the "Messianic Mission of Christ"; the "Apocalyptic Sufferings of Christ;" the "Eschatological Resurrection of Christ;" the "Cosmic Christ," and the "Parousia of Christ"—with consistent emphasis on Christ's participating in, addressing, and redeeming suffering and oppressed human beings and nature. Moltmann argues that Christian ethics is Christological ethics. Faith in Christ requires following Christ by practicing the public, alternative ethic of Jesus; participating in Christ's sufferings for creation; living out the resurrection by living lives of "expectant creativity" for the liberation of a suffering creation; and working for the Kingdom of God through commitment to justice and peace.

133 Moore, Robert J. "A New Christian Reformation." In *Ethics of Environment and Development: Global Challenge, International Response*, edited by J. Ronald Engel and Joan Gibb Engel. Tucson: University of Arizona Press; London: Belhaven Press, 1990: 104-13.

After reviewing the historical roots of a Christian distrust of nature, Moore details the steps being taken to restore an opposite theological approach that values creation. This includes rediscovering the indwelling Holy Spirit, retrieving the Biblical symbol of gardener and of a God who on the Sabbath glories in creation. It also includes retrieving the covenantal link between justice and harmony with nature.

134 Ogden, Schubert M. "Subtler Forms of Bondage and Liberation." In his *Faith and Freedom: Toward a Theology of Liberation*, 99-124. Nashville: Abingdon Press, 1979.

Ogden points out that the homocentric belief that nature acquires value solely through human beings is characteristic of post-Christian humanism generally; and that the goal of unlimited growth through science and technology is shared from evolutionary Baconianism through modern socialism. Liberation theology, whatever its orientation—political, economic, cultural, racial, or sexual—is consequently also homocentric. Ogden finds it impossible to dismiss the argument that Christianity has been important in homocentrism's development, but insists that theology must be freed from it because its presupposed dualism between history and nature is theoretically false—since humans emerged from nature and are subject to nature's laws; vicious in practice—since it fosters damaging attitudes toward the environment; and inappropriate to the Christian witness of faith—since all things are created out of nothing by God and therefore difference between creatures can be only a matter of degree. Thus dominion means ruling over creation so as to recognize both difference in intrinsic value and also the unity by which all creatures are bound. He argues that process metaphysics is a conceptual resource for overcoming dualism because it expresses this combination of unity and difference.

135 Peters, Ted F. *Futures—Human and Divine*. Atlanta: John Knox Press, 1978.

Peters explores the implicitly and explicitly religious character of the various forms of emerging "future consciousness." He contrasts secular understandings of the future, which extrapolate the future from past and present (*futurum*), with Christian eschatology, which evaluates the present in light of the future transformation of society and nature by God (*adventus*). He argues that the futurists' humanism, which tends to be relativistic and anthropocentric, is inadequate to provide a holistic vision of sufficiently deep ultimate concern to integrate the world for the survival and fulfillment of all; it requires completion by the vision of the Kingdom of God. He goes on to elaborate a philosophical foundation for a responsible Christian eschatology. Jesus' crucifixion and resurrection anticipates the future of society and the cosmos; living as resurrected people now means incarnating God's future in selfless love and concern. Although God is not yet fully actual, God's future reality is effective in the present, freeing creatures from the determinism of the past; redemption is continuing creation. Hope for God's future is a stimulus; love of God and of the creation are interdependent. He concludes by proposing six basic tasks of teaching and action for the Christian church.

136 Rasmussen, Larry L. "Honoring Creation's Integrity." *Christianity and Crisis* 52 (18 November 1991): 83-87.

Maintaining that the ecocrisis requires a cosmology that does not limit intrinsic value to human beings and that places mind and history within nature, Rasmussen offers a "sacramentalist liberationist" perspective that views humans as a unique, self-conscious expression of the cosmos which God is "in, with and under," one that asserts a preferential option for suffering human and nonhuman creation. Portions of this essay appeared as "Mindset and Moral Vision" in *Technology and Religion*, vol. 10 of *Research in Philosophy and Technology*, edited by Frederick Ferré, 119-28 (Greenwich, CT: JAI Press, 1990).

137   Rasmussen, Larry L.   "Returning to Our Senses: The Theology of the Cross as a Theology for Eco-Justice."   In *After Nature's Revolt: Eco-Justice and Theology*, edited by Dieter T. Hessel, 48-56. Minneapolis: Augsburg Fortress Publishers, 1992.

As an ethic to address the massive public suffering, human and extrahuman, of our time, Rasmussen proposes Luther's theology of the cross. This ethic is summarized as stating that being with the gracious God means "loving the earth"—turning toward God as creation's priest, trustee and servant, "loving Jesus"—who shows that healing comes from entering into creation's suffering for the sake of empowering victims, and "going home"—analyzing our context, which is marked by a self-destructive quest for mastery. Focusing on the human, crucified Jesus as the point where God's cosmic power is concentrated is essential if ecological justice and social justice are to be kept together.

138   Rasmussen, Larry L.   "Theology of Life and Ecumenical Ethics."   In *Ecotheology: Voices from South and North*, edited by David G. Hallman, 112-29.   Geneva: WCC Publications; Maryknoll, NY: Orbis Books, 1994.

In this essay Rasmussen seeks to outline a theological framework for discussing various particular approaches to a "theology of life" (a theme of the World Council of Churches' follow-up initiative for the "Justice, Peace, and Integrity of Creation" process). An ecumenical theology and ethic of life continues the biblical affirmation of human responsibility before the God who is the power in and of creation and the transcending power that beckons creation toward compassion and justice. From science it takes an awareness of the unity of life, both in shared destiny and in the "common creation story" of evolution, and the urgency to formulate a life-centered ecumenical ethic. That ethic, for Rasmussen, turns on power—as cosmic energy, expressed in religious and other symbols, and as social arrangements—and is served by norms of sustainability, participation, sufficiency, and solidarity.

139   Rasmussen, Larry L.   "Toward an Earth Charter."   *Christian Century* 108 (23 October 1991): 964-67.

Asking what the churches can contribute to the discussions at the Rio "Earth Summit," Rasmussen reviews the different theological-cosmological models evident in discussions at the World Council of Churches' Canberra Assembly: dominion, stewardship, partner, sacramentalism, prophet-teacher (more a stance than a cosmology), and evolutionary, with special attention to the social justice implications of the second, third and fourth models. Rasmussen favors an evolutionary sacramentalist model infused with a profound earth-oriented asceticism.

140   Rayan, Samuel.   "The Earth Is the Lord's."   In *Ecotheology: Voices from South and North*, edited by David G. Hallman, 130-48.   Geneva: WCC Publications; Maryknoll, NY: Orbis Books, 1994.

Rayan, a Roman Catholic priest and theologian from India, begins by elaborating on the theme "the earth is the Lord's" in poetic terms, drawing on the Bible and Indian thought. The earth is also ours, to be shared among all God's children and to be respected and cherished as something precious. Rayan then focuses on Christian traditional teachings condemning private property and holding up the ideal of common ownership and on three areas of contemporary concern: the commercialization of the earth, the unequal distribution of population, and the ecological crisis. Originally published in *Vidayjyoti Journal of Theological Reflection* 54 (March 1990).

141 Rockefeller, Steven C. "Faith and Community in an Ecological Age." In *Spirit and Nature: Why the Environment is a Religious Issue*, edited by Steven C. Rockefeller and John C. Elder, 139-72. Boston: Beacon Press, 1992.

In this essay delivered at the 1990 Middlebury College Spirit and Nature Symposium, philosopher of religion Rockefeller draws together the bases for an ecological worldview from ethics, the world's faiths, and twentieth-century philosophy. He considers the environmental crisis "a crisis in our understanding of and commitment to community" requiring a transformation of values and attitudes that is religious in nature and bound up with the struggle for social justice. He emphasizes the effort to find a way of life directed away from "egoism, having, and subjugation" and toward the creation of a community embracing other life forms as well as humanity.

142 Rolston, Holmes, III. "Does Nature Need to Be Redeemed?" *Horizons in Biblical Theology* 14 (1993): 143-72.

Skillfully crossing the language barriers of separate disciplines, philosopher Rolston maintains that the worldviews of biologist and theologian on the question of the necessity of nature's redemption are not as far apart as they initially appear; that a knowledge of biology helps clarify the theological issues at stake, while the unique evolutionary attainments of humanity introduce the necessity of religious categories of description. While biology illustrates that suffering is a universal fact throughout the evolution of organic life and not a novelty introduced by human sin, the Genesis story of the Fall points to a break between humans and other organic life introduced by humanity's acquisition of moral choice—the choice of living by the animal law of eat-or-be-eaten, or rising to the possibility of imaging God in love, justice, and freedom. The Genesis story also agrees with the innate selfishness biology finds within humans—when humans desire to *be* God rather than to *be like* God their sin pollutes the world, and nature does need to be redeemed. The article also appears in *Zygon* 29 (June 1994): 205-29.

143 Ruether, Rosemary Radford. "Ecology and Human Liberation: A Conflict Between the Theology of History and the Theology of Nature?" In her *To Change the World: Christology and Cultural Criticism*, 57-70. New York: Crossroad Publishing Co., 1981.

Maintaining that the ecological crisis is linked to social domination, Ruether explains its origins and evaluates three responses—the liberal progressive response, which stresses civil freedom, social equity, education, and progress, but which has led to exploitation by dominant White males; the Marxist revolutionary response, which acknowledges the social-domination aspect of wealth and argues for social ownership, but still stresses the importance of unending progress; and the romantic response, which argues for a return to nature and for the wisdom of indigenous peoples and women, while failing to recognize complementary roles of East and West, male and female, Black and White. She concludes with an outline of "a new worldview of eco-justice" that replaces Western concepts of ever-expanding power and wealth, hierarchical power structures, and linear models of history with a Hebraic sense of mortal limits and periodic revolutionary conversion to a more equitable and harmonious state.

144 Santmire, H. Paul. *Brother Earth: Nature, God, and Ecology in Time of Crisis.* New York: Thomas Nelson Publishers, 1970.

This, one of the first books on ecological theology, is still useful, especially for understanding the background of the tensions between advocates of ecology and those of social justice. Santmire shows how American history includes the opposing ethics of (1) adoration of nature and withdrawal from the city; and (2) exploitation of nature in the service of civilization. Both persist in the political and internal life of the church; both attempt to escape the anxiety of historical existence, including the demands of justice. As an alternative, Santmire proposes an ethic of responsibility based on a vision of the Kingdom of God as "creative rule" (God's establishing, shaping and valuing in the divine history with nature) and "created realm" (of which the natural and the human are two dimensions). Human life is not only "in" nature but also "above-and-with" nature as overlord, caretaker, and wondering onlooker. Christ overcomes human estrangement from nature and makes present the final future of the whole universe. The ethic of responsibility, which finds its criterion in the Kingdom (rather than in civilization or nature) attends to both the needs of the poor and the rights of nature. A version of chapter 1 appeared separately as (017).

145 Santmire, H. Paul. "Ecology and Ethical Ecumenics." *Anglican Theological Review* 57 (January 1977): 98-102.

This review of Thomas Derr's *Ecology and Human Need* (174) welcomes his emphasis on social justice, but asks whether it requires an anthropocentric focus on human dominion that excludes substantive theological attention to the value of nature apart from humanity.

146 Santmire, H. Paul. "Healing the Protestant Mind: Beyond the Theology of Human Dominion." In *After Nature's Revolt: Eco-Justice and Theology*, edited by Dieter T. Hessel, 57-78. Minneapolis: Augsburg Fortress Publishers, 1992.

Santmire provides a significant critique, at once revisionist and traditional, of the Protestant "the-anthropocentric" theology of dominion underlying most calls for eco-justice and responsible stewardship. He finds that it too easily becomes a theology of anthropocentric domination even as it asserts nature's intrinsic value. He proposes "a new ecological paradigm," appropriating Barth's thought in terms of a universal divine ecology rather than a narrow divine-human economy. The divine purpose is to initiate and shepherd a cosmic history and bring it to fulfillment in the eternal Sabbath rest: thus, nature has its own independent history with God; humans are to cooperate with nature; and the work of Christ and the Spirit is cosmic in scope.

147 Santmire, H. Paul. "Is Christianity Ecologically Bankrupt? The View from Asylum Hill." In *An Ecology of the Spirit: Religious Reflections and Environmental Consciousness*, edited by Michael Barnes, 11-26. The Annual Publication of the College Theology Society, 1990, vol. 36. Lanham, MD: University Press of America, 1994.

Santmire critiques what he perceives as a dangerous and erroneous Christian response to the ecological crisis—that of creation-centered spirituality as proposed by Matthew Fox. Although appreciative of creation spirituality's affirmation of nature, he finds fault with its failure to adequately account for the place of evil and suffering in human life. He compares Fox's writing to Henry Thoreau's *Walden*, which he considers an elitist escape fantasy. Santmire argues instead for an Augustinian theology which celebrates "God's overflowing and immanence in nature" while still advancing a Fall/redemption theology which "speaks to the realities of death and estrangement in human experience."

148 Santmire, H. Paul. "The Liberation of Nature: Lynn White's Challenge Anew." *Christian Century* 102 (22 May 1985): 530-33.

Santmire revisits Lynn White Jr.'s "Historical Roots" essay (026), finding deepest significance in its challenge to consider the liberation of nature as a theological theme and to end the theological legitimization of *any* structure of domination. The critique of humankind's domination of nature, as the last extension of St. Paul's vision of universal liberation, belongs to the prophetic tradition of the critiques of slavery, anti-Semitism, and patriarchy.

149 Schaeffer, Jill. "The Liberation of Creation." *Ecumenical Review* 42 (January 1990): 621-67.

These reflections stress God's "preferential option for the poor," human and non-human, and are based on what Birch and Cobb (065) refer to as "outward" and "inward" liberation. The former is described with reference to the biblical stories of creation, the flood, and the sabbatical year, emphasizing human dependence on nature and God's concern for the whole. The latter is related to Jesus' mission to save the whole cosmos and to free human beings to act on behalf of the whole.

150 Schulze, Bernd, ed. *Reintegrating God's Creation*. Church and Society Documents, September 1987, no. 3. Geneva: World Council of Churches, 1987.

This slim booklet consists of condensed presentations by scientists, theologians, and others assembled in Amsterdam in May 1987 to discuss "the integrity of creation," a side of the Justice, Peace, and the Integrity of Creation (JPIC) process which was not at the time being attended to, according to editor Schulze. The opening section, "The Disintegration of Creation," is by James Lovelock (whose "Gaia" hypothesis views Earth as a self-regulating system), Adebisi Sowunmi, and Darryl D'Monte (who describes links between environment and poverty). A theological section, "The Integrity of Creation" follows. Adelbert Schloz critiques contemporary views regarding creation—including nature as primarily a consoling, aesthetic object—which he sees as serving the interests of the privileged and leading to neglect of creation's disintegration and of human suffering. Douglas John Hall analyzes the meanings of "integrity of creation" and proposes three metaphors for the human role which finds its definitive paradigm in Christ: steward, priest, and poet. "The Reintegration of Creation" gives concluding remarks by Lovelock, Sowunmi, D'Monte (who again affirms the social justice dimension) and Schloz. Mady A. Thung, Rolando Mendoza, and Schulze give examples of how churches can respond to environmental and social justice issues. Thung and Schulze provide a "Postscript" on working for social change.

151 Sittler, Joseph. "Called to Unity." *Ecumenical Review* 14 (January 1962): 177-87.

This is Sittler's landmark address to the 1961 Assembly of the World Council of Churches in New Delhi. He claims that Christology is irrelevant unless it is related to our earthliness—which includes hunger, war, and the care of the earth. Western Christendom has inherited a dualism of nature and grace that has shrunk Christ to personal and historical categories. However, in Colossians and Irenaeus we have a model for a Christology of nature commensurate with the cosmos we now inhabit, and which can lead the churches to true Christian unity.

152   Sittler, Joseph.   "Christian Theology and the Environment."   In his *Essays in Nature and Grace*, 112-22.   Philadelphia: Fortress Press, 1972.

Concluding his slender but seminal book, Sittler relates the doctrine of grace to the "environmental problem," noting that Christian ethics must speak to a culture in which the scope of the known universe and of human powers to alter and perhaps destroy the earth have reached unprecedented magnitudes.   He suggests that the theology of grace is ethically "verified" by the fact that the world must be dealt with graciously if it is to continue to exist.   A footnote in response to Richard J. Neuhaus (see 300), argues that abuse of persons and of nature are both rooted in the failure to regard creation as grace.

153   Sittler, Joseph.   "Ecological Commitment as Theological Responsibility."   *Zygon* 5 (June 1970): 172-81.

Sittler argues that God, as the source of all reality, loves and gives meaning to the *whole* of reality.   All reality is ecological for it is relational: we must "behold" in relations, meaning we must honor the integrity of other beings and "think" in relations, that is, recognize human beings as both natural and historical.   The relation of theology and ecology is best understood within the doctrine of grace as created and uncreated.   Grace as creating the variety of the world can also be applied to ethical relations between humans such as race relations.

154   Spretnak, Charlene.   *States of Grace: The Recovery of Meaning in the Postmodern Age*.   San Francisco: HarperSanFrancisco, 1991.

In seeking answers to what humans can do to change their attitudes toward nature in time to save the planet, the author argues against the deconstructive postmodernist worldview with its claims of inherent disconnection, and for the present-day relevance of the wisdom traditions, especially in their emphasis on practices that encourage awareness of the sacred and of the concept of grace.   She singles out Buddhism for its insights into the nature of mind; native peoples' spirituality for its relationships with the natural world; contemporary Goddess spirituality for an ecologically-grounded response to the body of earth and the personal body; and the Semitic traditions (Judaism, Christianity, Islam) for social justice and a sense of community.   Chapter 5, "Who Is the Other?" considers not only the positive tendencies of the Semitic traditions to see the divine manifest in human history, to respond to injustice with prophetic anger and social legislation, and to show concern for the poor and disadvantaged, but also their negative tendencies to harshly limit the divine community to adherents of the faith and to cast women in inferior roles.   Spretnak discusses structural injustice in the world and in the United States which takes the forms of war, inequality of wealth, and ever-increasing use of "resources."   She maintains that the religious motivation to combine faith with social justice brings about social change, and she calls for liberation theologians to root themselves in the communitarian decentralist tradition of Catholic social teaching which would place the movement closer to emerging Green economics.   Spretnak also calls for children to be educated in an awareness of their inseparable relatedness to each other and to Earth.

155   Tinker, George E.   "Creation as Kin: An American Indian View."   In *After Nature's Revolt: Eco-Justice and Theology*, edited by Dieter T. Hessel, 144-53.   Minneapolis: Augsburg Fortress Publishers, 1992.

Contrary to the order implied in "justice, peace, and the integrity of creation," Tinker argues that justice and peace flow from genuine concern for the integrity of creation—understood in American Indian terms as a balanced, harmonious community of humans and other creatures. He relates this idea to Christianity by interpreting the proclamation of the Kingdom of God in Mark's Gospel in spatial, rather than temporal, terms—as a call to return to a proper relationship with Creator and creation which generates action for justice and peace.

156 Tinker, George E. "The Full Circle of Liberation: An American Indian Theology of Place." In *Eco-Theology: Voices from South and North*, edited by David G. Hallman, 218-24. Geneva: WCC Publications; Maryknoll, NY: Orbis Books, 1994.

This essay critiques liberation theology as represented by Gustavo Gutierrez in hopes of greater mutual understanding and solidarity between Third World and Fourth World (indigenous) peoples. According to Tinker, Marxist class analysis, by overlooking the cultural discreteness and personhood of native peoples, threatens to continue the "spiritual genocide" perpetrated by European colonialism. Likewise, insistence on the primacy of God's revelation in history and time excludes Native American spirituality's priority on creation and place. Tinker argues that an American Indian reading of 'repentance' and '*basileia*' (Kingdom) in terms of place can generate a more immediate and attainable vision of justice and peace and mandates social structures different from either capitalism or socialism. Previously published in *Sojourners* 21 (October 1992): 12-17 and *SEDOS Bulletin* 25 (15 January 1993): 9-13.

157 United States Conference of Catholic Bishops. "Renewing the Earth." *Origins, NC Documentary Service* 21, 27 (12 December 1991) 425-32.

The bishops' statement is significant as a clear and comprehensive call to eco-justice by a major Christian body, and as signalling a deepening of ecological sensibilities in traditional Roman Catholic social thought. It claims that the health of the planet requires justice within and between nations as well as a sustainable economy, spells out poverty-environment linkages, and cites Catholic responses. It reviews relevant themes from Catholic social teachings: a sacramental universe, respect for human and other life, and an ethic of global justice and solidarity which includes an "option for the poor" and a norm of "authentic development." Problems caused by rapid population growth are acknowledged, but concentration on Third World fertility rather than First World consumption is criticized, and population coercion, incentives, disincentives, and abortion are condemned. Theological and pastoral concerns are raised regarding tendencies to worship the earth, reject science, and pit the environment against the poor. The statement suggests actions to be taken by various groups and professions, and ends with a call to conversion and a word of hope.

158 Westhelle, Vítor. "Creation Motifs in the Search for a Vital Space: A Latin American Perspective." In *Lift Every Voice: Constructing Christian Theologies from the Underside*, edited by Susan Brooks Thistlethwaite and Mary Potter Engel, 128-40. New York: HarperCollins Publishers, 1990.

Admitting that theology in Latin America has been ambivalent about creation, first because creation appears detached from the immediate problems of the displaced peoples of the world, and secondly because creation discourse is infused with the language of "order" and thus associated with repression and the state, Brazilian theologian Westhelle discusses three ways in which scriptural creation motifs are meaningful in a liberation context. Creation motifs that praise the Creator as maker of all things new, of *creatio ex nihilo*, of a God not bound to what exists, inhabit memory and prepare the brain for liberation. At the ecological level of the relation between human beings and nature, an analogy exists between human labor and God's creative activity. The worker is embedded in the land, and both land and worker change in the process of meaningful work. The third motif of creation, *imago Dei*, Westhelle sees as "community inter-relatedness that affirms the fundamental solidarity of God with the displaced and dispossessed whom God empowers."

159 Westhelle, Vítor. "The Weeping Mask: Ecological Crisis and the View of Nature." *Word and World* 11 (Spring 1991): 137-46.

Brazilian theologian Westhelle focuses on the need to change the vision of nature and the cultural values that have "oriented the present hegemonic civilizations of the world" and led to the ecological crisis. Reorientation requires an act of repentance, breaking with three fundamental myths of modernity: the atomic indi-vidual, progress through accumulation, and private piety. The needed ecological consciousness—which will come from those who are powerless, dispossessed, and outside official religion—is one that embraces community solidarity, views labor as a metabolic relationship between humans and nature, and beholds nature as the mask of God, now "weeping and groaning in travail." Westhelle notes the inseparability of justice and environmental concern, affirms the intrinsic rights of nature, and interprets references in Genesis to "image of God" and "dominion" as mandates for equality among humans and peaceful coexistence with animals.

160 Wilkinson, Loren. "Gaia Spirituality: A Christian Critique." *Evangelical Review of Theology* 17 (April 1993): 176-89.

Wilkinson presents a generally careful and balanced discussion of "Gaia" from three viewpoints: as a scientific hypothesis (that the earth as a whole is a self-organizing and self-regulating entity); as a monistic spirituality invoked to sup-port a global environmental ethic (in evidence at the Global Forum at Rio); and as supported by ecofeminist principles (women as nurturers, critique of patriar-chy, and Goddess-worship). Cautioning against uncritical acceptance or fearful rejection, Wilkinson allows that the Gaia hypothesis coheres with the biblical pic-ture of a harmonious creation, but that reductionistic or monistic interpretations are inconsistent with human environmental responsibility.

In addition to the works annotated in this chapter, readers interested in theological and philosophical perspectives may wish to consult the following entries located elsewhere in the bibliography: 005, 018, 023, 048, 166, 174, 193, 195, 216, 225, 230, 237, 238, 239, 241, 243, 248, 251, 284, 309, 326, 331, 332, 376, 377, 414, 434, 459, 465, 480, 487, 488.

4

Ethical Analysis

Moving from a theological affirmation of eco-justice to judgments and recommendations on environmental policy requires ethical analysis. Items in this section attempt to clarify and interrelate ethical concepts such as "justice," "love," "rights," and "the common good"; propose norms for decision-making; argue for (or against) particular ethical stances (e.g., "responsible stewardship") and diagnose moral failure. Applications of eco-justice norms to specific policy issues or areas (e.g., energy, agriculture, economics, war, racism) have been assigned to later sections; works that ethically address multiple environmental and social issues are found here. Discussions of "animal rights" appear in this section because the question of our duties to other creatures is a fundamental issue for ethical theory.

161 Abraham, K. C. "A Theological Response to the Ecological Crisis." In *Ecotheology: Voices from South and North*, edited by David G. Hallman, 65-78. Geneva: WCC Publications; Maryknoll, NY: Orbis Books, 1994.

Indian theologian Abraham regards ecological issues as integral to the struggle of the poor for liberation. He sees the ecological crisis as a justice issue in which economic exploitation and environmental degradation are connected. Justice, which includes justice to the planet and to future generations, is a matter of care rather than of balancing rights and duties. The ecological crisis requires a new sense of interdependence, a new spirituality, and a new scale of values based on "enabling power" rather than "dominating power." He outlines three models for the church's response: the ascetic, monastic model, which cannot effect structural, systemic changes; the sacramental/eucharist model, too often confined to ritual observance; and the liberative solidarity model, which adds the liberation of creation to political and economic liberation and draws on the biblical idea of covenant. Abraham asserts that people of all faiths can work together on behalf of ecological concerns.

162 Adams, Carol J. "Feeding on Grace: Institutional Violence, Christianity, and Vegetarianism." In *Good News for Animals? Christian Approaches to Animal Well-Being*, edited by Charles Pinches and Jay B. McDaniel, 142-59. Maryknoll, NY: Orbis Books, 1993.

Adams argues that the eating of animals is a form of institutional violence, unjust because unnecessary and cruel, involving injurious physical force, the denial mechanism of false naming, and pricing that discounts environmental depletion. This institutional violence is harmful to society because of its substantial contribution to land, air, and water pollution; its consequences for consumers of flesh and dairy products; its effects on slaughterhouse workers, and its manipulation of consumers. Whether or not Jesus ate animal flesh is not important; a Christology of vegetarianism involves the "acquisition of an ability to discern justice-making according to the Christological revelation" and requires knowledge of farm animals and the conditions under which they are raised.

163 Altner, Günter. "The Community of Creation as a Community in Law: The New Contract between the Generations." Translated by John Bowden. *Concilium* 4 (August 1991): 54-64.

The author believes that humans are creatures distinguished primarily by their sharing of God's knowledge of the goodness of all creation and by their responsibility for creation. Viewing creation as a community in which human and nonhuman creatures alike participate requires extending legal rights to non-human creation and future generations, thus admitting them to the democratic constitutional state, as disadvantaged groups of people have been admitted. To do so will require cooperation among churches and nation-states as well as binding international commitments.

164 Baer, Richard A., Jr. "Poverty, Pollution, and the Power of the Gospel." *Engage/Social Action* 3 (January 1975): 49-57.

Baer claims that the gospel can enable affluent American Christians to adopt a life-style that is more environmentally sound and more open to sharing with the rest of the world than that practiced today. The gospel provides insight into the sins of the "righteous" and the insecurity that motivates the exploitation of nature. Alongside the supportive fellowship of the church, the gospel frees the individual from societal values based on production, consumption, and control. Focused more on God's grace than on human sin, the Christian's stance is that of the forward-looking "planner," full of praise and a sense of the mystery of life beyond human control. Originally published in *Stewardship* 26 (1974), this article also appears in N. C. Murphy, ed., *Teaching and Preaching Stewardship: An Anthology*, 233-31 (New York: Commission on Stewardship, National Council of the Churches of Christ in the USA, 1985).

165 Board of National Ministries of the American Baptist Churches in the USA. "Ecological Wholeness and Justice: The Imperative of God." *Foundations* 17 (April/June 1974): 133-57.

This article is of particular interest because of its attempt to integrate the independent results of separate task forces on "justice" and "ecology." Its conclusions are that ecology and justice together demand that: identity and self-worth be found in interdependence, decisions address the well-being of all parts of "Spaceship Earth," resources be viewed as a trust for all creatures in all generations, and God's creatures be viewed as things of beauty and subjects of adoration. It correlates existential questions about self-worth, the meaning of life, unity and diversity, relationships and survival, change, guilt and redemption with biblical witness, and it formulates "signposts" and a vision of the "Promised Land" to guide and be tested in action. Because Christians care about the world, they must work to see that the poor are fed, the right to life of all creatures is respected, and the economic system is balanced.

166 Bube, Paul Custodio. *Ethics in John Cobb's Process Theology.* Atlanta: Scholars Press, 1988.

In one of the most fully developed treatments of the relationships between ecology, justice, and theology in this bibliography, Bube interprets John B. Cobb Jr.'s thought in terms of two major periods. Prior to 1969, the major category of Cobb's ethics was the notion of "Christian existence"—an awareness of responsibility for the choice of the center from which one organizes the self. After 1969, when he concluded that the radical self-transcendence of Christian existence tended to widen the gulf between humans and other living creatures, Cobb developed a Christology of "creative transformation"—the universal process by which God lures the world toward a richer and more inclusive future, and the norm which shows how ethical principles of rights, equity, justice, and liberation apply to both human and non-human creation. Faith in Christ as creative transformation means faith that the goals of justice, liberation, and sustainability ultimately serve one other.

167 Byron, William J. *Toward Stewardship: An Interim Ethic of Poverty, Power, and Pollution.* New York: Paulist Press, 1975.

Byron presents an ecological interpretation of the biblical theme of stewardship. He states that while neither the Old nor the New Testament presents an unambiguous doctrine regarding the use of land for the good of humanity, the early texts of the teaching church indicate that faithful stewardship requires not only avoidance of avarice but assistance to the needy. Destruction of the environment is avaricious behavior, and since the fundamental idea of stewardship is that "wealth possessed is held in trust for others," environmental responsibility for the sake of the poor and future generations is an implied moral responsibility.

168 Campolo, Tony. *How to Rescue the Earth without Worshiping Nature.* Nashville, TN: Thomas Nelson Publishers, 1992.

Discussing the importance of environment, Campolo highlights, not only standard ecological problems, but also related issues of justice, including animal rights and the plight of the poor as he seeks to develop an environmental ethic that addresses these concerns while remaining true to evangelical Christianity. He draws from a variety of sources, including Christian mystics such as Francis of Assisi and Benedict, early church reformers such as John Calvin and John Wesley, and more contemporary thinkers such as C. S. Lewis and Teilhard de Chardin. Advocating a new Christian lifestyle, Campolo offers practical suggestions for both individual and church action aimed at improving the environment, while he firmly warns against the dangers of being drawn into the New Age movement.

169 Cobb, John B., Jr. "Christian Existence in a World of Limits." *Environmental Ethics* 1 (Summer 1979): 149-58.

Cobb describes several diverse and appropriate Christian responses to limits, from "Christian realism"—a style of action described by Reinhold Niebuhr which aims at maintaining relative justice by motivating others to see their own self-interest attained as they foster justice, to "the way of the Cross"—involving lone witness, and possibly poverty, without expectation of appreciation. For a similar treatment of this same issue see Cobb (170). Reprinted in *Religion and Environmental Crisis*, edited by Eugene Hargrove, 172-187 (Athens: University of Georgia Press, 1986) and in (339), pp. 17-19.

170   Cobb, John B., Jr.   "Eco-justice and Christian Salvation." In his *Sustainability: Economics, Ecology, and Justice*, 20-33. Maryknoll, NY: Orbis Books, 1992.

This essay consists of questions about the acceptability of various courses of action that Christians might support in light of the fact of limits. The choices are difficult, and Cobb pushes the reader to see just how difficult it is to maintain a belief in the possibility of eco-justice, or of Christians knowing how, or being able to, adjust their understanding of Christian faith in response. For a similar treatment of this same theme see Cobb (169).

171   Cobb, John B., Jr.   "Envisioning a Just and Peaceful World." *Religious Education* 79 (1984): 483-94.

Cobb critiques the Vancouver Assembly of the World Council of Churches for focusing on peace and justice without lifting up the values of participation and sustainability. While acknowledging that "peace with justice" can be understood as implying these other values (and vice versa), he insists that they will be overlooked if they are not explicitly named. Like science and technology, education and global interdependence have not in practice brought nearer a peaceful, just, participatory, and sustainable world, but religious educators especially can help to envision one.

172   Comstock, Gary L.   "Pigs and Piety: A Theocentric Perspective in Food Animals." In *Good News for Animals? Christian Approaches to Animal Well-Being*, edited by Charles Pinches and Jay B. McDaniel, 105-27. Maryknoll, NY: Orbis Books, 1993.

This argument for vegetarianism and against the slaughtering and eating of pigs derives its unique quality from the use its author, a Mennonite with Iowa farm relations, makes of personal acquaintance with and research into the life history of pigs. Among the many internally-debated points, of particular relevance to justice is his answer to the criticism that Jesus said nothing against vegetarianism and was most likely an eater of fish. Comstock sees an analogy to the owning of slaves, also implicitly condoned in the Bible, but wrong "because the overall themes of the Bible are freedom, liberation, justice, and mercy." The biblical authors erred in a point of fact concerning the rational abilities of darker-skinned individuals. Once this fact was corrected, darker-skinned individuals fell within the Bible's moral protection. Once mammals are recognized as conscious, sentient individuals, justice must be done them.

173   Daly, Lois K.   "Ecofeminism, Reverence for Life, and Feminist Theological Ethics." In *Liberating Life*: *Contemporary Approaches to Ecological Theology*, edited by Charles Birch, William Eakin, and Jay B. McDaniel, 88-108. Maryknoll, NY: Orbis Books, 1990.

In a helpful summary of ecofeminism and an intriguing retrieval and critique of Albert Schweitzer, Daly presents Schweitzer's ethic of reverence for life as a resource for feminist theological ethics. She sees Schweitzer providing a consistently non-dualistic and non-hierarchical understanding of God, human beings, and nature in terms of the will-to-live, but faults his focus on individuals as a neglect of issues of justice and social analysis.

174 Derr, Thomas Sieger. *Ecology and Human Need*. Philadelphia: Westminster Press, 1975.

This work, originally published as *Ecology and Human Liberation: A Theological Critique of the Use and Abuse of Our Birthright* (Geneva: World Student Christian Federation, 1973), argues that the biblical view of human dominion over a desacralized, historicized nature is not the sole or direct cause of the destructive exploitation of the environment. Instead, it supports a socially just but exclusively theo-anthropocentric environmental ethic in which nature must be used wisely for the survival and betterment of human beings. Derr discusses and rejects the more radical views of Conrad Bonifazi, Joseph Sittler, H. Paul Santmire, process theologians, and countercultural "remystifiers." He argues for recognition of obligations to future generations, socially responsible management of possessions, improvement of the quality of life (especially the material condition of the poor), and the need to halt population growth. He strongly criticizes "lifeboat ethics" and "no-growth" proposals. For a critical review of this neo-orthodox approach to eco-justice, see Santmire (145), pp. 98-102.

175 Donahue, James A. "Environmental Ethics and Contemporary Moral Discourse." In *An Ecology of the Spirit: Religious Reflections and Environmental Consciousness*, edited by Michael Barnes, 11-26. The Annual Publication of the College Theology Society, 1990, vol. 36. Lanham, MD: University Press of America, 1994.

This broad survey of major debates in contemporary moral discourse, focusing on their relation to environmental awareness, begins by outlining the necessary components for an adequate Christian environmental ethic grounded in the realization "that all life constitutes the arena of God's creation and activity." Examining the major debates of communitarianism versus liberalism, universalism versus particularism, and classicism versus revisionism in natural law, Donahue shows how these different positions help or hinder the development of such an ethic. Throughout, he stresses the importance of the human imagination in deciding these debates.

176 Dumas, André. "A Society which Creates Justice: Three Themes but One Development." *Ecumenical Review* 30 (July 1978): 211-19.

Dumas argues for taking justice as the central hinge of the "Just, Participatory and Sustainable Society" as well as for the priority of history and the personal in the biblical revelation and the Christian understanding of God. Humanity is related to nature through legitimate domination, respectful cultivation, wonder, and meditation. While technology increases domination, it diminishes the other two relations and works against participation and justice.

177 Engel, J. Ronald. "Ecology and Social Justice: The Search for a Public Environmental Ethic." In *Issues of Justice: Social Sources and Religious Meanings*, edited by Warren R. Copeland and Roger D. Hatch, 243-63. Macon, GA: Mercer University Press, 1988.

Engel maintains that ecocentric and resource conservation ethics, the two most prominent sorts of environmental ethics today, do not adequately address the full range of social and environmental values at stake in such issues as tropical deforestation; nor do they deal with the complex relationships between environmental and social justice. An adequate vision of eco-justice requires a democratic environmental ethic guided by the pluralistic moral principle of maximizing richness of experience of all life forms through maximizing the freedom, equality, and community of all forms of life. The belief that such an ethic is rooted in the nature of things is in fundamental continuity with biblical prophetic faith.

178 Engel, J. Ronald. "Introduction: The Ethics of Sustainable Development." In *Ethics of Environment and Development: Global Challenge, International Response,* edited by J. Ronald Engel and Joan Gibb Engel, 1-23. Tucson: University of Arizona Press; London: Belhaven Press, 1990.

Engel suggests that the ecological, social, political, and personal values of "sustainable development" need to be carefully examined before it is accepted as the *true* ethic for humans to follow. He asks whether sustainable development is only a new term for the kind of economic activity that now dominates the world, or whether it is a new moral conception of "the kind of human activity that nourishes and perpetuates the historical fulfillment of the whole community of life on Earth." If the latter, it is an ethical paradigm with the potential to bring together advocates of alternative development and advocates of ecological integrity, one that may require the transformation of both modern science and the historic religions, as it will also necessitate the development of a greater mutuality between them. Engel finds ethicists agreeing that "individuals-in-community" describes the reality and ideal of life on Earth. This suggests to him that the meaningful choices are not between individuals and community, or environment and people, but between different kinds of "mixed communities of people, animals, plants, and minerals"—those "whose development path is ecologically sustainable and socially just and those whose path is not." He sees a need for ethicists to reconceptualize inherited moral ideals so that they include the values of the natural world, and he calls on them to work with concerned citizens in the public arena to help in forming coalitions between advocates of ecological integrity and those of social and economic justice.

179 Engel, J. Ronald. "Landscape of the Future: The Challenge of a Global Ethic." In *The Benedictines of Lisle: Centennial Celebration of a Monastic Land Ideal,* 74-87. 1985-1986 Humanities Lecture Series. Lisle, IL: Illinois Benedictine College, 1986.

Engel sees "hitherto unexplored and unrecognized continuities between the root metaphors and symbols of the great faiths of the world and the new forms of eco-centric religiousness which have emerged in modern times." He identifies six major strands of environmental awareness, the "scientific/democratic environmental traditions," that have emerged in the United States since the 18th century and matches them with six traditions within the biblical faith. Thus he pairs the modern ethic of the wilderness experience and the biblical wilderness/paradise motif, both involving rebirth, a sense of transcendence and a prophetic posture toward human injustice. He matches the ecological environmental tradition associated with Aldo Leopold to the biblical theme of covenant; the agrarian environmental tradition represented by Wendell Berry to stewardship; and the Enlightenment-based animal rights or animal liberation traditions to the perception of kinship between man and beast illustrated in the book of Genesis. He links the idea that nature has potentialities which are waiting for the grace of human artistic transformation and the notion of co-creatorship that is seen in Genesis when God charges Adam with the unfinished task of naming the animals. Finally, he links resource conservation or utilitarianism, associated with Gifford Pinchot, to the biblical doctrine of dominion, seeing both as demanding sustainable and just interventions into natural processes. Because of the fact that in each of these environmental traditions, secular and biblical, "human beings participate with nature in ways that realize the values of nature and the ends of human existence together," making these continuities explicit would, Engel asserts, contribute toward healing the separation of social justice and ecological concerns in the modern world.

180 Faramelli, Norman J. "Eco-Justice: Challenge to the Churches in the 1970s." *Foundations* 17 (April/June 1974): 124-32.

Faramelli, an engineer, minister, and former director of the Boston Industrial Mission, argues that eco-justice will result in a society respectful of the natural order, one that realizes the full potential of all persons. Conflicts between ecology and justice must be overcome by transforming profit-oriented minds and institutions that exploit both people and environment and set them against one another, and by initiating "total environmental planning" that takes account of the environmental needs of both the poor and the well-off.

181 Ferré, Frederick. "Obstacles on the Path to Organismic Ethics: Some Second Thoughts." *Environmental Ethics* 11 (Fall 1989): 231-41.

Although it says little about theology, this article is a necessary postscript to Ferré's *Shaping the Future* (263). Ferré summarizes his argument for organismic ethics as an alternative to modern mechanistic consciousness, but also notes its shortcomings—it cannot distinguish between better and worse types of internal relations and homeostatic controls, and it permits the subordination of individuals to wholes. He proposes a "personalistic organicism" that recognizes the distinctive value of persons without restricting intrinsic value to persons (although he acknowledges that this position also has its difficulties).

182 French, William C. "Catholicism and the Common Good of the Biosphere." In *An Ecology of the Spirit: Religious Reflections and Environmental Consciousness,* edited by Michael Barnes, 11-26. The Annual Publication of the College Theology Society, 1990, vol. 36. Lanham, MD: University Press of America, 1994.

This essay discusses the strengths and weaknesses of the doctrine of natural law in both its classical and revisionist interpretations. French desires that the classical notion of the "common good" not only be retained but be expanded beyond humans to include the entire biospheric community. He discusses the historical reasons why the doctrine was limited to humans, and he details the modern social constructions, including industrial development and consumption patterns, that mitigate against its expansion. French demonstrates how the idea of common good has been expanded by Popes John XXIII and John Paul II, but he recognizes their work as still anthropocentric and thus insufficient. Identified as Catholic resources that support an expansion of the common good are the Noachic covenant, Stoic tradition, and Thomas Aquinas.

183 Fritsch, Albert J., and Science Action Coalition. *Environmental Ethics: Choices for Concerned Citizens.* Garden City, NY: Anchor Press/Doubleday, 1980.

Although the term "eco-justice" is limited to "the need to deal justly with the environment," this book as a whole assumes a comprehensive ethical perspective. It suggests that "the unique contribution of the prophetic voice today" lies in the continuity between eco-justice and social justice, and it sees this broadened view of justice as based on a fusion of the ecological worldview with an enlightened view of human self-interest: because our species stands atop an interdependent ecological pyramid "we enrich ourselves when enriching other inhabitants of this earth." This fusion is theologically congruent with the simultaneous recognition of humankind's creatureliness and special calling to give "Christlike service to other creatures." It leads ethically to the need for simpler lifestyles; to an interpretation of stewardship that synthesizes human responsibilities for caring for the earth and sharing its fruits with those less fortunate; and to a call to participate in bringing to birth a "new heaven and a new earth" by improving the quality of life of all persons, plants, and animals. In chapters on endangered species, nuclear safety, coal extraction, hazardous chemicals, and economic growth, these moral principles are translated into specific sets of value priorities. Unfortunately, the book's method of associating particular values—survival, technological optimism, eco-justice, prudence, human fulfillment—with particular issues blurs and obscures its holistic theological ethic and considerable practical wisdom regarding environment/justice relationships.

184 Gibson, William E. "Confessing and Covenanting." In *Shalom Connections for Personal and Congregational Life*, edited by Dieter T. Hessel, 11-27. Ellenwood, GA: Alternatives, 1986.

Gibson, who has long been associated with the Eco-Justice Project of the Center for Religion, Ethics, and Social Policy at Cornell University, applies biblical themes of confession and covenant to the eco-justice crisis, a crisis he interprets as God's judgment on unsustainable, unjust systems and requiring a confession of our failure to respect nature and to distribute its goods to all people. He suggests that in renewing our covenant relationship, the most appropriate norms are solidarity, sustainability, and sufficiency—or "sustainable sufficiency for all." A shorter version of this essay appeared as "Three Norms for Our Time," *The Egg* 6 (Spring 1986): 1-4.

185 Gibson, William E. "Eco-Justice: Burning Word: Heilbroner and Jeremiah to the Church." *Foundations* 20 (October/December 1977): 318-28.

Gibson interprets the signs of an eco-justice crisis—the suffering of the poor and environmental deterioration—as the "burning word" of divine judgment and a call to transformation. Comparing Robert Heilbroner (*An Inquiry into the Human Prospect*) and Jeremiah in their attacks on human resistance to change in the face of global inequity and impending catastrophe, he proposes that the church assume as its role the critiquing of industrial society and that it provide the vision, supporting programs, and leadership for a sustainable society wherein the needs of all are met. See Gomes (444) for a response appearing in the same issue.

186 Gibson, William E. "Eco-Justice: New Perspective for a Time of Turning." In *For Creation's Sake: Preaching, Ecology, and Justice*, edited by Dieter T. Hessel, 15-31. Philadelphia: Geneva Press, 1985.

This article, which discusses some of the history of attempts to combine ecology and justice since 1970, including the strategic planning of the Board of National Ministries of the American Baptist Church, argues the need for an eco-justice perspective combining sufficiency, stewardship, cooperation, community, and work that meets aesthetic, spiritual, and material needs. It suggests that effective eco-justice preaching will result in individual lifestyle change.

187 Gore, Al. *Earth in the Balance: Ecology and the Human Spirit.* Boston: Houghton Mifflin Co., 1992.

Although it is not insignificant that its author was at the time of its publication a United States senator and a vice-presidential candidate, this book stands on its own as a serious attempt to elucidate the spiritual component of the environmental crisis. Spiritual matters figure in every aspect of the work, from the explanation of its inception to its conclusion that faith is the starting point for ecological restoration, and that healing the relationship between civilization and the earth—"the real solution" to the global environmental threat—requires a sustaining faith. Justice is also an integrated component—in the linkage of hazardous waste facilities to race, the connection between a "throwaway culture" and "throwaway children," and the repeated pointing to the mountains of debt and pollution imposed on future generations. In the chapter entitled "Environmentalism of the Spirit," Gore decries the relative silence of the religious denominations toward the environmental crisis, seeing the religious right and left as having lost an opportunity to embrace a common vision.

188 Gustafson, James M. "Ethical Issues in the Human Future." In *How Humans Adapt: A Biocultural Odyssey*, edited by Donald J. Ortner, 491-516. Washington, DC: Smithsonian Institution Press, 1983.

Gustafson argues that the anthropocentrism of Western morality and ethical thought must be revised in light of scientific knowledge of the place of humans in the history of the earth and their interdependence with other life forms, and that this redescription must be done with care so as to not to destroy the concepts of human dignity, value, justice, and rights with which anthropocentrism is associated. The redescription must take into account the fact that humanity is not ruler of or ruled by nature but is a consenter to nature, and must acknowledge limitations and the necessity of cooperation, participation in nature, and (within limits) directing nature. The concepts of common good and justice need to be extended to cover human societies and nature and the relations between them. Commentaries by Roy Branson and Wilfred Beckerman and an open discussion follow.

189 Gustafson, James M. "Interdependence, Finitude, and Sin: Reflections on Scarcity." *Journal of Religion* 57 (April 1977): 156-68.

The author suggests that human dependence and interdependence and the finitude of human and earthly resources calls for an extension of human concern to include future generations and the larger community of humanity and the rest of creation. This requirement entails as well an extension of two traditional concepts of ethics—distributive justice and the common good—extensions complicated by the human condition of sin, that is, by the resistance to overcoming narrow self- and group-interests, the violation of interdependence, and the failure to acknowledge finitude.

190 Hall, Douglas John. *The Steward: A Biblical Symbol Come of Age.* Revised edition. Grand Rapids, MI: William B. Eerdmans Publishing Co.; New York: Friendship Press, 1990.

The 1980 edition of this work was the first of three studies on stewardship written by Hall for the Commission on Stewardship of the National Council of the Churches of Christ in the USA. The new edition a decade later, has, in the author's words, "been completely rewritten and reworked from start to finish." Yet it is significant how basically unchanged the new version is, a tribute to Hall's anticipation of the integration of ecology, justice, and peace. Between editions Hall was involved in the World Council of Churches' Justice, Peace, and the Integrity of Creation process, and the revised version adds material from this development. In both editions the author argues that the times are ripe for the biblical symbol of the steward to emerge as the basis of a new Christian reformation. Christ is the authentic steward who empowers us to become trustees of the life of the world. A theology of stewardship "must be hammered out in the context of an awareness both of the humiliation of humankind and the degradation of nature." Such a theology of eco-justice will be grounded in axioms implicit in the Gospel of the Cross and its message that the world is our "ultimate concern": we are together responsible for the whole earth, non-human as well as human. This responsibility must be exercised in light of both present and future and take political form. Given the frequent, and often very loose, appeal to "stewardship" as the basis for eco-justice ethics, this clear and challenging analysis of the symbol and its biblical and contemporary meanings is a significant contribution to the literature. See *Christian Mission: The Stewardship of Life in the Kingdom of Death* (New York: Friendship Press, 1985) and *Imaging God: Dominion As Stewardship* (100).

191 Harakas, Stanley. "The Integrity of Creation: Ethical Issues." In *Justice, Peace and the Integrity of Creation: Insights from Orthodoxy*, edited by Gennadios Limouris, 70-82. Geneva: WCC Publications, 1990.

Harakas gives as the elements of Orthodoxy's understanding of "the integrity of creation" that: the material and the spiritual are in continuity because humanity, as microcosm, includes both; integrity is not complete because both microcosm and macrocosm are fallen; the sacramental life of the church is a foretaste of restored integrity; and restoration depends on humans exercising their priestly and kingly functions. In Orthodoxy's holistic perspective, all issues—peacemaking, justice, and the ecological crisis—are interconnected.

192 Hough, Joseph C., Jr. "The Care of the Earth." *Quarterly Review* 1 (Summer 1981): 3-22.

Concerned for the conservation and restoration of rapidly depleting soil, Hough outlines three moral bases for land conservation: empirical natural law; the mystical basis of Albert Schweitzer; and the biblical basis. The empirical natural law argument—that human survival entails preserving soil, and that right of land access and land use follow—is criticized for lacking a base for universal altruism and for leading to the misuse of nature when human values are not at stake. In Schweitzer's ethical mysticism based on the intrinsic value of all created beings, the moral obligation to conserve soil rests on soil's being the basis for all life. Schweitzer's ethic is criticized for lacking a basis for the ordering of concrete moral choices and for evading questions of public policy. The biblical foundation for soil conservation is derived from both creation, which is a conditional gift from God limited by the claims of God and entailing rights of nature and the requirement to work for harmonious relationships with the whole world, and from the terms of covenant which require good husbandry and care of the land as well as concern for future generations who are also of the covenant.

193 Jensen, Franklin L., and Cedric W. Tilberg, eds. *The Human Crisis in Ecology*. Christian Social Responsibility Series. New York: Board of Social Ministry, Lutheran Church in America, 1972.

An outcome of a study called by the Fifth Biennial Convention of the Lutheran Church in America meeting in Minneapolis in the summer of 1970, this work is important as an early denominational product with an eco-justice perspective. Paul E. Lutz, H. Paul Santmire, Franklin L. Jensen, Cedric W. Tilberg, and Joseph Sittler share primary responsibility for its writing. The work begins by explaining the interrelationships of the various systems that constitute the ecosystem. Chapters 2 and 3, authored primarily by Santmire, develop the need for an ecological theology within a secular culture that questions the meaningfulness of theology, wants action without the delay of religious reflection, finds Christianity to be a major part of the problem, and sees ecology as an escape from social responsibility. Admitting an "unecological" religious inheritance compounded by the "pitfall" of a romantic view of nature that shunned the problems of the city, the chapters develop the cosmic vision of God's future as community and the duties placed upon the individual who would respond to God's vision. Among these is the development of a public policy that pays reparations not only to nature but to slum dwellers also. Subsequent chapters detail the ecological crisis and the social realities underlying it and list ten "imperatives of survival"—appropriate actions that the Christian church should take for the wholeness of creation. The final chapter, for which Sittler is primarily responsible, links God, justice, and the environment in a vision of the New Creation.

194 Jung, L. Shannon. *We Are Home: A Spirituality of the Environment*. Mahwah, NJ: Paulist Press, 1993.

Calling humans and phytoplankton "fellow travelers" who constitute "home," Jung stresses embodiment, sociality, and spirituality and says that humans are called upon to be homemakers, to relate to God, self, and other species so as to repair broken connections. He believes that one of the causes of the present environmental crisis is a lack of the power to work together fostered by individualism and reflected in Christianity's view of individual salvation and personal choice of a relationship to Jesus. Although he also uses biblical themes to set out a spiritual vision of Earth as home, he finds a religion of environmental appreciation apart from explicit Christian categories, and states that the environment has not been a central concern of Christianity. In broad terms he calls for redirecting the economic system to include the well-being of all life. Specific recommendations for individual and church activities seem weak given the scope of the book.

195 Larsen, Dale, and Sandy Larsen. *While Creation Waits: A Christian Response to the Environmental Challenge*. Wheaton, IL: Harold Shaw Publishers, 1992.

The Larsens articulate a Christian response to the environment that avoids what they consider to be the two extremes in the environmental debates. On one extreme is the anthropocentric or "technological" approach which misinterprets the biblical mandate of dominion and thus advocates wanton exploitation of Earth's resources. The other extreme is the biocentric "mystical" approach which calls for an Earth-centered religious ethic. The Larsens believe that both of these positions become idolatrous by taking something other than God and Christ as their center. They emphasize the need for a relationship with a "Person" (God) as opposed to a "Force" or "the All" or even an abstraction such as the "Divinity." They link their Christian ethic to ecological and justice issues such as the exploitation of developing nations and the need for simple living.

196 "Liberating Life: A Report to the World Council of Churches." [The Annecy Report.] In *Liberating Life: Contemporary Approaches to Ecological Theology*, edited by Charles Birch, William Eakin, and Jay B. McDaniel, 273-90. Maryknoll, NY: Orbis Books, 1990.

This report to the World Council of Churches, prepared for the WCC by an internationally representative group of theologians meeting in Annecy, France in September, 1988, and consequently known as "the Annecy Report," represents an attempt by a Christian body to speak to questions concerning the moral treatment of animals. It is premised on the notion that the exploitation of humans and the destruction of other forms of life are inseparable and are the result of inadequate Christian perspectives. Also appended in (206), pp. 235-52.

197 Longwood, Merle. "The Common Good: An Ethical Framework for Evaluating Environmental Issues." *Theological Studies* 34 (September 1973): 468-80.

While helping to clarify the conceptual grounds of conflicts between environmentalists and civil rights advocates, this essay criticizes liberalism for focusing upon distributive concerns such as justice, equality, and rights to the exclusion of the aggregate concerns of society as a whole, particularly its environmental concerns. Longwood argues that the aggregate concepts of common interest and public interest are less appropriate to environmental issues than that of the common good which embraces the total well-being of a person or community, including the biotic community. The common good reflects the fact that community is a gift from God and the pathway of human fulfillment.

198 Longwood, Merle. "Toward an Environmental Ethic." In *That They May Live: Theological Reflections on the Quality of Life*, edited by George Devine, 47-68. Proceedings of the National Convention of the College Theology Society, held in St. Paul, MN, 12-14 April 1971. Staten Island, NY: Alba House, 1972.

Longwood discusses theological and ethical aspects of the environmental crisis, arguing that the minor biocentric theme in the Western tradition must be strengthened to suit a Christian ethic that directs us to relate to each other and to nature in a manner befitting God's cosmic creation and redemption. He spells out the framework for such an ethic in terms of responsibility, meaning the conscientious relating of actions to a continuing community of beings, including past and future generations and all members of the biosphere, and in terms of the common good of the total biotic community.

199 McDaniel, Jay B. "A God Who Loves Animals and a Church That Does the Same." In *Good News for Animals? Christian Approaches to Animal Well-Being*, edited by Charles Pinches and Jay B. McDaniel, 75-102. Maryknoll, NY: Orbis Books, 1993.

The experience of howling like a wolf at a Paul Winter concert led the author to a realization of both the spiritual need to feel connected with animals and the failure of Christian religion, despite its incarnational nature, to encourage this connection. He suggests that the ideal Christian community, despite its traits of caring for each individual, encouraging full participation of its members, and respect for differences, is yet inadequate to a God perceived as covenanting with animals and the earth and must be expanded to include both these categories. It is morally problematic to limit the idea of community to human beings, for what is considered to be outside the community is often also considered expendable "as far too many Jews, Muslims, witches, heretics, and animals can attest."

200 Miller, Alan S. "The Environmental and Other Bioethical Challenges for Christian Creation Consciousness." In *Cry of the Environment: Rebuilding the Christian Creation Tradition*, edited by Philip N. Joranson and Ken Butigan, 380-400. Santa Fe, NM: Bear and Co., 1984.

Miller analyses the critical problems of population, food distribution, resource use, industrialization, and pollution to show that distributive justice at the global level is at the center of environmental ethics, and that science and technology are directed by political and corporate imperatives rather than by social needs. He suggests that Christianity may have to move from traditional preoccupations with eschatology and salvation history to a new symbol system reflecting the inseparability of humankind and the other natural orders so as to be in a position to work out new dimensions of political and economic life.

201 Murphy, Charles M. *At Home on Earth: Foundations for a Catholic Ethic of the Environment*. New York: Crossroad Publishing Co., 1989.

Examining how traditional and contemporary Catholic theology address the environmental crisis, Murphy explores the writings of the Second Vatican Council and a variety of thinkers including Pascal, Teilhard de Chardin, Johann Baptist Metz, and John Cobb. He begins with an historical synopsis of the environmental movement, then critiques the limits of science and philosophy (as distinct from religion) in ethical discourse. He explores the importance of the book of Genesis in the formation of a Catholic environmental ethic, looking particularly at St. Ambrose's and St. Augustine's understandings of Genesis. A chapter on the theology of Pope John Paul II shows its foundation in Genesis and demonstrates John Paul's radical social teachings regarding both the common good as it relates to the environment and the dignity of all peoples.

202 Nash, James A. "Biotic Rights and Human Ecological Responsibilities." *Annual of the Society of Christian Ethics* (1993): 137-62.

Calling biotic rights "an expression of fidelity to God's universal covenant of justice," Nash argues that standards of justice be extended to include nonhuman individuals and species in an ecological context. He takes up most of the contentious animal-rights issues, including that of the criteria for recognizing rights-holders which he believes is conation. Nash's reasoned approach avoids absolutes while offering specific rights formulations. Thus, rather than a "right to life" he suggests a "right to participate in the natural dynamics of existence"; rather than moral absolutes, he suggests prima facie claims; and he upholds the superiority of human values while denying their exclusivity. An adequate conception of biotic rights is defined as one "that finds its fullest practicality in the quest of the ecological common good."

203 Nash, James A. "Human Rights and the Environment: New Challenge for Ethics." *Theology and Public Policy* 4 (Fall 1992): 42-57.

Nash defends and elaborates the concept of human rights at some length before proposing a "Bill of Environmental Rights." Against critics of "rights" language, he argues that the ethical category of human rights provides essential standards for justice. Rights can be held by groups as well as individuals and require governments and other agencies to enforce them. Individual human rights may be limited by the rights of nonhumans or future generations or by the common good. For Christians, human rights are grounded in God's valuing of human beings. From the propositions that human rights spell out the "basic necessities for lives expressive of human dignity in community" and that environmental health is essential for human life, Nash concludes that environmental rights are the precondition for any other human right.

204 Nash, James A. *Loving Nature: Ecological Integrity and Christian Responsibility*. Nashville, TN: Abingdon Press, 1991.

This work constitutes an important presentation of an eco-justice theology and ethic. After reviewing, both in terms of social justice and environmental values, the different aspects of the ecological crisis and the ethical issues they raise, Nash presents a list of needed ecological virtues. Critiquing charges of Christian culpability for the ecological crisis, he notes elements of ecological sensitivity within Christian history, Christianity's need for repentance, and its potential for reformation. Two chapters explore the ecological implications of creation, covenant, divine image, dominion, incarnation, sacraments, the presence of the Spirit, sin, judgment, redemption, and the church. Nash argues that these provide a solid, ultimate grounding for a strong ecological ethic, which he proceeds to develop through analyses of how a multidimensional understanding of Christian love can be applied in an ecological context with justice yielding both human environmental rights and prima facie biotic rights for species and their members. The final chapter offers public policy guidelines based on this ethic in six areas, including the economics-ecology dilemma and the linkages among justice, peace, and ecological integrity.

205 Peters, Ted F. "Creation, Consummation, and the Ethical Imagination." In *Cry of the Environment: Rebuilding the Christian Creation Tradition*, edited by Philip N. Joranson and Ken Butigan, 401-29. Santa Fe, NM: Bear and Co., 1984.

Peters proposes an ethics based on "proleptic eschatology"—the idea that God is freeing us from the past and drawing all things into the eschaton, which is proleptically revealed in Christ. This ethics tries to realize in present action the future promised by God, beginning from a provisional vision of that future as a harmonious global community. Such an ethic includes care for nature and posterity, defense of human dignity, and distinction between needs and wants. Peters compares his view to process thought.

206 Pinches, Charles, and Jay B. McDaniel, eds. *Good News for Animals? Christian Approaches to Animal Well-Being*. Maryknoll, NY: Orbis Books, 1993.

This anthology of essays, many of which were first presented at a 1990 conference sponsored by the International Network for Religion and Animals held at Duke Divinity School, is organized into four sections: what has been said about animals in the past; what is being said about animals today; should Christians eat animals; and how should Christians respond to current concerns about animals. The contributors are concerned to extend justice to animals; several of the essays point to the human consequences of animal mistreatment. Appended are a description of the current state of animals, both domesticated and wild, prepared by Richard M. Clugston, and the text of "Liberating Life: A Report to the World Council of Churches" (196). See Adams (162), Cobb (338), Comstock (172), French (089), McDaniel (199), Regan (212), Ruether (215), and Walker (222).

207 Pitcher, Alvin. "Energy as a Moral and Religious Issue." In *Energy Ethics: A Christian Response*, edited by Dieter T. Hessel, 33-55. New York: Friendship Press, 1979.

Declaring that the North American failure to use energy in ethically and politically defensible ways is basically due to a religious failure to find an adequate "way of being" in the world, Pitcher presents an alternative Christian eco-justice ethic, the "belief that the resources of the earth are part of creation, gifts of God for all life, present and future, human and otherwise," as a way of life in which "limits" are constitutive of the meaning of being rather than something reluctantly to be adjusted to. This ethic must be made manifest in enduring religious communities which are structured by forms of order that respect the givens of creation, and in which the whole has priority over the parts. Such communities will serve as prophetic alternatives to the dominant culture which emphasizes the autonomy of parts, freedom from limits, newness, change, and perpetual growth.

208 Preston, Ronald H. "The Integrity of Creation: Issues of Environmental Ethics." In his *The Future of Christian Ethics*, 74-98. London: SCM Press, 1987.

Allowing the reality of environmental threats, but skeptical of more extreme claims about limits to growth, Preston defends the biblical concept of responsible stewardship and argues that our main ethical concern is how the more affluent one-third of the world should use its increasing wealth with the two-thirds world in mind. Looking at recent literature on Justice, Peace, and the Integrity of Creation, he critiques the static and monistic (and thus socially conservative) view of nature implied therein, the extension of rights to non-sentient beings, and the use of apocalyptic language about "a new heaven and earth." An appendix critiques Moltmann, *God in Creation* (130).

209 Preston, Ronald H. "The Question of a Just, Participatory, and Sustainable Society." *Bulletin of the John Rylands University Library of Manchester* 63 (Autumn 1980): 95-117.

Preston discusses individually the terms 'just', 'participatory', and 'sustainable'. Among his observations are that ecumenical discussion has not furthered basic Christian reflection on justice as much as it has illuminated present injustice, that problems resulting from wider participation in social decisions—which is needed—have not been fully confronted, and that pessimism surrounding sustainability is unwarranted. He briefly discusses the theological issues of science and faith, man and nature, and responsibility to the future; and he warns against homeostatic ecological conservatism. He stresses that more work is needed on finding a way to move from sweeping theoretical calls for change to influencing national governments. Reprinted in Preston's *The Future of Christian Ethics* (London: SCM Press, 1987), pp. 53-73

210 Rasmussen, Larry L. "Creation, Church, and Christian Responsibility." In *Tending the Garden: Essays on the Gospel and the Earth*, edited by Wesley Granberg-Michaelson, 114-31. Grand Rapids, MI: William B. Eerdmans Publishing Co., 1987.

Rasmussen explores key terms for responding to the gift of creation: 'creation' as one household and humanity as steward; 'neighbor love' as applied to nonhuman others; 'justice' as rendering whatever is needed for the fullest possible flourishing of creation; '*shalom*' as the sum of God's hopes and dreams for creation; 'church' as "communities of visibly redeemed creation." He believes that reflection on these terms will promote the acceptance of creation as the basic unit of reality, an identification with the welfare of future generations, conservation and preservation, and a recognition of the church's vocation to demonstrate the possibilities of this environmental ethic.

211 Rasmussen, Larry L. *Moral Fragments and Moral Community: A Proposal for Church in Society.* Minneapolis: Augsburg Fortress Publishers, 1993.

Rasmussen sees "moral community" as answering to a critical lack in the modern world and as defining the nature of the churches' response to that lack. Technology has replaced the common reference points of nature, culture, and social relations with machinery, and neither the model of the market nor the model of the state is able to provide humans with the experience needed to learn civic morality. Citing research indicating that privatized religion dampens concern for others, he calls for a church that excludes no one, functioning "as if the entire planet's fecund variety were all part of the same covenantal intimacy it knows in God."

212 Regan, Tom. "Christianity and the Oppression of Animals." In *Good News for Animals? Christian Approaches to Animal Well-Being*, edited by Charles Pinches and Jay B. McDaniel, 206-19. Maryknoll, NY: Orbis Books, 1993.

On the basis of taped remarks made by the president of the American Feed Industry, Regan claims that the World Council of Churches (WCC) yielded to pressure by industry lobbyists and withdrew its condemnation of factory farming, even though factory farming had been criticized in "Liberating Life: A Report to the World Council of Churches" (the Annecy Report). Regan, one of the report's authors, finds this incident "one chapter in a larger political story . . . Do what needs to be done to protect vested interests in animal exploitation." He argues that how nonhuman animals are treated should be a matter of strict justice, independent of human interests, and that the WCC needs to recognize its involvement in a politics of depreciation of the work and aims of animal rightists.

213 Robb, Carol S., and Carl J. Casebolt, eds. *Covenant for a New Creation: Ethics, Religion, and Public Policy.* Maryknoll, NY: Orbis Books, 1991.

The thirteen essays in this collection apply theological and environmental ethics to questions of environmental public policy. Major sections address: new models of ownership; re-visioning relationship with the rest of nature; and reconstructing justice for environmental ethics. In their introduction, Robb and Casebolt assert that the degradation of the biosphere is the result of an ownership mentality similar to that which justified slavery; that sexism, racism, and class oppression serve to justify privileged access to Earth's goods created for all. They suggest that covenantal relationships are the way to meet the current environmental crisis, and they point out ways in which a new covenant for environmental ethics connects to and draws upon the Biblical covenants. See Bahr (032), Christiansen (073), Daly (340), Lockman (118), Robb (423), and Stortz (221).

214 Rolston, Holmes, III. "Environmental Ethics: Some Challenges for Christians." *Annual of the Society of Christian Ethics* (1993): 163-86.

Rolston posits reasons for Christians to embrace an environmental ethics. Lacing his argument with numerous examples of conflicts between environmental ethics and biblical tradition, he suggests that religious insights and scientific knowledge can broaden and deepen each other. Discussed are the inappropriateness of the Christian ethic of compassion toward individuals applied to questions of animal welfare; the wisdom inherent in archaic biblical stories such as that of Noah's ark; the biblical land ethic as meaning broadly that all peoples dwell on promised lands; and the danger of worshiping Earth rather than seeing it as a gift of God. Of particular concern to Rolston is the often alienated response of Christians toward nature as a result of its inherent and seemingly unjust cruelty, when, he believes, the insights of Christianity and the linked processes of genesis and death found in nature are mutually instructive. "The nature that is grace is also cruciform. . . . Things perish in tragedy. But things perish with a passing over in which the sacrificed individual flows in the river of life."

215 Ruether, Rosemary Radford. "Men, Women, and Beasts: Relations to Animals in Western Culture." In *Good News for Animals? Christian Approaches to Animal Well-Being*, edited by Charles Pinches and Jay B. McDaniel, 12-23. Maryknoll, NY: Orbis Books, 1993.

In an historical look at treatment of animals, the author points to the connections of animals and dominated sectors of society, especially women. Also discussed is what needs to be done to move to an ethic of treating animals humanely.

216 Santmire, H. Paul. "Catastrophe and Ecstasy." In *Ecological Renewal*, edited by Paul Lutz and H. Paul Santmire, 75-153. Philadelphia: Fortress Press, 1972.

Santmire proposes a three-dimensional understanding of love as the "valuational fuel" for Spaceship Earth—as eros (interpreted by Norman O. Brown), philia (James Cone) and agape (Teilhard de Chardin), combining joyful vitality with a passion for justice and devotion to universal reconciliation. These three dimensions correspond to God as living, holy, and gracious and Christ as life-giving, judging, and reconciling, and to childlike, adolescent, and adult characteristics of a new lifestyle and politics. The church can provide a communal and liturgical matrix in which this new lifestyle can grow.

217 Santmire, H. Paul. "Ecology, Justice, and Theology: Beyond the Preliminary Skirmishes." *Christian Century* 93 (12 May 1976): 460-64.

In this programmatic essay, Santmire argues for moving beyond preliminary disputes between ecological and political theology by acknowledging the priority of justice over survival, the independence of ecology from conservative organicism, and the seriousness of the environmental crisis. Sustained, critical reflection is required on the more fundamental issues of: the relation of Western religious traditions to environmental problems; the relationship between nature and history; root-metaphors for embodying both ecological and political concerns; the intrinsic value of nature before God; and sexual dualism and our understanding of God.

218 Schweitzer, Albert. *The Teaching of Reverence for Life.* New York: Holt, Rinehart and Winston, 1965.

The six sermonic chapters of this little book follow a logical progression—from an historical survey linking ethics with life affirmation and individual conduct, to a plea in the final chapter that humanity act as ethics demands and save life from the annihilation of atomic war. Schweitzer sees reverence for life as an enlargement of the virtue of love of humanity developed in both Greco-Roman philosophy and Christianity. It is an ethics in conflict with the phenomenal world and cannot be deduced through scientific investigation, yet its practice brings humanity into a spiritual relationship with the universe, and implies that all life is sacred and no distinctions in value between one life form and another or between persons can be made—when necessity demands distinctions, humanity is accountable for the resulting sacrifice of life. The ideology of inhumanity is at the root of atomic warfare, but an ethics concerned only with human issues does not have the strength or vision to combat it; reverence for life does.

219   Snow, John H.   "Fear of Death and the Need to Accumulate." In *Ecology: Crisis and New Vision*, edited by Richard E. Sherrell, 45-58. Richmond, VA: John Knox Press, 1971.

A seminal analysis of how greed, the drive to accumulate things and convert matter into energy through modern technology, is a reaction to the fear of death and leads to social and environmental destruction. Protestant doctrines of total depravity and the view of mortality as punishment for sin have encouraged the accumulation of goods as a means of justification. Only a new sense of the trustworthiness of the universe and the God who made and keeps it can break this pattern.

220   Stivers, Robert L.   *Hunger, Technology, and Limits to Growth: Christian Responsibility for Three Ethical Issues*. Minneapolis: Augsburg Publishing House, 1984.

Stivers sees poverty, hunger, alienation, and limits to growth as challenges to standard assumptions about growth, progress, and consumption. He identifies the biblical foundation for dealing with these problems in the dynamics of gift, openness, and response found in both Israel's theology of covenant and Jesus' proclamation of the Kingdom. He argues that our response should be to work for the "Just, Participatory, and Sustainable Society," guided by the core values of justice (freedom and equality); participation (community, the common good); and sustainable sufficiency (timely satisfaction of basic needs with care for the earth and people), plus guidelines derived from them. He calls both "rigorous discipleship" and the more moderate course of "responsible consumption" valid choices for Christians, and outlines general social policy recommendations, including the priority of "sufficiency" until basic needs are met.

221   Stortz, Martha Ellen.   "Ethics, Conservation, and Theology in Ecological Perspective." In *Covenant for a New Creation: Ethics, Religion, and Public Policy*, edited by Carol S. Robb and Carl J. Casebolt, 196-211. Maryknoll, NY: Orbis Books, 1991.

Stortz suggests the need for a "Copernican revolution" that moves beyond speciesism in ethics, conservation, and theology to see the moral universe as including things human and not human, conservation as embracing the whole of the biotic community, and theology as the divine provision of the cosmic Christ who repairs fractures to the whole of creation. Stortz's proposal includes a critique of both eco-justice and stewardship. She refers to Carol Gilligan's notions of "male" and "female" patterns of development—the male pattern one of thinking in terms of a hierarchy of rights and duties using justice as the norm, the female pattern one of thinking in terms of affections and loyalties using caring as the norm—and finds the male pattern similar to environmental ethics with its references to eco-justice, the female pattern similar to biblical notions of stewardship. Both put humans at the center and direct energy toward the application of a rule, principle, or norm, and neither is able to address the earth's needs as well as does the ecofeminist notion of a nonhierarchical web of relationships with energy directed toward attending to the whole.

222 Walker, Theodore, Jr. "African-American Resources for a More Inclusive Liberation Theology." In *Good News for Animals? Christian Approaches to Animal Well-Being*, edited by Charles Pinches and Jay B. McDaniel, 163-171. Maryknoll, NY: Orbis Books, 1993.

The author locates aspects of traditional African life that are sustainable and liberating of other life as he criticizes the "racial and racist aspects of modern White ecological/animal rights thinking" which stand in the way of African-Americans' wholehearted support of the environmental agenda. Cited as an example of the latter are the shoot-to-kill orders of an anti-poaching unit in Kenya that pertain to Black elephant hunters but not to White buyers and distributors of ivory. Ecological gains will not be achieved "until it becomes financially profitable to be ecologically responsible."

223 West, Charles C. "Justice within the Limits of the Created World." *Ecumenical Review* 27 (January 1975): 57-64.

West defines justice in the face of limits as including not only just distribution, but also unlimited possibilities for humanization and reconciliation—for creating a new covenantal community which includes the poor. He argues that the task requires recasting human hope in terms that will guide technology and science, and that nonhuman creation is to be enhanced by being drawn into history and cared for out of faithfulness to its maker. He identifies several policy implications relating to public and private goods, values and goals, the poor, and the role of Christians.

224 Winter, Gibson. *Liberating Creation: Foundations of Religious Social Ethics*. New York: Crossroad Publishing Co., 1981.

Winter delineates the creative, artistic process through which divine and human powers may collaborate to "liberate creation" from the destructive consequences of the Western technological project. He cites three root metaphors which compete for the interpretation of our foundational religious symbols and the meaning of contemporary human dwelling: mechanistic, organicist, and artistic. The mechanistic and organicist metaphors directly conflict, as modern technological societies destroy traditional peoples and the environment, but the emerging artistic metaphor incorporates the transformative power of mechanism and the bonding power of organicism and offers ethical guidelines for the creation of just and ecologically whole communities. Those guidelines specify universal archetypal directionalities, including mutuality of Self and Other, equality, dialogue, and creative participation. He calls "communitarian socialism" the most appropriate political expression of the artistic paradigm. Winter's proposal is illustrated by an analysis of the struggle over land rights in the Canadian Northwest precipitated by the construction of the Mackenzie Valley Pipeline (450).

In addition to the works annotated in this chapter, readers interested in ethical analysis may wish to consult the following entries located elsewhere in the bibliography: 062, 065, 071, 073, 075, 089, 103, 120, 152, 157, 225, 226, 233, 236, 241, 243, 246, 280, 290, 293, 309, 317, 387, 429, 444, 465, 466, 483.

5

Feminist Criticism

Feminist critiques of received theological and ethical traditions and feminist efforts to reconstruct or replace them form a sufficiently important and cohesive body of literature to warrant a separate section. Items included here are also cross-referenced to the subject category of the critique. For example, after an analysis of the theological justifications for male/female dualisms, the reader is referred to the chapter on theological perspectives. Many works within other subject categories include feminist perspectives; those included in this section give prominence to a feminist critique.

225 Adams, Carol J., ed. *Ecofeminism and the Sacred*. New York: Continuum Publishing Co., 1993.

These expressions of various forms of ecofeminist spirituality are linked by a belief that, in order to change the patriarchal power structures which dominate both women and nature, society must recognize the interdependence of all things, the immanence of spirit, and the aliveness of the earth. Part 1 explores attempts to revision mainline spiritualities in ecofeminist terms, part 2 envisions different forms of ecofeminism, and part 3 discusses methods by which to embody ecofeminism. See Adams and Proctor-Smith (226), Caputi (229), Keller (111), and Riley (245).

226 Adams, Carol J., and Marjorie Proctor-Smith. "Taking Life or 'Taking on Life'? Table Talk and Animals." In *Ecofeminism and the Sacred*, edited by Carol J. Adams, 295-310. New York: Continuum Publishing Co., 1993.

A reflection on the theological and social issues of vegetarianism from an ecofeminist viewpoint. The authors see various relationships between the oppression of women and that of animals, including the way in which both are considered nonentities and the fact that economically poor women are the ones employed in slaughterhouses and chicken factories. They suggest that feminists have not embraced vegetarianism, as they say ecofeminists have, because feminists wish to remake women into transforming agents rather than have them identified with "nature." Theology, in order to be true to its requirement to listen to the voice of the oppressed "Other," must recognize the Other as including animals, and recognize also that humans benefit from animal oppression, as rich people benefit by gaining wealth at the expense of the poor. The authors suggest that the Christian emphasis on the "word" of God confirms the object status of animals who have no speech, and that the symbol of the Passover lamb acts to sanctify literal lamb eating.

227 Berry, Thomas F. "Patriarchy: A New Interpretation of History." In his *The Dream of the Earth*, 138-62. San Francisco: Sierra Club Books, 1988.

Berry incorporates the critique of patriarchy into his quest for a new "mutually enhancing human-earth relationship." While noting the existence of an ancient European culture which was matricentric, egalitarian, democratic, and peaceful, he focuses on later "patriarchal" establishments—empire, church, nation state, and corporation—which control Western history, oppressing women and bringing Earth to the brink of ecological disaster. The ecological and feminist movements have a common enemy and share a commitment to more feminine, nurturing values.

228 Brennan, Margaret. "Patriarchy: The Root of Alienation from the Earth?" In *Thomas Berry and the New Cosmology*, edited by Anne Lonergan and Carol Richards, 57-63. Mystic, CT: Twenty-Third Publications, 1987.

Brennan believes Thomas Berry does not see the connections between his cosmic ecological vision and feminism. She argues that patriarchy must be eradicated in order to end human exploitation of nature; that the domination of women and of nature are linked in the symbolism and language of the modern scientific worldview; and that we must work toward an economy that recognizes and values not only the earth's economy, but also women's dignity and their contribution to the nonmonetary economy. See Berry (227).

229 Caputi, Jane. "Nuclear Power and the Sacred: Or Why a Beautiful Woman is Like a Nuclear Power Plant." In *Ecofeminism and the Sacred*, edited by Carol J. Adams, 229-50. New York: Continuum Publishing Co., 1993.

After recounting previous investigations of nuclear metaphor, undertaken by herself and others, that have revealed its associated religious and sexual imagery (such as Oppenheimer's code name "Trinity" for the first atomic explosion), and after acknowledging that her previous response, as well as that of other Euro-American feminist writers, was to condemn nuclear force, Caputi suggests that a better and ultimately healing strategy is that of several Native American writers who attempt to "reclaim the atom from its immurement in phallocentric language, sexuality, and religion, and to recall its repressed sacred gynocentric face."

230 Carmody, Denise Lardner. *Feminism and Christianity: A Two-Way Reflection.* Lanham MD: University Press of America, 1982.

In a double critique of Christianity and feminism, Carmody attempts a centrist position. With self-expressed "contemplative absorption in God and firm work for social justice," she deals with theology, psychology, sociology, and ecology. She sees Goddess religion as helping women believe in themselves, but faults it for identifying divinity with the natural world, for having an undeveloped notion of sin, and for not attempting a systematic theology. She believes that feminism needs to turn from expansionist economics to steady-state economics; that, dedicated to ecological sanity, social justice, and simple living, women could be decisive in preserving the planet; that women should massively enter into agricultural economics so that social factors become a part of its calculus. She also points out that both nature and human history embrace tragedies that call for a theodicy.

231   Chung Hyun Kyung.   "Ecology, Feminism, and African and Asian Spirituality."
In *Eco-Theology: Voices from South and North*, edited by David G. Hallman, 175-78.
Geneva: WCC Publications; Maryknoll, NY: Orbis Books, 1994.

This summary of a consultation on African and Asian spirituality in Sri Lanka in
June 1992 states that eco-feminism has its basis in the opposition to "power over"
relationships that lead to the rape of women and the rape of the earth.   It promotes instead "power from within" and "power with" other beings; a non-
dualistic and non-hierarchical cosmic spirituality (as found among indigenous
people in Asia and Africa); and a web of mutual, non-exploitative, intimate relations between God, people, and nature.   Chung (and the consultation participants,
who reviewed and affirmed this statement) commit themselves to incarnating this
vision in their struggle for the liberation of nature and the Third-World poor.

232   Cromie, Thetis R.   "Feminism and the Grace-Full Thought of Joseph Sittler."
Christian Century 97 (9 April 1980): 406-8.

Cromie applies Joseph Sittler's environmental theology with its organic and relational understanding of grace in all of creation as an antidote to the Self/Other
dualism that is the root of sexism as well as of racism and environmental abuse.
See Sittler (153) and (152).

233   Gnanadason, Aruna.   "Women, Economy and Ecology."   In *Eco-Theology:
Voices from South and North*, edited by   David G. Hallman, 179-85.   Geneva: WCC
Publications; Maryknoll, NY: Orbis Books, 1994.

Gnanadason offers a perspective from India where the environmental and
women's movements have revitalized concern for creation.   Although Indian
women are the primary victims of environmental degradation, because they have
the primary responsibility for obtaining water and fuel for their families, they are
also active in movements to protect the environment from the onslaughts of
"development."   Gnanadason says that while women's intrinsic bond with nature
has been broken and abused by patriarchal Indian culture, that bond also gives
them an understanding of the sacredness of all creation and enables them to contribute creative actions for sustaining life.

234   Gray, Elizabeth Dodson.   "A Critique of Dominion Theology."   In *For Creation's Sake: Preaching, Ecology, and Justice*, edited by Dieter T. Hessel, 71-83.
Philadelphia: Geneva Press, 1985.

In an analysis of the problems of eco-justice in terms of a critique of patriarchy,
Gray argues that the "anthropocentric illusion" of Western scientific-industrial
civilization (which includes the myths of a hierarchical cosmos, human dominion,
and the femininity of nature) is largely based on Jewish and Christian tradition.
Hierarchical rankings of value must be rejected, and "attunement" substituted for
dominion in defining humanity's relation to nature.

235   Gray, Elizabeth Dodson.   *Green Paradise Lost*.   Wellesley, MA: Roundtable
Press, 1982.

Originally titled *Why the Green Nigger? Re-Mything Genesis* (Wellesley, MA:
Roundtable Press, 1979), this influential work articulates a radically egalitarian

and ecological view of nature as a web of functional interdependencies of which humans are a part. Positing that hierarchicalism, anthropocentrism, and the fear of physicalness (sex, the body, death, woman) are rooted in aspects of male psychosexual experience and have led to sexism and the ecological crisis, and that women alone have the bodily basis for an awareness of relatedness to nature, inescapable limits, and care for future generations, Gray calls for a restorative symbiosis of male and female perspectives. Environmentalism must be based, not on a paternalistic idea of responsible stewardship, but on an expanded sense of identity with the vast natural systems of which humans are a part. Men and women together need to "remyth" Genesis, understanding God's continuing covenant in creation, the humanness of both sexes, and the diversity, equality, and value of the Eden that is Earth.

236   Gray, Elizabeth Dodson. *Patriarchy as a Conceptual Trap.* Wellesley, MA: Roundtable Press, 1982.

By means of a litany of global problems Gray articulates the importance of examining the patriarchy inherent in our society. She believes that patriarchy is a conceptual trap, which she likens to a black hole that once inside cannot be escaped. She asserts that a system wherein men control culture and myth is ubiquitous in every society on earth, including those of the Judaic and Christian traditions. Patriarchy makes maleness the human norm, thereby silencing an important alternative perspective that women offer. It reinforces as norms detrimental ways of thinking—that reality is hierarchical, that humans are separate from one another, the rest of creation, and God, and that man has dominion over nature. "The result has been incredible anthropocentric illusion and our now fast-approaching ecological disasters. Repentance involves taking off our Wizard-of-Oz hierarchical glasses and allowing ourselves, for once, to perceive the systemic reality in which we actually live as earth-creatures."

237   Halkes, Catharina J. M. *New Creation: Christian Feminism and the Renewal of the Earth.* Louisville, KY: Westminster/John Knox Press, 1991.

This wide-ranging work by a Dutch feminist theologian deals with the images of 'nature' and 'woman', especially the stereotypical images that have been damaging to women and the environment and to the relationships of men and women, nature and humanity, poor and rich. Making extensive use of Carolyn Merchant, Evelyn Fox Keller, and Gerhard Liedke, Halkes draws connections between the environmental and feminist movements, seeing them as having in common an egalitarian perspective. Although Halkes speaks from a Christian background, her emphasis is on a spirituality that needs not be limited to any particular faith. She writes positively of Sallie McFague's image of the world as God's body, finding it closer to present day reality than the image of the kingdom of God.

238   Jantzen, Grace M. "Healing Our Brokenness: The Spirit and Creation." *Ecumenical Review* 42 (April 1990): 131-42.

After identifying the various oppressive dualisms underlying Christian theology—God/material universe, mind/body, male/female—and showing them to be irrational, Jantzen asks if this oppression is innocent or the result of vested interest by the dominant groups of society. She concludes that ruling-class males do have a vested interest in providing a theological justification for these dualisms which keeps them from being replaced by a theology of justice and integration. She sees this as originating in "alienation of the bodily dimension of male selfhood that has not been welcomed." To correct it requires models of living in a diversity of concrete situations. Jantzen suggests that the story of St. Francis's embrace of a leper who turns out to be Christ is a profound model that illustrates the need to make a healing commitment to the "underside" of our dualisms.

239 Johnson, Elizabeth A. *Women, Earth, and Creator Spirit.* New York: Paulist Press, 1993.

In this lecture Johnson links Earth's exploitation, women's marginalization, and neglect of the Trinity's Creator Spirit in Western religious consciousness. She blames hierarchical dualism stemming from an androcentric view of Earth for all three. Neglect of the Spirit has a symbolic affinity with the marginalization of women, in part because the work of the Spirit—bringing forth and nurturing life, keeping life connected, and renewing it when broken—is analogous to "women's work." She speaks of being "converted to the earth" which entails prophecy, including active non-violent resistance to halt aggression against vulnerable Earth and its creatures, and the exercise of responsibility for a new project of eco-justice since "structures of social domination are chief among the ways that exploitation of the earth is accomplished."

240 McCoy, Marjorie Casebier. "Feminist Consciousness in Creation: 'Tell Them the World Was Made for Woman, Too.'" In *Cry of the Environment: Rebuilding the Christian Creation Tradition*, edited by Philip N. Joranson and Ken Butigan, 132-47. Santa Fe, NM: Bear and Co., 1984.

McCoy reviews feminist scholarship on the linked domination of women and nature. She urges eliminating those references to human beings and the environment which reflect sexual stereotypes (e.g. "Mother Earth") and stressing instead those elements of the creation tradition which support the partnership of women, nature, and men within the unfolding of creation.

241 McDaniel, Jay B. "Four Questions in Response to Rosemary Ruether." In *An Ecology of the Spirit: Religious Reflections and Environmental Consciousness,* edited by Michael Barnes, 11-26. The Annual Publication of the College Theology Society, 1990, vol. 36. Lanham, MD: University Press of America, 1994.

In a response to Rosemary Ruether's essay, "Ecofeminism: Symbolic and Social Connections of the Oppression of Women and the Domination of Nature" (246), McDaniel focuses on the ecofeminist alternative that Ruether proposes. He questions whether ecofeminism is concerned with the individual animals that make up Earth's interdependent web, how open ecofeminism is to cultural and native beliefs in supernatural phenomena, and how ecofeminism addresses the "tragic dimension" of nature. He also questions whether ecofeminism allows God to be seen as dependent upon creation.

242 Peck, Jane Cary, and Jeanne Gallo. "JPIC: A Critique from a Feminist Perspective." *Ecumenical Review* 41 (October 1989): 573-81.

The authors charge that, while feminists affirm the goal of "justice, peace, and the integrity of creation," women and women's issues have not been central to the JPIC process, and thus the process has lacked essential contributions from the feminist experience. These include stress on interconnections and a method of beginning with the concrete suffering of women. They propose that women be the majority of participants and leaders in the JPIC process, women's issues the central foci, and women's materials the primary data. The test for the process and its results is its material contribution to transforming the suffering, injustice, and threats to women, other oppressed, and the earth.

243 Primavesi, Anne. *From Apocalypse to Genesis: Ecology, Feminism, and Christianity*. Minneapolis: Augsburg Fortress Publishers, 1991.

Using an ecofeminist lens, Primavesi outlines an ecological paradigm of the inter-relatedness and interdependence of creation while criticizing the dominant hierar-chical, dualistic paradigm of Christianity. She calls for recognition of the role of the Spirit in the renewal of creation—Spirit understood as existing independently of the Father or Son, springing from God and creation united. Many of her examples and prescriptions have to do with ways of thinking about food—its biological necessity, its blessing, the justice of its sharing. Primavesi examines the roots of the current understanding of Genesis 1-3 and provides an ecological reading that has to do with food procurement rather than with notions of original sin and the fall from grace. She provides a view of Jesus as a sinner who lived and died with sinners, a signification that divinity is embedded in the immanent.

244 Primavesi, Anne. "A Tide in the Affairs of Women?" In *Eco-Theology: Voices from South and North*, edited by David G. Hallman, 186-98. Geneva: WCC Pub-lications; Maryknoll, NY: Orbis Books, 1994.

Primavesi reflects on some developments in science, philosophy, and theology which may foster inclusion of "the women's dimension" into decision-making in environmental policy as well as academic and ecclesiastical institutions. Those developments include: the constructivist model of science; contextualism in theology; and ecological and feminist philosophies based on a relational, non-violent worldview. She concludes that a constructivist-environmental approach to knowledge-building, which emphasizes personal experience and its role in con-structing the world, shares a common agenda with the kind of knowledge-building women can and must bring to decision-making processes. This essay originally appeared in a different version in *Ecofeminism and Theology* [Yearbook of the European Society of Women in Theological Research], edited by Mary Grey and Elizabeth Green (Mainz: Gruenewald; Kampen, Kok Pharos, 1994).

245 Riley, Shamara Shantu. "Ecology Is a Sistah's Issue Too: The Politics of Emergent Afrocentric Ecowomanism." In *Ecofeminism and the Sacred*, edited by Carol J. Adams, 191-204. New York: Continuum Publishing Co., 1993.

Riley argues that a womanist, "a culturally identified woman of color who also critically analyzes the sexual politics within her respective ethnic group," must, in order for the planet to survive, see herself as interconnected with both nonhuman nature and other women. She discusses the origins of Western dualism in Jewish and Christian thought and the resources of pre-colonial African spirituality which ecowomanists may draw on in their efforts to relate to the natural world, and she questions the wisdom of feminists who appropriate non-Western earth-bound spiritualities when they might better reclaim their own pre-Christian European traditions.

246 Ruether, Rosemary Radford. "Ecofeminism: Symbolic and Social Connections of the Oppression of Women and the Domination of Nature." In *An Ecology of the Spirit: Religious Reflections and Environmental Consciousness*, edited by Michael Barnes, 45-56. The Annual Publication of the College Theology Society, 1990, vol. 36. Lanham, MD: University Press of America, 1994.

After defining ecofeminism as the confluence of deep ecology and feminist ideologies, Ruether briefly traces the history of patriarchy from pre-Hebraic thought through the Reformation and scientific revolution, concentrating on the correlation between the domination of women and the domination of nature in the symbolism and social constructions of each of these time periods. She sees a broad range of injustices as the legacy of the industrial revolution—the gap between rich and poor, exploitation of developing nations, monopolizing of resources by the West, and militarization aimed at maintaining unjust social constructions. She calls on humanity to redefine its relations to itself, nature, and God, using ecofeminism's ideals of cooperation and nurturance rather than competition and domination. This essay also appears in (225), pp. 13-23. See McDaniel (241) for a response.

247 Ruether, Rosemary R. "Eco-feminism and Theology." In *Eco-Theology: Voices from South and North*, edited by David G. Hallman, 199-204. Geneva: WCC Publications; Maryknoll, NY: Orbis Books, 1994.

Ruether argues that the roots of the ecological crisis are found in the common perception of women and nature as spirit-less tools to be exploited by dominant males, a view reflected in both Greek and Hebrew cosmogony. The crisis itself, she sees as sparked by modern industrialism and colonialism. Positive elements of biblical culture, such as the concept of the covenant between God, humanity, and nature, and the concept of the cosmos as the body of Christ, can contribute to creating a new eco-feminist culture. Such a culture requires the transformation of relationships of domination and exploitation into relationships of mutual support and a new view of God as the supporter of those relationships.

248 Ruether, Rosemary Radford. *Gaia and God: An Ecofeminist Theology of Earth Healing*. San Francisco: HarperSanFrancisco, 1992.

This major work analyses the roots of destructive relations between men and women, ruling and subjugated groups, humans and the earth. The first section examines ancient creation stories and their Christian cosmological syntheses for their roles in sacralizing male domination, class hierarchy, and a spirit/nature split. It also looks in detail at modern science, especially at what is to be learned from ecology about the web of natural interdependencies. Herein lies a new creation story, Ruether suggests, one that has not as yet fostered the ethic necessary to prevent human damage to the environment. The second section examines stories of destruction from the prophetic and Christian apocalyptic traditions, revealing the reification of good and evil and the tribal hatreds such stories exhibit, and reflecting on the continuing attraction of the apocalyptic as a way of escape from overwhelming chaos. Ruether stresses the need to shape an alternative spirituality and ethic to better channel these fears, so as to deal with environmental damage, expanding poverty, and "a militarization that is aimed at retaining unjust advantage over the world's resources for a wealthy elite." A third section examines narratives of sin and evil and the Christian concept of the Fall, along with their legacy of male domination, religious intolerance, Earth-fleeing, and phobic attitudes toward death and decomposition. A "new fall story" emerging from the ecofeminist movement is also critically examined. This section broadly traces the social and cultural patterns of domination from Mesopotamian origins through industrialization. Within biblical thought and Western Christian tradition Ruether also finds elements that are positive for ecological ethics and spirituality, and the final section explores what Ruether terms the covenantal (linked to the law-making voice of God) and sacramental (linked to Gaia who "beckons us into communion") traditions. Ruether suggests that both are needed as humans rebuild society for a sustainable Earth starting with a vision of universal equity.

249 Ruether, Rosemary Radford. "Mother Earth and the Megamachine: A Theology of Liberation in a Feminine, Somatic, and Ecological Perspective." In her *Liberation Theology: Human Hope Confronts Christian History and American Power*, 115-26. New York: Paulist Press, 1972.

Ruether discusses the psycho-social history of the domination of women and the connections of that domination to the technological domination of the natural and social worlds. She finds the alienation of the masculine from the feminine primary among many dualities transmitted through Christianity to shape the modern technological environment and a model for the subjugation of men to machinery, for identifying women with bodily existence, and for political suppression of social groups by technological elites. She suggests that the women's revolution has an important role to play in healing the dualities that have caused women's subjugation and in helping to reconcile spirit and body, build a social order free from hierarchy, rule, and competitiveness, free men for creativity, and create a mutuality among humanity and nature.

250 Ruether, Rosemary Radford. "New Woman and New Earth: Women, Ecology, and Social Revolution." In her *New Woman, New Earth: Sexist Ideologies and Human Liberation*, 186-214. New York: Seabury Press, 1975.

Ruether develops the need for, and provides a new model of, socio-ecological relationship in this chapter which is divided between a broad-stroked history of sexism and the domination of nature and a future-oriented description of an ideal society. She calls the nineteenth-century concept of "progress" a materialization of the Judeo-Christian God concept and the end result of patriarchal religion's having "sought to deny that the spiritual component of humanity was a dimension of the maternal matrix of being." Modern industrial society intensified patterns of sexism and ecological destructiveness by separating production from the home, confining women to domesticity, eroticizing the private sector, and privatizing morality and religion. An ideal society would not be antitechnological, but would democratize decision-making and assure the equalization of its benefits. Ruether envisions the development of local communitarian societies with communalized housekeeping, child-raising, and food production and procurement, thereby freeing women from exclusive domesticity, allowing men to develop affective roles, conserving natural resources by reducing duplication of equipment, and promoting a state of "reciprocal interdependence" with others and the earth.

251 Ruether, Rosemary Radford. *Sexism and God-Talk: Toward A Feminist Theology*. Boston: Beacon Press, 1983.

This feminist critique and re-interpretation of traditional Christian doctrines draws from biblical, heterodox, orthodox, pagan, and modern resources in accordance with the critical principle that only what promotes the full humanity of women is authentic and redemptive. On this basis, classism, ethnocentrism, Christian-ism, anthropocentrism, and hierarchical relations are criticized, and a mutuality that affirms different ways of being is upheld. Most directly relevant to eco-justice are chapters 3 and 10. Ruether argues that, because Western culture has symbolically linked women and nature, the critique of the domination of women by men requires the critique of the domination of nature by humans. An ecological ethic must take into account structures of social domination and exploitation that mediate the domination of nature and prevent concern for the welfare of the whole community. The proper model for hope and change is *metanoia*: the continuing effort to realize the basic ingredients of a just and livable society, and the constant recovery of *shalom* defined as blessedness and "holy being" within the mortal limits of covenantal existence.

252 Williams, Delores S. "Sin, Nature, and Black Women's Bodies." In *Ecofeminism and the Sacred*, edited by Carol J. Adams, 24-29. New York: Continuum Publishing Co., 1993.

Williams describes the relation between the use of Black women's bodies in the nineteenth century and the use of nature today, and says that using either the land or human beings inappropriately destroys the natural order. Although such use denies that Black women and nature are made in the image of God, many Christians have believed it to be their God-given right.

In addition to the works annotated in this chapter, readers interested in feminist criticism may wish to consult the following entries located elsewhere in the bibliography: 013, 046, 062, 112, 113, 173, 269, and 292.

6

Science and Technology

Eco-justice literature has roots in earlier inquiries into the social impacts and ethical implications of rapid advances in science and technology. Concerns about the potential of technology for dehumanization, social disruption, and concentration of wealth and power predated issues of environmental limits and violence against nonhuman nature, and they remain central to the eco-justice discussion. This section includes eco-justice critiques of modern science and technology, explorations of the implications of "postmodern" scientific developments for eco-justice, and proposals for promoting more just and environmentally sound technologies.

253 Abrecht, Paul. "Impact of Science and Technology on Society: New Directions in Ecumenical Social Ethics." *Zygon* 12 (September 1977): 185-98.

In this examination of the fundamental ethical questions raised by the World Council of Churches' five-year (1969-74) inquiry into "The Future of Man and Society in a World of Science-Based Technology," Abrecht comments that a greater number of persons in Western Christendom have worried about justly distributing the fruits of technological and economic growth than about growth itself. Increasingly, however, he finds scientists, technologists, theologians, and social theorists raising questions about the environmental limits and risks of technological development and about the connections between science and society. He claims that these problems will not be solved in isolation from policy issues relating to sustainability, technology, democracy, and life-style, and that the churches must point to possibilities for new and responsible life in community. This essay previously appeared (with slight differences) in *Christianity and Crisis* (28 April 1975): 92-8.

254 [Abrecht, Paul]. "Science and Technology in the Struggle for a Just, Participatory, and Sustainable Society." In *Faith, Science, and the Future*, edited by Paul Abrecht, 2d ed., 1-7. Philadelphia: Fortress Press, 1979.

This paper reviews the emergence of the theme of a "sustainable society" alongside more traditional concerns for social justice within the World Council of Churches after 1970, including the planning of the 1979 conference at the Massachusetts Institute of Technology on the theme of a "Just, Participatory, and Sustainable Society." It underscores the lack of consensus on the proper role of science and technology in creating such a society.

255 Abrecht, Paul, ed. *Faith, Science, and the Future.* 2d ed. Philadelphia: Fortress Press, 1979.

This collection of papers (some previously published) was prepared for the 1979 World Council of Churches General Assembly at the Massachusetts Institute of Technology on the theme of "The Just, Participatory, and Sustainable Society." Most deal with some issue or aspect of the relation of technology to society (genetics, food, energy, technology transfer, appropriate technology, etc.), and only a few refer to religious beliefs or communities. See (254).

256 Barbour, Ian. "An Ecological Ethic." *Christian Century* 87 (7 October 1970): 1180-84.

This essay represents a condensed presentation of ideas that Barbour develops in *Technology, Environment and Human Values* (258) and *Ethics in an Age of Technology* (257). Describing both environmental deterioration and poverty as products of a "thing-oriented" technological mindset and a lack of adequate social controls over technology, Barbour suggests that a new ecological ethic and a new theology, along with decision-making mechanisms for redirecting technological development, can help bring about a person- and life-oriented culture. The population explosion must be halted, however, if efforts against pollution and poverty are to succeed.

257 Barbour, Ian. *Ethics in an Age of Technology.* Gifford Lectures 1989-1991, vol. 2. New York: Harper Collins Publishers, 1993.

This essay is essentially a revision of *Technology, Environment, and Human Values* (258), with some new topics and updated discussions. Part 1 sets up the value framework for analyzing several "critical technologies." Arguing that technologies are the product of individual and social choice, Barbour draws on science, philosophy, and religion to spell out individual, social, and environmental values for appraising them. He notes that the biblical heritage offers resources for a "distinctive synthesis" of environmental and social justice concerns. Part 2 examines policy choices relating to agriculture, energy, and computers in light of these values, with examples primarily from the United States, but also from the Third World, Europe, and Japan. Justice, participation, and sustainability are most often at stake—but always in combination with other values—and priority is given to social justice in matters of food and health access. In the final part, Barbour turns to the risks posed by technology's "unprecedented powers" (environmental degradation, genetic engineering, and nuclear weapons) and argues for the possibility of redirecting technology through political participation, more appropriate and efficient technologies, frugal lifestyles, education, new perceptions provoked by crises, and alternative visions of the good life.

258 Barbour, Ian. *Technology, Environment, and Human Values.* New York: Praeger Publishers, 1980.

Barbour offers an interdisciplinary study of conflicting material, social, and environmental values and political forces involved in the "hard choices" the United States faces regarding policies for scarce resources and environmental quality. After opening with a survey of attitudes toward nature and technology and a discussion of social and environmental values, he summarizes the state of discussions in many areas (land use and pollution, cost/benefit analysis and technology assessment, energy, food and population, economic growth) and gives his own views. A process theologian, Barbour is concerned not only to balance but also to combine environmental preservation and distributive justice. He argues that all organisms have some degree of intrinsic value and that ecological diversity has value for God; ecosystems have only instrumental value for the individual organisms they support. He affirms the ability of individuals to work for change through political action and lifestyle. The range, organization, and thorough bibliographical references make this a virtual handbook to the issues. This book is revised and updated as (257).

259 Barbour, Ian, ed. *Western Man and Environmental Ethics: Attitudes Toward Nature and Technology.* Reading, MA: Addison-Wesley Publishing Co., 1973.

The role of attitudes toward nature and technology both in leading to the environmental crisis and in contributing to survival and the quality of life is examined in this collection of essays in theology, the humanities, and the social and biological sciences. Barbour's introduction traces contrasts and convergencies in the views offered by the essays. He argues for redirecting technology in accordance with the values of survival, human fulfillment, freedom, justice, and nonhuman welfare, and claims that both the principles of "ecological wisdom" and social justice can be applied to technology, development, and resource issues. See Faramelli (348), Moncrief (014), Santmire (017), White (026).

260 Beach, Waldo. *The Wheel and the Cross: A Christian Response to the Technological Revolution.* Atlanta: John Knox Press, 1979.

This work aims at awakening the Christian lay person to the "religion of scientism" dominating life in the United States, to the ecological costs of a consumer-driven lifestyle and artificially-induced wants, and to the inequities in world-resource distribution. Beach calls for Christians to promote both an ethics of stewardship in relation to nature and a move to world equity as part of an authentic reading of what Christian love requires.

261 Berry, Thomas F. "Technology and the Healing of the Earth." In his *The Dream of the Earth*, 50-69. San Francisco: Sierra Club Books, 1988.

Berry weighs the benefits of technological civilization against its destructive effects on the earth community. He divides responders to technology into four groups: entrepreneurs "entranced" with the prospect of continued progress; social reformers critical of technology's human costs and the unjust distribution of its fruits but not of its environmental impact; those who criticize technology's disruption of nature's integrity; and those working on the alternatives needed for healing the earth. He proposes seven principles for the development of more benign technologies.

262 Birch, Charles. "Nature, Humanity, and God in Ecological Perspective." In *Faith and Science in an Unjust World: Report of the World Council of Churches' Conference on Faith, Science, and the Future,* vol. 1, *Plenary Presentations,* edited by Roger L. Shinn, 62-73. Geneva: World Council of Churches, 1980.

Birch argues that the dominant mechanistic, technocratic worldview reflects its origins in a society bent on mastering nature, and that Christianity has accommodated itself to this unecological, dehumanizing worldview which is now challenged by personal encounter with the wonder and mystery of the universe. He suggests the need for a new partnership of faith and science, such as that found in process theology, which acknowledges the oneness of nature, humanity, and God and implies an ethic embracing all life and supporting an ecologically sustainable and socially just society.

263 Ferré, Frederick. *Shaping the Future: Resources for the Post-Modern World.*
New York: Harper and Row, 1976.

In a pluralistic position, based on philosophical theology but nontechnical, Ferré
attempts to locate resources for a "post-modern" religious consciousness that
preserves the values of science and technology without scientism and technolatry.
He suggests that, while it is doubtful whether any great metaphysical and religious synthesis such as process theology can be widely accepted in this time of
transition, a possible stance for those who are between religious models is
"polymythic organicism"—an openness to the full range of religious symbols,
embracing both nature and society, which express the values of homeostasis (self-
limitation), holism (mutuality among well-differentiated parts), and creativity
(human dignity and autonomy).   He believes that Judaism and Christianity
embody these values to the degree that institutional religion *may* be able to help
guide us into the post-modern world. Ferré applies these three values to the
reform of education, politics, and economics. See Ferré (181) for a postscript to
these thoughts.

264 Gilkey, Langdon.   "Robert L. Heilbroner's Vision of History." *Zygon* 10
(1975): 215-33.

Gilkey critiques Robert Heilbroner's argument (*An Inquiry into the Human Prospect*) that environmental limits to growth will require an authoritarian, ascetic,
and tradition-bound society and so will overturn the Enlightenment belief in progress and in values of freedom, individualism, and scientific creativity. He maintains that, while Heilbroner's analysis shows the ambiguity of human creativity,
in a Christian view, problems are caused not by creativity itself but by the glut-
tony and selfishness which taint it. Although a "new Dark Ages" is possible, it is
not certain, and God continually offers new possibilities in even the most tragic
historical situation.

265 Gilkey, Langdon.   "Technology, History, and Liberation." *Anticipation* 16
(March 1974): 14-19.

This paper considers the deeply entrenched problems technology poses for the
moral and religious consciousness. Although Gilkey makes a division between
problems centering around nature and those he chooses to discuss having to do
with human interactions, the issues raised are germane to eco-justice concerns.
Gilkey asks how a just society handles the problems of order and freedom raised
by technology. He stresses two issues: the vastly increased social and political
control over the shape of humanity that those with technological knowledge can
exercise, and the deep conformity technology demands. Because it consists of a
plurality of uncoordinated systems, technology seems to require centralized control, thus jeopardizing the possibility of a plurality of free communities. Gilkey
suggests that technology "threatens to become a 'fate' that controls and
determines us" because technological growth is itself largely the result of a lack
of self-control on the part of lustful human beings.

266 Gill, David M. *From Here to Where? Technology, Faith, and the Future of
Man.* Report on an exploratory conference, Geneva, 28 June - 4 July 1970. Geneva:
World Council of Churches, 1970.

This summation of the content and foci of the World Council of Churches'
(WCC) exploratory conference on "Technology and the Future of Man and
Society" is written by the Secretary of the WCC Department on Church and
Society and includes a foreword by Samuel L. Parmar of India, the conference

Chair, expressing the connection of environmental and justice issues. It explains how 'environment' differs in meaning depending upon socio-economic status: for persons from developed nations it refers to pollution and ecological imbalance; for those of undeveloped nations, to the need for structural reform. The conference was divided into five working groups addressing ecology and population, the human implications of discoveries in the biological sciences, the future of industry and urban life, systems and ideologies in a world perspective, and the use of computers to anticipate the future. Each group reflected on its area in light of what it foretold for the future of humanity; to what degree that future would be determined by the continuance of present trends, planned choices, moral choices, Christian faith, and ideology; and the role of Christians and the church. Among the trends that emerge from the working groups are skepticism about the Western assumption of links between technology, Christianity, and modernization; an expression of the inadequacy of the "usefulness to man" criterion of conservation; questions as to the relevance of theological reflection for addressing the environmental crisis; a feeling of the inadequacy of technical solutions to such questions as an acceptable quality of the environment and duties to future generations; skepticism about the "population explosion panic"; and an agreement that the paramount goal must be a commitment to global economic justice. According to Gill, a final panel relating technology to theology sparked frustration among participants, and made it clear that "theologians and scientists are still far from sharing a common language."

267 Gosling, David, ed. *Technology from the Underside.* Report of the Consultation on New Technology, Work, and the Environment. *Tugon* 6, no. 1 (1986).

This report contains the papers and recommendations of the participants to a Southeast Asian consultation sponsored by the World Council of Churches Subunit on Church and Society and the National Council of Churches in the Philippines that took place in Manila on 10-15 January 1986. The chapters reflect various interests and include five that address the nuclear threat in Asia and the Pacific. An address by Kim Yong Bock adds to the nuclear theme the description of Korean *Minjung* who, as conscripted prostitutes and forced laborers working in Japan, were victims of nuclear bombs. Other environmental problems in the Asian region addressed include deforestation, marine pollution, otter board trawler fishing, and the promotion of monosodium glutamate. Technology is viewed mainly from the standpoint of its victims, as is especially clear in the chapter on the Bhopal disaster. The consultation's recommendations address the exploitation of labor, with special attention to the exploitation of women; the root causes of exploitation in imperialism and a destructive work ethic; and the responsibility of the church.

268 Hessel, Dieter T. "Now That Animals Can Be Genetically Engineered: Biotechnology in Theological-Ethical Perspective." In *Eco-Theology: Voices from South and North*, edited by David G. Hallman, 284-99. Geneva: WCC Publications; Maryknoll, NY: Orbis Books, 1994.

Hessel argues for evaluating animal biotechnology (especially transgenic technology) in terms of what is appropriate to the larger eco-social good. As a basis for biotechnology policy, he delineates a theology that affirms God's continuing presence in and with creation and the role of human creatures as earthkeepers responsible for respecting and caring for otherkind as well as humankind. Over against this view of human vocation is the Baconian project of increasing human power over nature which now guides biotechnology. Hessel lists as ethical imperatives for biotechnology: shifting to a more appropriate eco-social paradigm; anticipating the social impacts of research and development; assessing the qualitative character of biotechnics; establishing criteria for eco-just biotechnics (including evaluating the expected pattern of justice or injustice); and implementing a standard of "appropriateness." Biotechnics is not necessarily ruled out, but requires deeper ethical and religious reflection, and more democratic social involvement to limit or direct it for the good of all. Originally published in *Theology and Public Policy* 5 (Summer 1993), pp. 40-54.

269 Ruether, Rosemary Radford. "A Feminist Perspective on Religion and Science." In *Faith and Science in an Unjust World: Report of the World Council of Churches' Conference on Faith, Science, and the Future*, vol. 1, *Plenary Presentations,* edited by Roger L. Shinn, 55-58. Geneva: World Council of Churches, 1980.

Arguing that the gods of scientific reason and of the Old Testament tradition stand outside the world of matter and dominate it as the tool of a Western White male ruling-class elite, Ruether says that women, who, like nature, have been an exploited resource, must look to the conversion of the world to the egalitarian "new humanity" that both Christianity and science promised—and betrayed.

270 Schumacher, E. F. "The Age of Plenty: A Christian View." In *Valuing the Earth: Economics, Ecology, Ethics*, edited by Herman E. Daly and Kenneth N. Townsend, 159-72. Cambridge, MA and London: MIT Press, 1993.

Taking as definitive of Christian faith that humanity was created to save its soul and the rest of creation to help humanity do so, the author of *Small Is Beautiful* utilizes a line from a poem by Ignatius Loyola as a criterion of resource use: "That man ought to make use of them [other things on the face of the earth] just so far as they help him to attain his end / And that he ought to withdraw himself from them just so far as they hinder him." Schumacher contends this purpose in life requires a technology that favors smallness, simplicity, capital saving, and non-violence.

271 Shinn, Roger L. *Forced Options: Social Decisions for the Twenty-First Century.* 3d ed. Cleveland: Pilgrim Press, 1991.

Society faces "forced options" regarding the "big problems" of energy, food, population, limits to growth, genetic technology, and war—problems involving both physical limits and issues of social justice which can neither be solved by technical "fixes" nor by the application of received ethical and religious wisdom. Yet, Shinn explains, religious faith can contribute effectively to bringing about the necessary social changes, including a new moral and pragmatic discipline. He sees decision-making as involving the distinguishing and relating of technical information and commitment to values within the framework of an ideology; ethical responsibility as including both care of the earth and human advantage so that concerns for ecology and social justice reinforce each other. Shinn proposes Christ the Suffering Servant as a powerful symbol in the present situation. An epilogue reviews developments since the first 1982 edition, including the shift from "limits to growth" to "sustainable development" and the growing recognition that environmental and social justice interests converge. For a retrospective on Shinn's thought and a bibliography of his writings, see Beverly W. Harrison, "The Quest for Justice," 289-310, and E. Richard Knox, "Bibliography of Writings," 311-55, in Beverly W. Harrison, Robert L. Stivers, and Ronald H. Stone, eds., *The Public Vocation of Christian Ethics* (New York: Pilgrim Press, 1986).

272 Sowunmi, M. Adebisi. "Giver of Life—'Sustain Your Creation.'" In *Ecotheology: Voices from South and North*, edited by David G. Hallman, 149-54. Geneva: WCC Publications; Maryknoll, NY: Orbis Books, 1994.

Nigerian scientist Sowunmi finds that both science and the Bible show that God created a perfect earth with awe-inspiring grandeur and diversity and abundant resources for humankind and all other creatures. Holding that the underlying cause of the ecological and economic crises is the domination of indigenous "cultures of life" by industrial and colonial "cultures of death," the author calls for the formulation of a radically new global political and economic order, informed by Christian and indigenous values, fully involving the oppressed, and requiring fundamental changes by the rich and powerful.

273 Swimme, Brian, and Thomas F. Berry. *The Universe Story: From the Primordial Flaring Forth to the Ecozoic Era—A Celebration of the Unfolding of the Cosmos.* San Francisco: HarperSanFrancisco, 1992.

Swimme and Berry present the evolution of the universe as a "sequence of meaningful irreversible events best understood as narrative" exhibiting intentionality characterized by differentiation, autopoiesis (self-manifestation), and communion. They believe that the present age is a critical period in this "universe story," one characterized by both a planet-destroying, commercial-industrial mystique and a dawning consciousness of the sacred dimension of the planet. Awareness of the universe story is itself a revelatory experience that entails working for the integral functioning of the sacred earth community. Among other things this means that such concepts as justice, progress, good, and evil need to be extended to include all creatures.

274 Tillich, Paul. "Has Man's Conquest of Space Increased or Diminished His Stature?" In *The Spiritual Situation in Our Technological Society*, edited by J. Mark Thomas, 185-95. Macon, GA: Mercer University Press, 1988.

Tillich's inquiry into the spiritual significance of space travel touches on humanity's relation to earth, economic justice, and democracy. Space travel is described as the fullest expression of the "horizontal" dimension of existence—the control and transformation of the cosmos. While it threatens to eclipse the "vertical" or spiritual dimension of transcendence, is linked to weapons technology, alienates humanity from the earth, diverts funds from other purposes such as population control, and promotes a scientific-technological elitism, these dangers do not warrant stopping it. Originally published in *Great Ideas Today 1963*, edited by Robert M. Hutchins and Mortimer J. Adler, 49-69 (Chicago: Encyclopedia Britannica, 1963), the essay also appears as "The Effects of Space Exploration on Man's Condition and Stature," in *The Future of Religions*, edited by Jerald C. Brauer, 39-51 (New York: Harper and Row, 1966).

275 West, Charles C. "God—Woman/Man—Creation: Some Comments on the Ethics of the Relationship." *Ecumenical Review* 33 (January 1981): 13-28.

West identifies two sets of issues involved in the relations between nature and human justice. First is the inability of the dominant humanist ideologies—technological humanism, analytical pessimism, and revolutionary humanism—to clarify the interaction of technology and society. Second is the question of nonhuman creation in light of what the church has said about the secularization of nature; reality as interpersonal and Christocentric; and God's will for historical transformation. West recommends addressing these questions by exploring knowing, participating, and transforming relationships in the context of covenant.

In addition to the works annotated in this chapter, readers interested in science and technology may wish to consult the following entries located elsewhere in the bibliography: 015, 020, 065, 124, 142, 160, 244-45, 280, 287, 357.

7

Social and Political Issues

Emergent environmental concerns have added a new dimension to long-standing social issues. Among those dealt with here are: race and ethnicity; labor and employment; urban planning and poverty; personal, sexual, and family relationships; population change; international relations; and militarism, war, and refugees. To respond collectively to these and more "purely" environmental problems, we need both an adequate public philosophy and effective political action. Thus, many of these entries grapple with the interactions of individuals and groups in the larger society; democratic decision-making and discourse; political power-structures and the role of government; and environmentalism as a social and political movement.

276 Abrecht, Paul. "The Future as a 'Religious' Problem." *Ecumenical Review* 24 (April 1972): 176-89.

Abrecht points out that the three revolutions whose outcome may determine our future each have a spiritual-ethical dimension. The political-economic revolution entails assumptions about nature and human welfare that are challenged by concerns about the moral and environmental problems created by economic growth. The technological revolution is increasingly criticized for its ambiguous consequences for the human spirit and social justice. Cultural revolutions challenge traditional values and raise problems of moral and cultural identity and social cohesion. New challenges thus face the two dominant Christian responses to the future—revolutionary millennialism (stressing political action as a Christian obligation) and eschatological 'realism' (stressing the finitude and ambiguity of human efforts)—each of which has strengths and weaknesses and must be in dialogue with the other.

277 Anderson, Terence. "Indigenous Peoples, the Land, and Self-Government." In *The Public Vocation of Christian Ethics*, edited by Beverly W. Harrison, Robert L. Stivers, and Ronald H. Stone, 159-78. New York: Pilgrim Press, 1986.

Anderson briefly sketches the background and present situation of native peoples' struggles to continue as distinctive peoples. He outlines some of the main policy goal options—subjection/protection, assimilation/integration, interdependence/independence—and argues that interdependence, that is, giving native peoples the option of maintaining their ethnic identity and distinctive political structures while controlling their economic development, best accords with the Christian principles of love of neighbor (which includes liberty and justice) and the stewardship of creation.

278   Baum, Gregory. "The Grand Vision: It Needs Social Action." In *Thomas Berry and the New Cosmology*, edited by Anne Lonergan and Carol Richards, 51-56. Mystic, CT: Twenty-Third Publications, 1987.

While admiring Thomas Berry's proposals, Baum criticizes his rejection of the whole Enlightenment project, his distinguishing of "green" politics from all existing politics, and his neglect of the "Christo-centric heart" of the Christian tradition. Baum argues that the Enlightenment's critical and ethical dimension must be recovered and affirmed, that environmental concerns must be integrated into a socialism built on solidarity with society's victims, and that radical visions can be politically effective only if they find a home within a tradition.

279   Blockwick, Jessma. "The Population/Food Equation: More than a Numbers Game." In *Beyond Survival: Bread and Justice in Christian Perspective*, edited by Dieter T. Hessel, 48-69. New York: Friendship Press, 1977.

Blockwick's response to the population issue based on human rights and Christian faith, seeks to honor both informed freedom of choice and the needs of the general welfare. She argues that because God created a world with limits and because life is sacred, Christians have a responsibility to ensure both that population does not exceed the level below which spiritual and physical well-being are possible and that the affluent reduce their consumption and pollution. Discussed are the population-control policies of China and India and the inadequacy of United States aid for population control.

280   Boff, Leonardo. "Social Ecology: Poverty and Misery." In *Eco-Theology: Voices from South and North*, edited by David G. Hallman, 235-47. Geneva: WCC Publications; Maryknoll, NY: Orbis Books, 1994.

Boff describes the agreement among liberationist, pacifist, and environmental critiques that the dominant societal model cannot generate wealth without also generating poverty, violence, and environmental destruction. He sees social ecology—the study of human systems in interaction with environmental systems—as necessary for understanding global capitalism's exploitation of nature. A social-environmental ethic is needed which avoids both static naturalism and anthropocentrism and which incorporates justice for the earth and common responsibility for the destiny of all human beings. As an example of a policy reflecting such an ethic, Boff cites debt-for-nature swaps, but cautions that they must involve representatives of social movements as well as governments and must be accompanied by technology transfers to promote less ecologically damaging means of production. An addendum to the essay presents examples from Latin America of problems affecting persons and the environment.

281   Bratton, Susan Power. *Six Billion and More: Human Population Regulation and Christian Ethics*. Louisville, KY: Westminster/John Knox Press, 1992.

This wide-ranging and detailed effort to introduce the subject to a Christian audience and to develop a Christian ethical framework for dealing with population, highlights caring for creation, justice for women and children, cultural context, and Christian responsibilities. After reviewing the principles of population dynamics, Bratton surveys biblical teachings on reproduction and the history of Christian responses to population problems, discussing population increase in relation to its environmental impacts and to the Christian responsibility to respect creation and to share its fruits with humans and nonhumans. She insists that Christians must provide alternatives to "lifeboat" and "triage" ethics and concludes that high per-capita pollution and consumption, rather than population decline, are the most crucial population issues within developed countries. Economic and social causes of exploding populations in developing nations are outlined to show that population is a distributive-justice issue and involves how cultures change. A range of issues relating justice to population—the role of individuals, governments, and families; cultural context; child welfare; women's roles; family planning; contraception; coercion; and abortion—are considered along with possibilities for action.

282 Chambers, Richard G. "Plant Breeders' Rights and the Integrity of Creation." In *Creation and the Kingdom of God*, edited by David Gosling, Gennadios Limouris, and Freda Rajotte, 36-42. Church and Society Documents, August, 1988, no. 5. Geneva: World Council of Churches, 1988.

In one of the few critiques of a denomination's engagement with a specific eco-justice issue, Chambers recounts the United Church of Canada's Agriculture, Fishery, and Food Committee's (AFF) opposition to legislation for patenting new varieties of plants. In opposition to AFF's pragmatic and economic arguments, he sees the need for a credible theology of nature (such as Douglas J. Hall's view of humanity as steward, priest, and poet) which links human freedom to freedom for all life and promotes production and distribution based on need. See Hall, "The Integrity of Creation," in Schulze (150), pp. 25-36.

283 Chapman, G. Clarke. *Facing the Nuclear Heresy: A Call to Reformation.* Elgin, IL: Brethren Press, 1986.

Chapman describes "nuclearism" as a covert religion and the threat of nuclear war as a religious heresy requiring action by a confessing church movement. He criticizes the "zero sum" view of resources, which he links to nuclearism, and questions whether it is not the image of scarcity combined with inequitable distribution of vital supplies, rather than real scarcity, that is the problem.

284 Clark, J. Michael. *Beyond Our Ghettos: Gay Theology in Ecological Perspective.* Cleveland: Pilgrim Press, 1993.

Demanding a broader vision than that provided by the "ghetto mentality" of gay liberation theology, the author declares that "the demands of relational justice and responsibility in gay theology also imply the demand of *ecological* justice and responsibility." He sees gay ecotheology as a natural extension of gay liberation theology, linked by a common valuing of diversity and difference, the result of experiencing homophobic "heteropatriarchy's" disvaluing of same. Clark defines gay ecotheology as a collaborative and creative extension of ecofeminism; his development of gay theology is informed by ecofeminist thought. He calls Christianity and mechanistic thinking "villainous compatriots" that have "joined the ecocidal force of patriarchy to help devastate the earth," and he deplores the human egocentrism of the biblical concept of dominion and the theological hubris of *imago Dei*. Throughout the short work Clark frequently connects the disvaluation of gays and lesbians, the exploitation of women, and the environmental destruction of the homes of minorities and peoples in less developed nations.

285   Curran, Charles E.   "Population Control: Methods and Morality."   In his *Issues in Sexual and Medical Ethics*, 169-97.   Notre Dame, IN: University of Notre Dame Press, 1978.

In this chapter of a larger work dealing with sexual and medical ethics, Roman Catholic theological ethicist Curran discusses the preliminary considerations that influence the approach taken to population control: the degree of harmony and order thought to exist in the world; the understanding of the state; the freedom of the individual couple in determining family size; and an adequate and objective understanding of the nature of the problem.   His treatment is based on a belief that a population problem exists that will become much more serious in the finite human world in which we live.   He suggests that the Roman Catholic Church's prohibition of artificial contraception might be understood to rest on a care for the species and could thus be reversed to call for a limitation of births.   He believes that the state can intervene to ensure that individuals act responsibly toward procreation, but it must do so in accord with justice.   Curran also evaluates specific proposals to population problems, emphasizing the necessity of holistic solutions that recognize the part played by the over-consumption of developed nations, the need for socioeconomic development among poorer nations, and the general need for changes in socioeconomic structures.

286   Fagley, Richard M.   *The Population Explosion and Christian Responsibility.* New York: Oxford University Press, 1960.

This full-length analysis of the relationship of Christianity and population, while it falls short of developing the environmental side of eco-justice, is nevertheless a significant stepping-stone in that direction.   Fagley defines the problem of population as a temporal matter stemming from a rate of human increase out of proportion to economic, social, and "absorptive capacities" of civilizations, and says it is not the increase of the human race that causes concern, but what the increase "portends for the quality of life on this planet."   He condemns as immoral the curtailing of crop production or the hoarding of surpluses by rich nations; discusses the expectations of poor nations for economic and social development and the obstacles that prevent their assuring a more adequate food supply through the accumulation of capital for industrialization; and discusses the problem of soil impoverishment, although not to link such practices with population pressure, but to show that the amount of land available for agriculture is a misleading statistic.   At the time of writing, the rainforests of the Amazon basin and Central Africa were being looked to as areas that could be put to use for crop production.   While stating that "no one has a right to dismiss out of hand the food potential in these fountains of verdure," Fagley emphasizes the difficulties and doubts about their development.   His discussion of food and population concludes that economic and social development alone without a means of curbing population growth cannot restore balance.   An extensive survey of religious doctrine on procreation, marriage, and contraception concludes that responsible parenthood is a Christian doctrine "whose time has come," and that Christian stewardship requires Protestant individuals and bodies to use political and economic means to convince others, including government bodies, of its necessity.

287   Faramelli, Norman J.   "The Manipulative Mentality: We Do to Nature What We Do to People."   In *Ecology: Crisis and New Vision*, edited by Richard E. Sherrell, 59-76.   Richmond, VA: John Knox Press, 1971.

The author rejects positions that identify the cause of environmental destruction and social injustice as technology or the technical mindset (Martin Heidegger, Jacques Ellul, Lewis Mumford) or that see environmental destruction and social injustice as intended by their perpetuators.   The common abuse of environment and people is a side effect of the drives for success and profit. These cannot, and should not, be eliminated, but need to be balanced by receptive, intuitive, and mystical human capacities.

288 Freudenberger, C. Dean, and Joseph C. Hough, Jr. "Lifeboats and Hungry People." In *Beyond Survival: Bread and Justice in Christian Perspective*, edited by Dieter T. Hessel, 19-47. New York: Friendship Press, 1977.

The authors condemn Garrett Hardin's "lifeboat ethics" and his prescription of triage for United States aid policy as an inaccurate description of the problem of world hunger as well as an ethically indefensible response, the latter because God created the world and called humankind to live together for the good of one another and the earth. They propose an inclusive principle of justice (a restatement of the World Council of Churches ideal of a "just, participatory, and sustainable society"): "The common good we seek is a world in which all people have access to the basic necessities of life, in which all people have some say about the shape of their future, and where decisions about resource use stand under the judgment of some assessment about the renewable carrying capacity of the earth." Applied to the global food crisis, this global principle of justice requires promotion of rural development, efforts to reduce population growth, environmentally sound economic growth, opposition to increased military expenditures, and less consumptive lifestyles in the Western world.

289 Geyer, Alan F., and Barbara G. Green. *Lines in the Sand: Justice and the Gulf War.* Louisville, KY: Westminster/John Knox Press, 1992.

Eco-justice, although not the authors' main focus, is an important element in this critique of the uses and limits of the just war tradition in Western and Christian thought and its application to the Persian Gulf War. The United States government, it is pointed out, previous to engaging in war, had shunned energy policies that would have made the nation less driven to a war for oil. Geyer, professor at Wesley Theological Seminary and a senior scholar at Churches' Center for Theology and Public Policy, and Green, Associate for Peacemaking Issues of the Presbyterian Church, USA, apply each of the just war criteria to the conflict and show the deep ambiguities involved. In summing up the consequences they write: "The enormity of Iraqi casualties and the unending suffering of the survivors, the environmental disasters, the lost peace dividend, the disdain for issues of domestic justice, the escalation of the arms trade, the seductive exhibitionism of high-tech weaponry, the deeper despair of the Palestinians, the aggravation of misery among the world's poorest peoples, and the implication of the United Nations in all these melancholy matters hardly add up to a vindication of, or by, the just war tradition."

290 Gustafson, James M. "Population and Nutrition." In his *Ethics from a Theocentric Perspective.* Vol. 2, *Ethics and Theology.* Chicago: University of Chicago Press, 1984.

Gustafson's magnum opus develops a perspective on ethics that rejects the assumption that God has ordered creation primarily for human well-being while it affirms that ethics is a matter of human participation in the patterns and processes of interdependence in the world. In this chapter Gustafson argues that nations and individuals have an obligation to reduce suffering due to starvation and malnutrition even though the causes of food shortage are not completely within human control. Voluntary giving of resources to meet the hunger of others he says is obligatory for Christians but an inadequate way to meet present and future needs. Among the possible ethical approaches nations may take to the problems of population growth and nutrition, he judges the Roman Catholic Church's position on birth control to be immoral because it does not recognize limitations, the ecological effects of agricultural technology required to grow more food, or the well-being of the whole of humanity and future generations. An ethical approach that requires a nation to develop its own agricultural capacities and control its own population before attending to the needs of other nations he judges more highly, but faults for its tendencies to be insensitive to innocent suffering and complacent to present patterns of consumption. Gustafson argues that the principle of distributive justice requires that the basic needs of each individual be met regardless of the individual's practice or non-practice of birth control, and that nations both increase food self-sufficiency and encourage birth control. At the same time, agricultural production must be sensitive to the needs of nature for the sake of nature's own flourishing as well as for humanity's sake.

291   John Paul II. *Laborem exercens*. Encyclical letter "On Human Work," 14 September 1981. Washington, DC: Office of Publishing Services, United States Catholic Conference, 1981.

This encyclical stresses labor as the key to social ethics and as the priority for economic production. The pope argues that the dignity of humanity resulting from the incarnation supports the dignity of labor, and that the Genesis mandate to Adam to "subdue the earth" shows the essential connection between work and humanity. He condemns the dehumanization of work by any system, capitalist or collectivist, which treats labor as a mere instrument. While recognizing problems of pollution and resource limitation, he affirms that work is the means for humans to exercise co-creatorship, cooperating directly with God in the sanctification of all creation. The complete text is included in Byers, ed. (334).

292   Keller, Catherine. "Chosen Persons and the Green Ecumenacy: A Possible Christian Response to the Population Apocalypse." In *Eco-Theology: Voices from South and North*, edited by David G. Hallman, 284-99. Geneva: WCC Publications; Maryknoll, NY: Orbis Books, 1994.

Keller argues that the frequent misuse of population concerns to support First World, White, or masculine self-interest is not an excuse to evade the issue; rather, feminists and liberationists should provide an interpretation of the problem which stresses the impact of overpopulation on poor women and its roots in poverty and sexism. She observes that the absence of the population issue from the Christian progressive agenda leaves the pope to speak, by default, for Christianity, articulating a pro-natalist synthesis of the Hebrew idea of procreation as blessing with a Hellenized Christian asceticism and imperial power. Keller presents a way of "recycling" Christian tradition to address population growth using the Hebrew prophetic priority of justice to structure the discussion, attending to the just distribution of resources, and affirming children as responsibly "chosen" rather than imposed by biological fate. She sees the apocalyptic sense of urgency awakened in the face of environmental threats directed toward the "counter-apocalypse" of "communities of resistance and solidarity." "Eco-asceticism" can combat consumer addiction to over-indulgence and its consequent self-detestation by heightening enjoyment of senses and relationships.

293   Kroh, Werner. "Foundations and Perspective for an Ecological Ethics: The Problem of Responsibility for the Future as a Challenge to Theology." Translated by John Bowden. *Concilium* 4 (August 1991): 79-93.

In a difficult but intriguing glimpse of eco-justice in contemporary German political philosophy and theology, Kroh describes Hans Jonas's "ethics of responsibility" as critiqued by Karl-Otto Apel's "ethics of discourse" and offers a theological response. While Jonas sees social and technological progress and democracy conflicting with the duty of preserving humanity and its environment, Apel argues that this duty requires them, for it is the duty to realize and preserve a "communicative community" characterized by solidarity, freedom, equality, rationality, and consensus. Kroh (following Johann Baptist Metz) argues that ethical responsibility for the future must also recognize irrational factors in human praxis (e.g., faith, sin) and be grounded in concrete recollections of past sufferings and the hopes that have emerged from them.

294 Lee, Charles. "The Integrity of Justice." *Sojourners* (February/March 1990): 22-25.

Lee, director and author of the United Church of Christ report, "Toxic Wastes and Race in the United States," argues that the environmental movement must be transformed by the recognition that there cannot be a healthy environment without justice. Alternative technologies will not be developed as long as there are poor minority communities in which hazardous waste can be dumped without political repercussions. The growing environmental activism among racial minority communities is an encouraging sign that this situation is changing.

295 Loy, R. Philip. "Politics and the Environment: Toward a New Public Philosophy." In *The Environmental Crisis: The Ethical Dilemma*, edited by Edwin R. Squiers, 209-26. Mancelona, MI: AuSable Trails Institute of Environmental Studies, 1982.

Loy names and critiques "pluralistic liberalism"—the identification of the public interest as the product of interactions between group interests—as the reigning public philosophy guiding American politics, including environmental politics. He proposes a new public philosophy based on civitas and civility in which self-interest is transcended for the sake of the larger community. Such a philosophy can be developed through civic education by, and participation in, intermediate institutions including the church.

296 Martin-Schramm, James. "Population Growth, Poverty, and Environmental Degradation." *Theology and Public Policy* 4 (Summer 1992): 26-38.

Noting the lull in population ethics since the mid-'70s, Martin-Schramm deftly re-introduces the issue. He reviews relevant statistics, factors, and ethical concerns, including the threat population growth poses to renewable resources and the greater danger posed by the destructive consumption of the rich. He argues that Christian ethics aims at justice as the restoration of right relation. The primary Christian response is to attack poverty—through social reform (especially by improving women's lives) and voluntary family planning, rather than by conventional Western economic development, disincentives, or coercion.

297 Meiring, Pieter G. J. "The Greens—Avant-Garde Missionaries?" *Missionalia* 19 (November 1991): 192-202.

Written by a South African, this article reports the activities of environmental groups, "the Greens," in Africa, as well as relations between Greens and South African Blacks. Meiring quotes a study by Mark Patzer which found that Blacks in South Africa consider the priorities of the Greens to be irrelevant and alienating. Patzer further found that Greens communicate primarily with affluent Whites. His list of Green priorities contrasted to the priorities of Blacks is reproduced by Meiring. Despite their shortcomings, Meiring considers Greens to be a missionary group whose holistic, spiritual message of healing for the earth should be taken seriously by the Christian church.

298 Meyer, Art, and Jocele Meyer. *Earthkeepers: Environmental Perspectives on Hunger, Poverty, and Injustice.* Scottdale, PA: Herald Press, 1991.

This Mennonite perspective views the overcoming of environmental degradation as integral to peacemaking as well as to combating poverty, hunger, and political oppression. Its short treatment of biblical ethical foundations focuses on land as a gift from God to be received and cared for as a trust, and on human redemption as an integral part of the redemption of the whole creation. Eco-justice is described as combining ecological living with economic justice for Earth and all its people. In addition to discussing the general problems of hazardous waste, water pollution, soil erosion, strip mining, acid rain, global warming, and deforestation, the Meyers recount their own story of reclaiming strip-mined property in Ohio through tree-planting, farming, and setting up a land trust. They discuss the environmental consequences of militarism and war, economics and development, population, genetic engineering, energy, and sustainable agriculture. Social justice dimensions highlighted include toxic dumping on the poor; family farms and the farm crisis; and environmental refugees. Examples draw from Haiti and the Philippines. Each chapter ends with "Earthkeepers' Response" to the issues raised, and each section ends with discussion questions and a resource list.

299 Mische, Patricia M. "Parenting in a Hungry World." In *The Earth is the Lord's: Essays on Stewardship*, edited by Mary Evelyn Jegen and Bruno V. Manno, 169-83. New York: Paulist Press, 1978.

This approach to intentional parenting aims to help children develop the values, worldview, habits, and skills essential for a positive contribution in the midst of realities such as world hunger. The author believes that concern for hunger belongs in the context of recognizing that what we do impacts the whole earth community—its soil, plants, animals, and humans. Children learn best by experiencing a family life style that questions the notion of ownership, recognizes dependence on others, and identifies with the need for food and celebration.

300 Neuhaus, Richard J. *In Defense of People: Ecology and the Seduction of Radicalism.* New York: Macmillan Co., 1971.

This early, influential, and controversial left-wing attack on the environmental movement as a diversion from social justice issues is written by a Lutheran pastor with a history of active participation in the civil rights and antiwar movements. According to Neuhaus, the vacuum produced by the failure of America's intellectuals and the disintegration of "the Movement" of the '60's allowed the ecology movement to emerge as a diversion from necessary political tasks, shifting attention from the conflicts of power to an organismic model of society in harmony with the imperatives of nature. As a result, its new values and myth for national existence and power are based on "survival"—actually the defense of a quality environment for the elite against the hostile force of the hungry poor. Claims of eco-catastrophe serve the interests of the well-off under the guise of scientific objectivity. In opposition to the ideology of the ecology movement, Neuhaus proposes a "Covenant with the Poor" based on commitments to the centrality of the human enterprise, an ethic of compassion and altruism, and the poor as the primary signal of the demands of justice.

301   Neuhaus, Richard J.   "In Defense of People: A Thesis Revisited." In *Environmental Quality and Social Justice in Urban America: An Exploration of Conflict and Concord among Those Who Seek Environmental Quality and Those Who Seek Social Justice*, edited by James Noel Smith, 59-72. Washington, DC: The Conservation Foundation, 1974.

In this excerpt of a conference presentation and its vigorous subsequent discussion, Neuhaus claims that the environmental movement arose as a way of sustaining the movement of the '60s at a time of discouragement and disarray. He charges that environmental/social justice coalitions are seriously blocked by recurring conservative or fascist themes in the environmental literature which run counter to the biblical and radical commitment to a new order brought about by and for the poor.

302   Neuhaus, Richard J.   "Resources and Global Development." In his *Christian Faith and Public Policy*. Minneapolis: Augsburg Publishing House, 1977.

Neuhaus offers judgments on a wide range of policy issues, demonstrating his suspicion of the environmental movement on the grounds of a biblically-based concern for justice for the poor and a mistrust of state-directed efforts to realize economic equality and distributive justice. He believes the "biblical stewardship mandate" should mean not only recognizing environmental problems and respecting extrahuman nature, but also that God wills nature to be used to benefit humankind. Issues he considers include lifeboat ethics, environmental pollution and risks, future generations, economic growth, sea bed resources, food, assistance to developing nations, trade, and population.

303   Noh, Jong-Sun.   "The Effects on Korea of Un-Ecological Theology." In *Liberating Life: Contemporary Approaches to Ecological Theology*, edited by Charles Birch, William Eakin, and Jay B. McDaniel, 125-36. Maryknoll, NY: Orbis Books, 1990.

The author criticizes the "division theology" which legitimates Korea's separation into North and South and the sexual, nuclear, and environmental exploitation of its people and land by military-industrial elites and global superpowers. He believes that a Jubilee theology of reunification and self-reliance for Korea is needed.

304   Nürnberger, K.   "Ecology and Christian Ethics in a Semi-industrialized and Polarized Society." In *Are We Killing God's Earth? Ecology and Theology*, edited by W. S. Vorster, 45-67. Proceedings of the Eleventh Symposium of the Institute for Theological Research (UNISA) held at the University of South Africa in Pretoria on 2 and 3 September 1987. Pretoria: University of South Africa, 1987.

Nürnberger provides a clear and helpful analysis of the environmental crisis at three levels and relates it to the South African situation. At the level of economic structures, he finds ecological destruction at both the affluent "centers" and the impoverished "peripheries." The internal processes of center and periphery and the imbalance of power and wealth between them lead to vicious cycles of prosperity, poverty, population increase, and environmental degradation. At the level of collective consciousness, he notes obstacles to environmental responsibility in both Western and traditional cultures, as well as domination of the latter by the former. South Africa, like other semi-industrialized countries, replicates the global pattern within itself, and racial polarization adds to the difficulties of dealing with the environment. Nürnberger identifies two ways Christians can contribute to a solution: by working out a new theological vision and the norms it implies as the basis for an overall strategy; and by showing how faith in Christ can overcome ideological legitimations of destructive self-interest.

305 Olivier, D. F. "Ecology and Mission: Notes on the History of the JPIC Process and Its Relevance to Theology." *Missionalia* 19 (April 1991): 20-32.

Olivier, of the University of South Africa, Pretoria, discusses the historical development of the JPIC (Justice, Peace, and the Integrity of Creation) process and its relevance in a South African context to the mission of the church. He points out that JPIC challenges the dominant worldview of endless economic development and more wealth for all which has shaped South Africa's expectations for the future. Furthermore, the concept of eco-justice means that any program of reform in South Africa must have a sound ecological basis or else it is "down-right dishonest and misleading" and will end in disillusionment as well as poverty, hunger, and death. The church, guided by JPIC, must "unmask such travesties of social justice." Olivier calls for accepting creation's finitude and seeing each historically-determined entity as morally bound to contribute to the well-being of the whole.

306 Owens, Owen D. "Interdependence." *Foundations* 19 (July/September 1976): 196-203.

Owens claims that limits to economic growth open new possibilities for valid ethnicity but also for systematic oppression and conflict between groups—even a new Holocaust. He proposes a lifestyle for coping with this crisis, based on the idea of interdependence as mutual reciprocity grounded in reverence for all creations of God, including nonhuman beings.

307 Owens, Owen D. "Salvation and Ecology: Missionary Imperatives in Light of a New Cosmology." *Foundations* 17 (April/June 1974): 106-23.

Owens delineates the new cosmology in terms of growing awareness of human interdependence on a finite planet. To survive and realize potentials for good in this situation, he argues, requires three values that emerge from the intersection of ecological wholeness and social justice: reverence, interdependence, and stewardship. Hope for change is grounded in faith in God, who intends our ultimate salvation while punishing us for our enslavement to limited goods. Owens discusses possibilities for structural change through political participation, comprehensive planning, self-sufficient "urban-ecological regions," new models for cities, and insight into human nature.

308 Pontificia Academia Scientiarum. "Study Week on a Modern Approach to the Protection of the Environment, 2-7 November 1987: Conclusions." Vatican City: *Pontificiae Academiae Scientiarum*, no. 23, 1988.

These conclusions by the participants to a week of study initiated by Pope John Paul II address transboundary pollution control, biological diversity, mountain environments, poverty, cultural diversity, and education. The participants conclude that a greater proportion of the poor need to enjoy the benefits of their own societies and of the global economy, and that greater equity in social and economic conditions, distribution of resources, and the development of forestry and farming techniques are essential to a sustainable global ecosystem. The introductory remarks of Giovanni B. Marini-Bettòlo warn that, while "science and the means of technology should offer solutions which are consonant with the continuous growth of the human populations," they cannot do so "unless they are supported by a new way of thinking about the environment based on ethical principles."

309   Preston, Ronald H.   "Humanity, Nature, and the Integrity of Creation." *Ecumenical Review* 41 (October 1989): 552-63.

Preston is concerned that much World Council of Churches' material on "the integrity of creation" regards nature as static and humans as obliged not to interfere with it.   He claims that subsuming humans in nature in this way can support conservative resistance to desirable social and technological changes.   WCC writings do not reflect sufficiently on the distinction between the personal and the less than personal, the ambiguity of nature, the positive possibilities for human intervention, and the need to develop an ethic of risk.   Humans are to respect nature and be responsible stewards of it, but its ultimate destiny, even if it could be known, is irrelevant for ethics.

310   Rasmussen, Larry L.   "The Planetary Environment: Challenge on Every Front." *Theology and Public Policy* 2 (Summer 1990): 3-14.

A presentation of the many challenges to social structures posed by the environmental crisis.   Politics is challenged to manage world politics in the face of global environmental issues, to test the indivisibility of justice, and to examine the meaning of democracy and the breadth of the democratic community.   The economic challenge is to live on a finite planet without economic growth.   The challenge to world religions is to embody their ancient claims of a global vision of human unity, of care of the earth, of generosity toward all creatures, of compassion, and of seeing all things as one and holy before or in the divine.   The European-American cultural challenge is to admit that there limits to natural resources and human ingenuity.

311   Riemer, Neal.   *The Future of the Democratic Revolution: Toward a More Prophetic Politics.*   New York: Praeger Publishers, 1984.

Riemer offers a promising proposal for a biblically-informed public politics for eco-justice.   He argues for a "prophetic politics" of "civilized survival, healthy growth, and creative fulfillment" as an alternative to the existing Machiavellian, utopian, and liberal democratic politics which he feels are incapable of dealing with urgent problems.   Prophetic politics draws on biblical prophetic tradition and constitutional and democratic principles (themselves partially rooted in biblical tradition), as well as on science and Greek and Enlightenment philosophy.   It measures the existing order against the values of life, peace, human rights, social justice, economic well-being, ecological health, and human excellence.   Prophetic criticism employs social science to show the gap between what is and what ought to be and to point to "constitutional breakthroughs" that will narrow that gap. Preston sees the need for continuous prophetic scrutiny of present achievements and possible future scenarios and of the weaknesses of prophetic politics itself, and he concludes that while prophetic politics is ethically necessary and theoretically possible, its practical realization is not assured.

312   Ruether, Rosemary Radford.   "Rich Nations/Poor Nations and the Exploitation of the Earth." *Dialog* (St. Paul, MN) 13 (Summer 1974): 201-7.

Characterizing the United States as a neo-colonialist empire, the author describes how it uses the raw materials and cheap labor of poor countries without contributing to their standard of living, and how it provides repressive juntas with so-called development aid to assure their longevity. She describes the rejection of this capitalist model by liberation thinkers in Latin America, yet faults the liberation movement for still embracing the nineteenth century myth of progress and thus clashing with the reality of dwindling resources. Admitting that drawing up an alternative plan for an ecologically viable society is far easier than finding an alternative power to counteract and reshape the military-industrial complex, she makes no attempt to tackle the latter but describes instead the desired scaling-down of development in advanced industrial nations and the necessity of rectifying the imbalance in the use of world resources between rich and poor countries. Ruether concludes on a theological note: what is needed "to make real a redeeming conversion to the Earth" is, she says, "a converted person" who accepts limits and relates to others in mutuality.

313 Rush, Susan M. "Hazardous Waste and Other Toxic Threats." *Church and Society* 80 (March/April, 1990): 41-52.

Declaring that "our ethical tradition calls us to examine our lifestyles as contributing factors in hazardous-waste problems," the author shows how consumer demand for products which produce hazardous wastes as by-products has generated a great deal of hazardous waste, the effects of which are little understood. Yet we have been slow to clean up hazardous waste sites, turning in recent years from land disposal to incineration, a shift that ignores the need to curb production. Hazardous waste becomes a social-justice issue when considered in terms of workplace contamination, eco-racism, industrial accidents, and export of hazardous substances to developing countries. She suggests that less hazardous waste would be produced if industrial economic externalities were internalized and hazardous waste export were taxed.

314 Schwartz, Joel. "The Rights of Nature and the Death of God." *The Public Interest* 97 (Fall 1989): 3-14.

This loosely argued rebuttal to legal theorists Christopher Stone and Lawrence Tribe expresses common conservative criticisms of nonanthropocentric environmental ethics, with some connections to theological ideas. Schwartz charges that claims that natural objects should have their legal rights represented by the judiciary or environmentalists is an attack upon representative government that is not unlike earlier attacks by priests who claimed special knowledge of God's purposes apart from the peoples' express desires. He finds Tribe's concern to limit human freedom with respect to nature (in the absence of checks once supplied by belief in God) inconsistent with his libertarian stance on constitutional issues such as abortion.

315 Schwartz, John C. "Population, the Church, and the Pope." *America* 168 (6 March 1993): 6-10.

Schwartz criticizes papal statements on population for rejecting scientific data and interpretations that conflict with church teaching—as the church did in the case of Galileo. He finds it wrong that, while the prohibition of artificial contraception is disputed by many Catholic theologians, the pope seeks to impose it on secular governments and agencies. He points out that the pope correctly condemns coercive population policies, overconsumption, and poverty, but says that those points do not discredit concerns about population growth or the need for artificial birth control as part of the solution.

316 Schwarz, Hans. "Towards a Christian Stewardship of the Earth: Promise and Utopia." In *The Environmental Crisis: The Ethical Dilemma*, edited by Edwin R. Squiers, 21-38. Mancelona, MI: AuSable Trails Institute of Environmental Studies, 1982.

Schwarz argues that conventional approaches to environmental problems (conservationist, aesthetic, individualist, collectivist) and current policies (resources as weapons or as natural heritage, triage) are inadequate. New policies are needed which balance production, distribution, and conservation and which distinguish between necessary and excessive consumption. But purely secular appeals for individual sacrifice for the common good (like Mao's) will fail. Only a metaphysical basis such as Christianity, with its teaching of ultimate salvation and a new creation, can provide a sufficient spiritual impulse.

317 Skillen, James W. "Ethics and Justice: What Should Governments Do for the Environment?" In *The Environmental Crisis: The Ethical Dilemma*, edited by Edwin R. Squiers, 227-34. Mancelona, MI: AuSable Trails Institute of Environmental Studies, 1982.

Skillen argues against applying a single universal ethical ideal to every situation and for using a variety of ethical and other "oughts" to interpret the different concrete roles and relationships in which we are involved, including the ecological web in which God has placed us as stewards. Based on theological arguments he has developed elsewhere, he proposes understanding the responsibility of government regarding the environment as a seeking of public justice for all interrelated creatures in their ecological context. Justice understood as securing personal freedom and property cannot take priority over this larger notion of justice because nonhuman beings and structures of creation are essential preconditions.

318 Soelle, Dorothee, with Shirley A. Cloyes. *To Work and to Love: A Theology of Creation*. Philadelphia: Fortress Press, 1984.

A thorough analysis of social justice as "community," with a suggestive but undeveloped treatment of ecology. Soelle argues that human beings affirm and participate in creation through work and love. "Good work" (as discussed by E. F. Schumacher) has three dimensions: self-expression; relatedness to society, and reconciliation with nature. Love has four dimensions: ecstasy, trust, solidarity, and wholeness. The dominance of monetary value in Western capitalist society produces distortion, frustration, and alienation in both love and work. Capitalism also promotes "exterminism"—the rape of the earth, the war against the poor, and the arms race. Soelle insists that creation can only be understood from the standpoint of liberation, and that the fate of the earth is equally in God's hands and ours. The liberating strands of the Christian tradition must be retrieved and developed to enable Christians to become co-creators with God and affirm creation over against exterminism. Baptism into Christ's death and resurrection empowers the Christian to participate in three biblically-based forms of creation: the renewal of the earth; liberation from bondage, and resistance against the death of our old egocentric, powerless being.

319 Squiers, Edwin R., ed. *The Environmental Crisis: The Ethical Dilemma*. Mancelona, MI: AuSable Trails Institute of Environmental Studies, 1982.

This uneven collection of papers is taken from the proceedings of the 1980 AuSable Forum. Although the book fails to take up the theological and ethical relationships between ecology and social justice in any systematic way, Squiers' introduction indirectly alludes to the mixture of justice and ecological dimensions in some of the major environmental issues with which the book is concerned, and several of the papers devoted to resource and policy problems grapple with eco-justice issues and principles, although not always with an explicit theological component. See Loy (295), Schwarz (316), and Skillen (317).

320 Summerton, Neil W. "Principles for Environmental Policy." *Evangelical Review of Theology* 17 (April 1993): 225-40.

Summerton, of the Department of Environment in the United Kingdom, carefully examines "sustainable development" as used in intergovernmental documents and the sub-principles associated with it: the "precautionary principle," the "preventionary principle," and "polluter pays." While raising but not pursuing questions of distributive justice, he notes their ambiguities and complexities, and argues that "sustainable development" presupposes absolute principles such as equity which lie outside the framework of utilitarian economics. Christians and non-Christians differ, not so much over policy goals, as over whether they can be achieved by autonomous human effort.

321 Todrank, Gustave H. *The Eden Connection: A Study in Cultural Euthenics.* Washington, DC: University Press of America, 1981.

In an idiosyncratic work, which argues that the world ecological crisis is directly related to and dependent upon widely shared world views including assumptions about the nature of God, human beings, nature, history, the good life, and future hope, Todrank highlights the myth of Eden as a concretization of the alienation of humans, God, and nature. He sees concerns for such issues as right-to-life and "special assistance to the weakling" as showing that humanity is not ready to deal with long-term ecologically-responsible solutions to its problems. He argues the overwhelming seriousness of population increase and the inadequacy of voluntarism to deal with it, so that some form of dictatorial population control will be an unfortunate necessity. The opposite approach, increasing the growth of population while decreasing its quality, is violence against the environment. Thus, "what man once deemed to be 'violence' may not really be violence at all; and what he once deemed to be equality, justice, or mercy, may be violence against the 'natural' environment in actual long-term consequences." Having stated that even if humans could solve their planet's ecological problems in theory, they may not be able to do so in practice, Todrank offers a bland and peculiar solution with no accompanying suggestions for its implementation. He stresses the importance of "awareness" and calls for a new Adam with a new body—suggesting that smaller, hairier persons would be ecologically desirable, "and the genetic engineers should work in that direction." Surprisingly, having found the biblical emphasis on stewardship a failure, Todrank calls for a New Eden with the Garden of Eden as a model and the ideal citizen a gardener.

322 Walther, Eric G. "Stewardship and the Food, Energy, Environment Triangle." In *The Earth is the Lord's: Essays on Stewardship,* edited by Mary Evelyn Jegen and Bruno V. Manno, 139-47. New York: Paulist Press, 1978.

Walther defines stewardship as living in dynamic equilibrium so that the world is handed to the next generation in as good or better condition than when received. He spells out a number of requirements for stewardship: limiting our individual good for the sake of the common good, changing the distribution of wealth and power, balancing competition with cooperation, and controlling population. Better stewardship of food requires better stewardship of land, water, seed, energy, and environmental quality. Stewardship can be fulfilled or violated with either private or public ownership.

323 Ward, Barbara. "Justice in a Human Environment." *IDOC International/North American Edition* 53 (May 1973): 25-36.

In this early, cogent analysis of the relationship of environmental and justice issues, Ward points out that for four centuries the rationale of the economic system has neglected the ethical, social, and moral context as well as the physical and natural context in which humanity lives, and has gotten away with it only because of a population growth held in check by death, the cushioning effects of colonialism, and stopgap social welfare. As social unrest and environmental risk again face the entire world, the two aspects of the problem have come together. Negative approaches suggest themselves: affluent nations may attempt to hold down the development of the rest of the world while maintaining an unjust standard of living; developing nations may pursue wealth without social controls in imitation of the nineteenth-century model of development. These approaches will not work for either rich or poor since both have to share the cumulative effect of what they do to the planet's life-support systems. Ward suggest a positive way forward in a moral approach that combines participation and justice. She includes a list of specific measures that address both ethical and environmental contexts. Ward further suggests that a positive way forward should be the temporal responsibility of the Christian community, since the dual responsibility of stewardship to the planet and to humanity is the essence of Christianity.

324 Ward, Barbara. *A New Creation: Reflections on the Environmental Issue.* Vatican City: Pontifical Commission on Justice and Peace, 1973.

Ward, an economist, argues that economics, nationalism, and science have engendered the environmental crisis and social injustice because they lack moral context. Christianity holds that injustice leads to death, that economics should be based on generosity, that nationalism should be based on peace, and that science should be based not only on dominion, but also on stewardship. All the perceptions which are disturbing to the status quo in the environmental revolution have a Christian basis.

325 Ward, Barbara. "Only One Earth." *Anticipation* 11 (July 1972), 27-32.

In this article, delivered at the Stockholm Conference on the Human Environment in 1972, Ward expresses a "modest hope" for planetary eco-justice, while maintaining that damage to the entire biosphere is possible, that resources are limited, that states must act in concert to avoid planetary disaster, and that these ideas require a "Copernican leap of the imagination" to truly comprehend. It is not possible, she maintains, to evade the issues of choice and justice, for given finite resources, the upward aspirations of some will be checked, and cuts will be made in either the luxuries of the rich or the necessities of the poor. Similarly, the need to check pollution can be satisfied by an unjust strain on the costs of development and modernization of poorer nations or it can be worked out in some fair way by nations acting in concert. Ward's hope for a just and timely solution to the environmental crisis is based on the meeting of the world's nations that she is attending, on the biologically based fact of planetary interdependence, and on the historical fact that perpetual striving toward moderation, compassion, and justice have always been a feature of human nature.

326   Wilkinson, Loren.   "How Christian Is the Green Agenda?"   *Christianity Today* 37 (11 January 1993): 16-21.

Wilkinson begins by discussing why the environmental movement is seen as anathema by so many evangelicals, most notably because it is often associated with syncretistic, earth-based religious ideas such as those espoused by Matthew Fox.   Briefly tracing the history of the ecological movement with regard to religion, Wilkinson notes that more and more Christians are articulating a biblical and theological environmental ethic.   He cites both individuals and organizations, such as the AuSable Institute for Environmental Studies, that are leading the Christian community in this field.   Wilkinson closes the article by discussing theological issues such as the Triune God, the Fall, eschatology, humanity's place in creation, and a biblical cosmic Christology.   In a subsection, he succinctly addresses the problem of over-population, including the extra burden that children in developed countries exert on the earth's resources, and New Testament views that support smaller families.

327   Young, R. V., Jr.   "A Conservative View of Environmental Affairs."   *Environmental Ethics* 1 (1979): 241-54.

In this perceptive critique, Young notes how "conservatives" now attack environmentalists by appealing to what was once a "liberal" concern: improving the lot of the poor through technological progress.   A genuinely conservative approach is lacking: both liberals and "conservatives" argue from consequences, rather than—in truly conservative fashion—from "the nature of things," while radicals oppose the traditional belief in the distinctive dignity of humans.   A genuinely conservative environmental ethic would return to values of humility, restraint, justice, order, and respect for creation out of reverence to the Creator.

In addition to the works annotated in this chapter, readers interested in social and political issues may wish to consult the following entries located elsewhere in the bibliography: 002, 034, 039, 041, 068, 110, 140, 178, 180, 246, 250, 252, 264, 330, 377, 401, 406, 416, 429, 439, 441, 471, 477, 479.

8

Economics and Sustainability

A major stimulus to eco-justice reflection has been the Club of Rome's thesis that unlimited economic growth threatens the resources and environment on which civilization depends. Since growth is widely believed essential for improving the lot of the poor, the thesis raises the question whether there can be an economic system that is both socially just and environmentally sustainable. This section includes both those who endorse limits to growth and those who doubt the limits thesis and see its adherents as undermining economic freedom or blocking the path to a just international economic order. Other issues include the redistribution of wealth and whether current economic theory and practice support such values as community and the well-being of nonhuman nature.

328 [Abrecht, Paul]. "Economics of a Just, Participatory, and Sustainable Society." In *Faith and Science in an Unjust World: Report of the World Council of Churches' Conference on Faith, Science and the Future*, vol. 2, *Reports of Sections*, 125-34. Geneva: World Council of Churches, 1980.

This section 8 report from the 1979 conference held at the Massachusetts Institute of Technology argues for linking economic analysis to the wider social goals of justice, participation, and sustainability. While the indivisibility of these goals is affirmed, justice is central, and participation and sustainability are its necessary, but not sufficient, conditions. Sustainability is treated briefly and primarily as a Western concern. Key issues are discussed and recommendations made.

329 Barney, Gerald O. "The Future of Creation: The Central Challenge for Theologians." *Word and World* 4 (Fall 1984): 422-29.

The vision which has guided human affairs—prosperity through development, and security through violence—has failed, Barney, coordinator of the Carter administration's *Global 2000 Report*, argues. Development is not sustainable and violence threatens to destroy the creation. Barney challenges theologians to formulate a viable alternative vision of the future of the creation by examining the prospects for a profound, creation-wide change in human behavior, sustainability, and violence and conflict resolution (including the role of Christianity and theology in causing conflict). He includes useful citations on global futures modeling and alternative visions.

330 Beisner, E. Calvin. *Prospects for Growth: A Biblical View of Population, Resources, and the Future*. Westchester, IL: Crossway Books, 1990.

The author believes that the "biblical view" supports a free-market economy, population growth, resource development, monetary reward for development, and the unrestricted use of private property; it does not support resource management, the concept of scarcity as a result of growth, or the concept of a fragile environment. Foundations for the biblical view include the "dominion mandate" and the biblical meaning of justice which is "rendering to everyone his due" according to the standard of the Ten Commandments.

331 Berry, Thomas F. "Economics as a Religious Issue." In his *The Dream of the Earth*, 70-88. San Francisco: Sierra Club Books, 1988.

Rather than examine the economy from the perspective of the religious quest for justice, Berry asks "the more basic question" of the sustainability of the industrial economy which is driving the whole earth system, and humanity with it, into deficit—a situation not fully appreciated by economics, business, politics, theology, or social reform movements. He argues that a "planetary socialism" that integrates the human economy with the earth requires a new religious orientation, based on a new cosmology, which regards the earth as the primary revelation of the divine and our primary object of loyalty. This chapter appears in slightly different form in (119).

332 Berry, Wendell. "Christianity and the Survival of Creation." In his *Sex, Economy, Freedom, and Community*, 93-116. New York: Pantheon Books, 1993.

This well-crafted essay is based on the premise that, while the indictment of Christianity by conservationists is deserved in the sense that Christian clergy and laity have been and continue to be indifferent to the destruction of creation, it is false to the Bible. Quoting biblical passages in support of the notion that creation is "the continuous, constant participation of all creatures in the being of God," Berry sees the destruction of nature as "not just bad stewardship, or stupid economics, or a betrayal of family responsibility," but as "the most horrid blasphemy." He finds life's holiness to be obscured by ideas of the church's exclusive sanctity and revelation's exclusive assignation to the Bible and by the dualism of body and soul. He labels both interest in the economy and daily work "religious practices" and decries the present situation in which Christians have no notion of an economy that is responsible to the holiness of life but have instead embraced the industrial economy, and wherein workers do not see their work as being connected to neighbor, God, and nature.

333 Birch, Charles. "Creation, Technology, and Human Survival: Called to Replenish the Earth." *Ecumenical Review* 28 (January 1976): 66-79.

In this paper presented at a plenary session of the World Council of Churches' Fifth Assembly in Nairobi in 1975, Birch argues that nations with a standard of living that the world cannot provide to all are, according to the criterion of justice, "overdeveloped." Development of poor nations requires "de-development" of rich ones. Steps in the right direction include promoting appropriate technology, self-reliance, and interdependence. Two connections need to be seen more clearly: that between human justice/injustice and environmental renewal/deterioration; and that between our image of nature and our manipulation of it.

334 Byers, David M., ed. *Justice in the Marketplace: Collected Statements of the Vatican and the United States Catholic Bishops on Economic Policy, 1891-1984.* Washington, DC: United States Catholic Conference, 1985.

Many of these statements—primarily by popes and United States Catholic bishops—touch on environmental issues in the context of Roman Catholic teachings on economic justice. Recurring themes include: God's purpose for creation as demanding the equitable sharing of earth's resources; human economic activity as the exercise of human dominion over the earth and as sharing in God's creative activity; local and national imbalances between population and productive land; the need to protect human dignity, especially the right to marry and procreate, from state efforts to restrict population growth; and the threat to human survival posed by environmental degradation. Included is the full text of John Paul II's encyclical on human work, *Laborem exercens* (291).

335 Chewning, Richard C., ed. *Biblical Principles and Economics: The Foundations.* Colorado Springs, CO: NavPress, 1989.

A work addressing the question: Are there biblical directives for the distribution of wealth? Chewning, series editor of *Christians in the Marketplace* of which this is volume 2, contributes preface, review, and comments after each of the six sections. His twelve "foundation principles" include human domination over the created order, the benefits of material wealth, and private property as an aspect of God's will. Except for Wayne A. Grudem and Richard V. Pierard, the contributors do not discuss environmental issues as part of economic justice, but Chewning's statements that "there is no fixed economic pie to be distributed but a flexible reservoir of economic resources and opportunities" and "the greatest economic problems we face are directly related to our human character and conduct and are not related to inanimate resources and conditions" reflect the volume's guiding principles. See Grudem (352) and Pierard (362).

336 Cobb, John B., Jr. "Can a Livable Society Be Sustainable?" In his *Sustainability: Economics, Ecology, and Justice*, 34-53. Maryknoll, NY: Orbis Books, 1992.

This essay attempts to deal candidly with the question of public willingness for needed change and suggests a reasonable course of action leading to economic sustainability along with the objections that will be made to it. As a very readable summary of much of *For the Common Good* (343) as well as a more up-to-date analysis of the directions in which the nations of the world are headed, it makes an excellent introduction to the economics of eco-justice.

337 Cobb, John B., Jr. "Economics and Ecology in the United States." In his *Sustainability: Economics, Ecology, and Justice*, 54-81. Maryknoll, NY: Orbis Books, 1992.

This essay exposes the fallacies of continuing on the path of growth, questions the freedom of free trade, and develops the economic goal of self-sufficiency. It constitutes a short course in economics to be placed beside currently prevailing models as a serious alternative.

338   Cobb, John B., Jr.   "Economics for Animals as Well as People." In *Good News for Animals? Christian Approaches to Animal Well-Being*, edited by Charles Pinches and Jay B. McDaniel, 172-86. Maryknoll, NY: Orbis Books, 1993.

Calling the goal of growth "a new ordering principle of society supplanting both nationalism and religion," Cobb contrasts growth-oriented contemporary economics, or "economism," to "planetism," or an economics based on reverence for the earth.   He says that Christians, who as a rule criticize materialism but not economism, must understand that growth bypasses animal welfare concerns and is at the expense of the environment and of future human beings.   Planetism is the only ideology with the potential to replace economism.   Planetism assumes persons are communal; economism that their lot increases along with their consumption "even if their communities are destroyed in the process."   Economism ignores justice to creation and to all future generations; planetism seeks to establish labor and environmental-impact rules to foster justice for all.

339   Cobb, John B., Jr.   *Sustainability: Economics, Ecology, and Justice*. Maryknoll, NY: Orbis Books, 1992.

This selection of Cobb's writings shows his longtime concern to integrate economics, ecology, justice, and Christian faith and demonstrates his readiness to consider the practical difficulties of attaining a sustainable worldview.   Cobb's introduction briefly summarizes the impact on his thinking of the writings and outlook of Paul Ehrlich, Lynn White Jr., Alfred North Whitehead, Bernard Meland, Charles Hartshorne, Paolo Soleri, and Herman Daly.   Each of the essays, which together span several decades, is relevant for eco-justice concerns; see (169), (170), (336), and (337).

340   Daly, Herman E.   "A Biblical Economic Principle and the Steady-State Economy." In *Covenant for a New Creation: Ethics, Religion and Public Policy*, edited by Carol S. Robb and Carl J. Casebolt, 47-60. Maryknoll, NY: Orbis Books, 1991.

With a concreteness that is characteristic of his thought, Daly not only argues that biblical authority prohibits unlimited inequality in the ownership of private property, but suggests a factor of ten as a reasonable maximum difference between the richest and poorest individuals.   He sees limits to inequality as a necessary correlate to limits to growth if poverty is to be reduced, future generations are to be provided for, and Earth and its creatures are to be sustained.

341   Daly, Herman E.   "The Ecological and Moral Necessity for Limiting Growth." In *Faith and Science in an Unjust World: Report of the World Council of Churches' Conference on Faith, Science and the Future*, vol. 1, *Plenary Presentations,* edited by Roger L. Shinn, 212-20. Geneva: World Council of Churches, 1980.

Daly maintains that ecological limits and the stewardship of creation require us to define our aggregate biophysical budget, live within it, and try to improve the efficiency with which we use resources.   Rather than "the greatest production of goods for the greatest number" our ethical dictum should be "sufficient per capita product for greatest number over time"—including some appropriate consideration for non-human life.   "Sufficiency" requires that economics deal with the question of "what is a good life?"   Three kinds of interdependent limits must be institutionalized: a financial counterpart to the real biophysical budget, a population limit, and a limit on the range of inequality in per capita resource consumption.   Mentioned is G. K. Chesterton's "distributism" as an alternative to growth-oriented capitalism and communism.

342 Daly, Herman E. "The Steady-State Economy: Toward a Political Economy of Biophysical Equilibrium and Moral Growth." In *Valuing the Earth: Economics, Ecology, Ethics*, edited by Herman E. Daly and Kenneth N. Townsend, 325-64, Cambridge, MA and London: MIT Press, 1993.

In this chapter Daly defines the concept of a steady-state economy and discusses the social controls needed to maintain it and the moral growth necessary for its adoption. Among the social controls considered are limits to wealth and income and Kenneth Bounding's transferable birth licenses. Daly suggests that standard economic theory makes human love less necessary by eliminating the need to face up to sharing a fixed total, and he likens the steady-state to the Sermon on the Mount, requiring attention to the evils of the day rather than looking to a larger total income tomorrow.

343 Daly, Herman E., and John B. Cobb, Jr. *For the Common Good: Redirecting the Economy toward Community, the Environment, and a Sustainable Future*. Boston: Beacon Press, 1989.

Daly, an economist, and Cobb, a process theologian, suggest a move from an economics which is an academic discipline to one in service of community; from chremanistics (short term gains of wealth by owners) to oikonomia (management of a household to benefit all of its members); from individualism to person-in-community; from cosmopolitanism to a community of communities; and from thinking of land in terms of matter and rent to thinking of it in terms of energy and biosphere. They advocate major policy steps regarding trade, population, land use, agricultural and industrial practices, governmental policies, and tax reform. They propose an alternative index of economic welfare based on measurements of education, health, and environmental quality. The attitude required to make such revolutionary changes lies, they suggest, in religion, for apart from God, there is no meaning, life, righteousness, truth, or value.

344 Daly, Herman E., and Kenneth N. Townsend, eds. *Valuing the Earth: Economics, Ecology, Ethics*. Cambridge, MA and London: MIT Press, 1993.

This latest version of the 1973 classic *Toward a Steady-State Economy* (edited by Herman E. Daly, San Francisco: W. H. Freeman and Co.) adds several papers and an index while retaining the format and most of the contents of the 1980 version, *Economics, Ecology, Ethics: Essays toward a Steady-State Economy* also edited by Daly, (San Francisco: W. H. Freeman and Co.). Influential in promoting the desirability of limits to growth and population, these collections constitute a departure from standard economics in both their ecological orientation and their concern with questions of ultimate value, and as a whole they contribute to a vision of a just and sustainable economics. In a new introduction the editors discuss economic goals in terms of optimal allocation, distribution, and scale, arguing that scale, or how big the economy should be, is a neglected and critical area of economics. They wish to demonstrate the impossibility of sustainable growth, the moral necessity of a non-growth outlook, and the practicality of policies consistent with steady-state economics. A tripartite arrangement organizes the twenty essays around ecology, ethics, and economics. In an introduction to the steady-state economy Daly clarifies the relationship of ends-based and means-based arguments about growth, explaining that it is only if continual economic growth is biophysically possible that distributive justice and intergenerational equity diminish as problems; also it is only with the moral exclusion of the poor, future generations, and non-human life, that biophysical constraints are said to be of little matter. See Daly (342) and Schumacher (270).

345 de Lange, Harry M. "The Jubilee Principle: Is It Relevant for Today?" *Ecumenical Review* 38 (October 1986): 437-43.

The author identifies the thrust of the jubilee principle (Lev. 25:10) as God's opposition to great divergences of wealth and poverty. Inequalities—persistent poverty, the ecological problem of inequality between present and future generations—call into question economists' claims to value-neutrality and their anthropology of acquisitiveness. Growth in production must be made to serve basic needs through the idea of "sufficiency" and its corollary, an upper limit to wealth.

346 DeWitt, Calvin B. "Ethics, Ecosystems, and Enterprise: Discovering the Meaning of Food Security and Development." In *Growing Our Future: Food Security and the Environment*, edited by Katie Smith and Tetsunao Yamamori, 6-26. West Hartford, CT: Kumarian Press, 1992.

DeWitt argues that halting the degradation of creation—the impoverishment of land, nature, and people—requires that ethics be consistent with ecosystem principles. He recommends that ethics include the principles of reflection (nurturing the earth as we are nurtured), leadership, fruitfulness, restoration, precedence (the priority of creation's wholeness and integrity), contentment, and action. In endnotes, he relates these principles to ancient Hebrew and Christian ethical teachings as recorded in the Bible. These principles also define the goal of development as the integrity of creation, which is the necessary prerequisite for food security.

347 Duchrow, Ulrich. *Global Economy: A Confessional Issue for the Church?* Translated by David Lewis. Geneva: WCC Publications, 1987.

Duchrow finds the global economy at fault in each of the problems facing humanity today, including the destruction of the environment, racism, neo-colonialism, the exploitation of women and of indigenous peoples, and militarism. Many agents are implicated, of which the churches of the affluent West are only one. But churches have been co-opted by economic interests such that pseudo-Christian arguments are used to buttress the present economic system. In the Lutheran tradition, the theological concept of "two kingdoms" is used to evade conflict with economic and political power. The church's institutional form has become assimilated to social, economic, and political forms of power. Economic theory and practice are also implicated. Alternatives exist which start with the idea of the human as inseparable from cultural and natural environments and which value the criteria of justice, participation, and sustainability. A final chapter deals with steps the churches can take to advance justice, peace, and the integrity of creation.

348 Faramelli, Norman J. "Ecological Responsibility and Economic Justice." *Andover Newton Quarterly* 11 (November 1970): 81-93.

Faramelli argues that concerns for justice and ecology must be combined by recognizing a common enemy in the military-industrial complex, introducing issues of distributive justice into ecology debates, and challenging the identification of material prosperity with the "good life." Ecological ethics cannot ignore the important role of human beings, especially the poor, in the Judeo-Christian tradition, nor human responsibility to transform as well as protect the earth. Reprinted in *Ecology: Crisis and New Vision*, edited by Richard E. Sherrell, 31-44 (Richmond, VA: John Knox Press, 1971); and Barbour, ed. (259), pp. 188-203.

349 Gibson, William E. "The Lifestyle of Christian Faithfulness." In *Beyond Survival: Bread and Justice in Christian Perspective*, edited by Dieter T. Hessel, 111-40. New York: Friendship Press, 1977.

Gibson defines the lifestyle of Christian faithfulness as the way in which individuals and societies reproduce in their actions toward others the quality and aim of the saving acts of God toward them. His claim is that contemporary economic systems, which produce poverty alongside excessive wealth and depend upon unsustainable exploitation of the earth, can be transformed by new lifestyles faithful to the biblical mandates of justice and stewardship. This requires a retrieval of Christian teachings on the danger of wealth and the Christian tradition of voluntary poverty or simple living, guided by the norm of sufficiency.

350 Goudzwaard, Bob. "Creation Management: The Economics of Earth Stewardship." Parts 1, 2. *Epiphany* 8 (Fall 1987, Winter 1988): 37-45, 67-72.

"Priced scarcity" is the basis for current market-oriented economic science, which studies the mechanical interaction of variables in the context of given, infinite ends and scarce means. The biblical and Aristotelian alternative, "careful administration" or stewardship, leads to studying the social interaction of responsible subjects in the context of chosen ends, means, and economic restraints. An economic system based on stewardship would reverse existing means-end relations: growth in income and consumption, rather than an end in itself, would be the means to achieving quantity and quality of labor, environmental quality, and the welfare of poorer nations. Goudzwaard is an economist and a former member of the Dutch Parliament.

351 Goulet, Denis. "On Authentic Social Development: Concepts, Content, and Criteria." In *The Making of an Economic Vision: John Paul II's "On Social Concern,"* edited by Oliver F. Williams and John W. Houck, 3-23. Lanham, MD: University Press of America, 1991.

Goulet situates the pope's encyclical *On Social Concern (Solicitudo rei socialis)* among critiques of development which go beyond technical analysis to relate economic development to larger human needs and ecological wisdom. He reviews French theorist L. J. Lebret's normative concept of development in which solidarity between rich and poor and the distinction between "having more" and "being more" are crucial. According to Goulet, environmental problems require extending solidarity to include the biosphere. He argues that seeing "the whole picture" overcomes the seeming oppositions between human freedom and natural necessity and between anthropocentrism and cosmocentrism. Neither nature nor human freedom are absolute values; thus, the values of resource conservation, species preservation, and protection of nature are on the same footing as the combating of poverty and injustice, and the developing of resources.

352 Grudem, Wayne A. "How an Economic System Can Be Compatible with Scripture." In *Biblical Principles and Economics: The Foundations*, edited by Richard C. Chewning, 27-52. Colorado Springs, CO: NavPress, 1989.

Grudem maintains that the Scriptures alone can define economic justice, although non-Christians can come to a right notion of God's will though natural law. He finds the Bible in support of stewardship of resources, but he also concludes that the Bible indicates that the earth has abundant resources without any limits. Because of earth's abundance, the large use of resources by a single individual or country is not unjust, and an economic system that rewards development and shuns resource rationing is superior to its opposite. The desire for property

should not be perceived as wrong, since God endorses the idea of private property in the commandments not to steal or covet, and since God owns and controls
all property. In an unequivocal statement of a perspective opposite to that which
has guided the faith/justice/ecology movement, Grudem states that humans should
not strive for equality of possessions either within the church or in society
generally, both because equality of possessions is not a biblical concept and
because material inequality is necessary for a well-functioning economy.

353   Hallman, David G.   *Caring for Creation: The Environmental Crisis, a Canadian
Christian Call to Action.*   Winfield, British Columbia: Wood Lake Books, 1989.

This work is provocative for its presentation of environmental problems from a
Canadian perspective.   In his discussion of the damage to Canadian soil, water,
and wildlife from acid rain, Hallman concentrates on Canadian sources of pollution while also revealing that eighty-five to ninety percent of acid rain originates
in the United States.   Other problems dealt with include garbage, nuclear power,
the ozone layer, the greenhouse effect, and the global environmental consequences of development projects in non-industrialized nations.   Although docu-
mentation of environmental problems takes up the greatest part of the book,
Hallman introduces his subject with a look at Christian theology's negative and
positive contributions to the environmental crisis, and he includes a section on
working together for eco-justice that calls "jobs versus the environment" a false
dichotomy.

354   Hallman, David G.   "Ethics and Sustainable Development."   In *Ecotheology:
Voices from South and North*, edited by David G. Hallman, 264-83.   Geneva: WCC
Publications; Maryknoll, NY: Orbis Books, 1994.

Hallman compares two statements of guiding principles regarding environment
and development—"The Rio Declaration" from the United Nations Conference
on Environment and Development and "One Earth Community" drawn up by the
World Council of Churches and the United Church of Canada—and judges that
the latter is the more ethically advanced.   He also looks at two issues in which the
churches have tried to move from guiding principles to practical norms and decisions about action: global climate change and the role of transnational corporations in environment and development.   Issues of justice, especially between
South and North, are central throughout.

355   John Paul II.   *Sollicitudo rei socialis.*   Encyclical letter "On Social Concern," 30
December 1987.   *Origins, NC Documentary Service* 17 (3 March 1988): 641, 643-60.

This key papal pronouncement embraces both justice and environmental concerns, although the latter remain somewhat peripheral.   Building on Paul VI's
encyclical *Populorum Progressio* (1968), John Paul II surveys the current situation, noting negative features, including the widening gap between rich and poor
and campaigns for birth control, and positive signs such as rising environmental
concern.   He argues that development is a moral and religious issue as well as an
economic one; it is an expression of human dominion, but must be limited by
respect for persons—as *imago Dei* and as destined for immortality—and for nonhuman nature.   Thus, development must take into consideration spiritual, social,
cultural, and ethical, as well as economic values.   He interprets the obstacles to
development as "structures of sin," rooted in idolatrous desires, which must be
overcome by solidarity and concern for the common good.   He presents
guidelines based on the church's social teachings and concludes by relating historical hope and achievement to the Kingdom of God and the Eucharist.

356 Johnston, Carol. "Economics, Eco-Justice, and the Doctrine of God." In *After Nature's Revolt: Eco-Justice and Theology*, edited by Dieter T. Hessel, 154-70. Minneapolis: Augsburg Fortress Publishers, 1992.

Johnston applies concepts of inherent relations and intrinsic value to God, human individuals, communities, economies, nature, and the relationships between them as she critiques modern thought, including economics, as being individualistic, reducing value to preferences, and promoting unsustainable growth. She offers an eco-justice perspective that values individual integrity in communal context; affirms power-sharing and the rights of nature; calls for development that respects the integrity of communities and the need to share the earth with other creatures; and recovers a relational, trinitarian understanding of God as preserving, liberating, and empowering all creatures.

357 Kim, Yong-Bock. "The Sustainable Society: An Asian Perspective." *Ecumenical Review* 31 (April 1979): 169-78.

Kim enters the debate about the relationship of ecological and social concerns with the viewpoint that sustainability must be subsumed under justice and participation, not the other way around. Discussions of the sustainable society have not sufficiently taken into account the Third World's experience of technocracy, science, and technology; criticisms of technocracy from within Western science and technology must be joined to an historical understanding of, and concern for, the experience of the victims of technocracy. The sustainable society must be understood in terms of the people's march into the Messianic kingdom of justice, *koinonia*, and *shalom*. Christians must open themselves to the wisdom and resources of non-Christians as all seek a concrete historical form of *shalom* between humanity and the cosmos.

358 Kurien, C. T. "A Third World Perspective." In *Faith and Science in an Unjust World: Report of the World Council of Churches' Conference on Faith, Science, and the Future*, vol. 1, *Plenary Presentations,* edited by Roger L. Shinn, 220-25. Geneva: World Council of Churches, 1980.

Although he claims no competence in Christian ethics, this Indian economist's biting critique is cited in many later discussions of a just, participatory, and sustainable society. He charges that slogans about "limits" and "sustainability" reflect anxieties of a pampered minority which are not shared by the poor majority who will not be affected by resource exhaustion. Nonetheless, he regards unlimited growth as impossible, and argues that just and sustainable societies will emerge only with the effective participation of *all* persons. Shinn's questions which follow the essay (pp. 229-30) are helpful.

359 McDaniel, Jay B. "Christianity and the Pursuit of Wealth." *Anglican Theological Review* 69 (October 1987): 349-61.

Starting with the premise that, given Earth's finite resources, it is impossible for all humans on the planet to live as do most middle-income Americans, McDaniel discusses the shifts in thinking about wealth that will be necessary to move to a just and sustainable future. Process theology suggests that wealth must be understood relationally rather than atomistically. "If wealth yields isolated egotism rather than a sense of connectedness with the world, we-they thinking rather than inclusive care, unnecessary exploitation of nature rather than a reverence for life, or, as all these problems imply, forgetfulness of God rather than faithfulness to God, then it is not 'wealth' in the Christian sense." Wealth is faring well in relation to the world. A person's wealth depends, in part, on an ability to have a democratic voice in community. God's call to justice is a call to be in relation with God, and is a form of wealth. Harmony, and therefore wealth, would exist throughout the world if all persons, present and future, could enjoy the same living standards.

360 Meeks, M. Douglas. "God and Land." *Agriculture and Human Values* 2 (1985): 16-27.

Asserting that Christians must critically retrieve the biblical origins of the understanding of God in order to understand themselves, not as dominators of nature, but as participants in nature, Meeks suggests focusing on the notion of *oikos*, or household—the root of economics, ecology, and ecumenics. Meeks finds that every land question has an ecological dimension of misuse caused by economic captivity to market law brought on by a distorted ecumenics in which some persons shape the world to exclude others. The body of this article is a clear explication of the theological relationships of justice and land in the Old Testament, ending with a "Christian consensus on land" that Meeks says held until the seventeenth century, in which God has absolute claim to the land, which has been created in common for all persons who have the individual right to only so much of it as they need, and which may be used for livelihood but not for domination. "The land and human beings, the land and the city, may dwell together in harmony if justice is done."

361 Meeks, M. Douglas. *God the Economist: The Doctrine of God and Political Economy.* Minneapolis: Augsburg Fortress Publishers, 1989.

Meeks again correlates God, economy, ecology, and justice by the term *oikos*, the Greek word for household management, appropriated in Old Testament traditions, and employed by Paul to describe God's plan for redemption of the world. In biblical traditions, Meeks maintains, God's oikic work not only concerns giving everyone in the household what it takes to live, giving nature its rights, and bringing about a supportive mutually habitable habitat in peace, the fact of God's justice and righteousness integrates these concerns so that economic justice includes justice for the land and justice for the peoples on the land. Modern definitions of *oikos* which assimilate it to the market fuel oppression. "It has to be asked whether racism, sexism, ecological rape, and denigration of democracy can be effectively combated without a simultaneous radical criticism of *oikos* in our society." Meeks is concerned to show that God concepts shape the economy despite the secularization of economics. Notions of a unitary, self-sufficient, self-possessing God have led to individual rights taking precedence over justice and individuals who believe they can ignore the suffering of others. Defining God as the Economist and the Trinity as an interdependent community which models love, faithfulness, and suffering, Meeks offers a trinitarian critique of modern market-society assumptions about property, work, and consumption. The book includes an extensive and rich bibliography.

362 Pierard, Richard C. "No Economic System Flows Directly from Scripture." In *Biblical Principles and Economics: The Foundations*, edited by Richard C. Chewning, 57-73. Colorado Springs, CO: NavPress, 1989.

In a contradictory note within a volume of essays otherwise supportive of free-market capitalism and a limitless resource base, Pierard states flatly that there are not enough resources to go around for everyone. "Christians should have serious reservations about any economic order that does not take seriously the necessity of protecting the physical environment. In this respect, virtually all modern-day systems are deficient." Also, "God's demand for justice lies at the heart of biblical ethics, and all economic systems are particularly vulnerable at this point because few of them even come close to the divine standard of justice."

363 Rasmussen, Larry L. "The Bishops and the Economy: Three Appraisals; III. On Creation, On Growth." *Christianity and Crisis* 45 (25 November 1985): 473-76.

Rasmussen criticizes the second draft of the United States Catholic Bishops' pastoral letter on the economy, maintaining that it wholly neglects the debate about economic growth, and constitutes an unacceptable, anthropocentric rendering of creation. He concludes with recommendations for pursuing justice and sustainability.

364 Rasmussen, Larry L. "The Future Isn't What It Used to Be: 'Limits to Growth' and Christian Ethics." *Lutheran Quarterly* 27 (May 1975): 101-11.

In an example of eco-justice reflection prompted by the limits-of-growth thesis, Rasmussen argues that "spill over" economics is no longer a viable solution to social inequities; rather, social justice must be sought in a setting where both limits and affluence exist. This requires an environmental ethic of responsible restraint along with equal global distribution of goods and services. Rasmussen believes that Christian ethics should promote social experimentation and the equipping of individuals attitudinally and in terms of character formation. Basic moral categories must be reshaped so that neighbor comes to mean future generations and non-human life, and so that the good of individuals and groups can no longer be assumed to equal common global good.

365 Rasolondraibe, Péri. "Environmental Concern and Economic Justice." *Word and World* 11 (Spring 1991): 147-55.

Rasolondraibe criticizes environmentalists for frequently ignoring the systemic causes of the environmental crisis and population problems. Developing countries need rapid economic development that meets the whole population's basic needs without putting more stress on the environment; this in turn requires that the global economy move toward sustainable development and the creation of technologies that produce more with less. Rasolondraibe traces the environmental crisis to Western society's doctrine of unlimited growth and the market mentality's spread to all areas of life. He proposes viewing the economy in terms of *shalom*, "an activity of mutual interdependence which aims at creating a 'just, participatory and sustainable' world community," rooted in the "shared otherness" of the triune God.

366 Rifkin, Jeremy, with Ted Howard. *The Emerging Order: God in an Age of Scarcity*. New York: G. P. Putnam's Sons, 1979.

Rifkin contends that resource limits and the law of entropy show the falseness of liberal faith in human fulfillment through unlimited material progress and require a rapid shift to a steady-state economy. He finds in the growing evangelical-charismatic movement hope for a new covenant vision that will enable the economy to be voluntary and cooperative rather than coercive and competitive. Although much in that movement leans toward the existing order, the role of evangelicalism in America in the eighteenth- and nineteenth-centuries suggests that charismatics could provide the liberating energy and evangelicals the new covenant vision for the "emerging order." In this new vision, based on the doctrine of creation and the law of entropy, human beings are to resist entropy increase by preserving the God-ordained integrity of creation until the coming of the Kingdom. All creatures have equal intrinsic worth, belong by mutual inter-dependence to a holistic natural order, and require a balance between energy release (work) and rest and replenishment for their well-being.

367 Sheldon, Joseph K. "Creation Rediscovered." *World Christian* (April 1990): 11-19.

In an article addressed to a popular audience and illustrated with photos from the Amazon rainforests, Sheldon underscores the health problems, loss of human cul-ture and species, and the disruption of global cycles that environmental stress is causing. He suggests that, in addition to a responsibility to address hunger directly, Christians have a responsibility to heal the damaged creation that is causing human hunger; that they cannot love the Creator without loving his crea-tion; that the redeemed in Christ are being called forth to rebuild planet Earth, today's ark.

368 Shigeko, Yamano. "Restoring Right Relationship Between Nature and People: Biblico-Theological Reflection II." *Tugon* 14 (1992): 379-81.

This paper is a brief critique from a Japanese perspective of the market economy and injustice that are driving environmental and human exploitation. Shigeko declares that "the land itself has become nothing unless it has money value in our part of the world." She deplores such existing practices as exchanging prawns for weapons and speaks of how the market economy is commodifying persons as well. She urges a holistic approach and a consideration of alternative forms of development.

369 Stivers, Robert L. "Justice, Participation, and Sustainable Sufficiency." In *The Public Vocation of Christian Ethics*, edited by Beverly W. Harrison, Robert L. Stivers, and Ronald H. Stone, 179-91. New York: Pilgrim Press, 1986.

Stivers identifies two questions underlying the issue of "limits to growth": the factual question of whether there are limits, and if so, how close they are; and the question of what kind of future humans want. Even if an immediate, wrenching social transformation is not warranted, Stivers argues, movement in the direction of justice, participation, and sustainable sufficiency is in order. These values are biblically-based and have been a focus of discussion within the World Council of Churches. Some modest suggestions for social policy follow.

370 Stivers, Robert L. *The Sustainable Society: Ethics and Economic Growth.* Philadelphia: Westminster Press, 1976.

This discussion of the ethical implications of the growth debate pursues a public ethic but also appeals to Christian resources for hope and norms of justice. According to Stivers, the thrust for growth arises primarily from material (eco-nomic and technical), rather than ideal factors. He identifies three parties to the debate about growth—"advocates," "critics," and "futurists." The advocates' case for continuing present forms of growth is strong but critics question whether the undesirable social costs of growth will exceed the benefits. Central to the debate between critics and advocates is the problem of justly distributing the benefits and costs of either continuing or slowing growth. Stivers recommends "differentiated growth" that respects criteria of environmental soundness and human welfare. While debate between advocates and futurists who question the possibility of continuing undifferentiated growth, is inconclusive, Stivers fears that the possible consequences of continuing growth make following the futurists a prudent course. Furthermore, pursuit of the sustainable society is desirable even if unnecessary because it subordinates the economic process to value considerations, including that of distributive justice.

371 Stivers, Robert L. "The Sustainable Society: Religious and Social Implications." *Review of Religious Research* 21 (Fall 1979): 71-86.

Stivers argues that "the sustainable society" meets Jacques Ellul's and Elise Boulding's criteria for a new vision which can replace the present spiritually empty technological worldview. The basis of this new ethic or worldview is care for persons, nature, and God, and suggests six principles: limits, appropriate size, holism (community), rough distributional equality and political freedom, diversity, and stewardship. Although this vision cannot now provide a blueprint for social change, it has implications for further research and policy-making.

372 Stone, Ronald H. "Ethics and Growth." *South East Asia Journal of Theology* 14 (1972): 40-55.

Addressing implications of the limits to growth from the standpoint of an ethic of the Christian church which takes love as its norm, hopes for the Kingdom of God, and accepts responsibility for action in a situation dominated by the "atheistic" economic systems of capitalism and Marxism, Stone argues that the church's tasks include promoting the raising of living standards in the developing world while reducing growth in the developed world, urging its members to reduce their birthrates, developing a corporate business ethic, and advocating more equal distribution of goods.

373 United Presbyterian Church in the USA. 188th General Assembly. "Economic Justice within Environmental Limits: The Need for a New Economic Ethic." *Church and Society* 67 (September/October 1976): 5-56.

This study and discussion document makes a case for a new economic ethic based on a theological perspective that economics is stewardship of the gifts of creation for the sake of all people. This ethic maximizes distributive justice, ecological responsibility, human freedom, and creativity. After criticizing the assumptions and effects of the United States' economic system, including those related to economic growth, the report deals with several specific issues. Among these are economic growth and technological change (redistributing growth to the most needy sectors is recommended), environmental quality, land use, and agriculture (where eco-justice is explicitly mentioned). A discussion guide and supplementary readings follow.

374 Wogaman, J. Philip. *Economics and Ethics: A Christian Inquiry.* Philadelphia: Fortress Press, 1986.

Wogaman argues that economic and social policies cannot be understood without ethics because they involve setting and evaluating priorities, tasks appropriate to neither the free market nor ruling elites, but tasks that should be done by and for the whole society through democratic processes. He sees a theological perspective helping to liberate the individual from economic illusions and idolatries across the ideological spectrum. Wogaman speaks of six entry points for relating theology to social and economic issues: physical existence as God's creation; priority of grace over works; physical well-being and social relationships; vocation; stewardship, and original sin. He proposes as the first priority for society, providing its members with the conditions necessary for participation along with a proper balance between incentives and security. Important economic realities from this perspective include expanded production, the gap between rich and poor, unemployment, resource depletion, military expenditures, and world economics. Specific priorities are adequate production, equality and security, employment and educational opportunity, environmental conservation, and a vision of a new world order.

375 Wogaman, J. Philip. *The Great Economic Debate: An Ethical Analysis.* Philadelphia: Westminster Press, 1977.

All decisions have a moral dimension, Wogaman affirms, and informed economic decisions are impossible without the guidance of an ideology. Because God transcends ideologies, a Christian set of criteria can be used to examine economic ideologies. He suggests five questions: To what extent does the ideology consider human and environmental well-being? Is the ideology committed to love of all members of the human family? Does the ideology include basic individual rights and freedoms? Does the ideology stress equality? Does the ideology take human selfishness seriously? Using these criteria, Wogaman examines five economic ideologies—Marxism, laissez-faire capitalism, social-market capitalism, democratic socialism, and economic conservatism (steady-state economics, "sustainable society," etc.)—each of which he finds to have particular strengths and weaknesses.

376 World Evangelical Fellowship Theological Commission and Au Sable Institute Forum. "Summarizing Committee Report of the World Evangelical Fellowship Theological Commission and Au Sable Institute Forum, 'Evangelical Christianity and the Environment' 26-31 August 1982." *Evangelical Review of Theology* 17 (April 1993): 122-33.

Following a review of creation's degradation (cf. DeWitt, "Assaulting the Gallery of God") (388), a subsection titled "Biblical and Theological Framework" stresses God as distinct from, yet involved in, creation, humans' "special task of caring for creation in a shepherdly manner," and personal relationship to Jesus Christ as keys to participation in God's purposes for creation. "The *praxis* of Sustainable Development" presupposes absolutes of justice and equity and requires attention to environment-poverty connections and cultural contexts. The tasks for the Christian community by which it takes part in and expresses the present and future Kingdom of Christ include forms of evangelism, political engagement, and education.

377 Wright, Nancy G. and Donald Kill. *Ecological Healing: A Christian Vision.* Maryknoll, NY: Orbis, 1993.

This book, a good basic introduction to environment and development issues from a Christian perspective, is presented by CODEL (Coordination in Development, Inc.), a consortium of church-related development aid agencies. It first reviews some interactions between poverty and the environment, including population growth and unjust land distribution, and then focuses on different human impacts on the biosphere. The ability of indigenous peoples to live sustainably in their environments, and the conflicts that arise between their sustainable ways of life and Western-style development, are the subject of one chapter, while another examines "what went wrong" in the Enlightenment values driving colonial and industrial models of development. The authors provide an alternative set of values in the scriptural view of Earth and its people, the writings of theologians including Thomas Berry, Sallie McFague, and Loren Wilkinson, and the statements of Orthodox, Protestant, and Roman Catholic church bodies. The last chapter outlines an understanding of sustainable development in accord with these values, and includes empowering women, sustainable agriculture, environmental restoration, population policies, local initiatives, and self-reliant communities. Discussion questions follow each chapter, and appendices provide further information on church statements.

In addition to the works annotated in this chapter, readers interested in economics and sustainability may wish to consult the following entries located elsewhere in the bibliography: 034, 099, 178, 228, 230, 290, 304, 323, 324, 416.

9

Land and Resource Use

Questions of sustainability and economic justice become concrete when they are applied to particular forms of resource exploitation and distribution. This section includes some of the most common topics in the literature of "applied" eco-justice: agricultural practices, energy production, and policies for the distribution and use of land. Other important issues covered here are management of ancient and tropical forests, the rights of indigenous peoples, and the integrity of rural communities.

378 [Abrecht, Paul]. "Technology, Resources, Environment, and Population." In *Faith and Science in an Unjust World: Report of the World Council of Churches' Conference on Faith, Science, and the Future*, vol. 2, *Reports of Sections*, 69-87. Geneva: World Council of Churches, 1980.

> This section 5 report from the 1979 conference held at the Massachusetts Institute of Technology asserts that while all creation has value for God, genuine basic human needs take priority in ethical decision-making. This general attitude, with attention to the norms of participation, justice, and sustainability, is applied to issues of renewable and nonrenewable resources, the "world commons" (sea bed resources, the atmosphere, etc.), environmental deterioration, and population.

379 Austin, Richard Cartwright. *Reclaiming America: Restoring Nature to Culture. Environmental Theology*, Book 4. Abingdon, VA: Creekside Press, 1990.

> Austin concludes his environmental-theology series with innovative and sensitive proposals for national policy and church practice. Recalling Thomas Jefferson's vision of a democracy of self-sufficient farmers, which he finds consistent with "biblical ecology" (cf. *Hope for the Land*) (030), Austin describes "good work" and "elegant frugality" as elements of an environmentally benign pursuit of happiness. After recounting the development of mechanized agribusiness in the United States, he defines the purpose of agriculture in terms of sustenance, conservation, and production and he envisions new forms of agriculture that serve these values while treating animals humanely, promoting justice, and producing sufficient food for all people. Three concepts are proposed to help reunite nature and American culture: recognition of the human right of access to nature; a strategy for land reform; and constitutional protection for species, ecological systems, and distinctive natural features. Austin urges churches to expand their self-understanding to embrace communion with nature as well as with God, to offer clear alternatives to patterns of behavior that oppress humans and nature, to

be prepared to respond with compassionate ministries to the devastation and suffering that lie ahead, and to labor in hope for the regeneration of the earth.

380 Austin, Richard Cartwright. *Spoil: A Moral Study of Strip Mining for Coal.* New York: Board of Global Ministries, United Methodist Church, 1976.

This five-session adult religious education program examines the ecological, political, economic, and moral issues of strip-mining. Each session begins with a scripture reading, testimonials of those involved in strip mining, and prayer; each ends with group discussion questions. Austin details mining procedures and their effects on the local environment and people, and he outlines strip-mining's connections to larger issues of energy use, the American democratic system, and Christian responsibility.

381 Austin, Richard Cartwright. "Three Axioms for Land Use." *Christian Century* 94 (12 October 1977): 910-11, 915.

Austin proposes a land ethic based on three principles: representation of the needs of the land-system in land-use decisions; humanity as the conscious, sensory element of the ecosystem; and land administration by those closest to and most dependent upon it. He urges land reform to reestablish as many people as possible on the land, and affirms that redeeming the land and redeeming humanity are not separate tasks.

382 Birkenfeld, Darryl L. "Land: A Place Where Justice, Peace, and Creation Meet." *International Review of Mission* 78 (April 1989): 155-61.

In an essay that illustrates the continuing value of biblical notions to illumine contemporary life, Birkenfeld, pastor of a Roman Catholic church in Hereford, Texas, applies the biblical concepts of the Promised Land and the Exile to the Texas Panhandle, a region of once "wondrous nourishment and promise" now both culturally and environmentally impoverished. In the Old Testament, the Promised Land entails a moral response—it is a place where justice and peace are to be accorded the neglected members of society, Earth, and Earth's creatures. Failure to exercise this moral responsibility results in exile. The settlers of the Texas Panhandle saw themselves as "chosen people" sent to drive out Native American tribes and subdue the land, and, Birkenfeld states, "similarities exist between an unfaithful Hebrew people in the Bible and our present generation in Texas" for whom the land has become "a locus of power and wealth, divorced from its original state as a gift that entailed social and ecological responsibility." The result is the physical and mental exile of Texans expressed as farm foreclosures, job layoffs, dissatisfied youth, economic and social disparities, and racism. The article ends with a somewhat sketchy proposal for a new church/land relationship centered in the idea of community.

383 Byron, William J. "The Ethics of Stewardship." In *The Earth is the Lord's: Essays on Stewardship*, edited by Mary Evelyn Jegen and Bruno V. Manno, 44-50. New York: Paulist Press, 1978.

Because by God's unmerited graciousness we are gifted with land, we are, the author maintains, bound to be grateful and so preserve it, share it, and use it in accordance with God's plan. We violate our trust when we neglect or needlessly destroy the land, or appropriate it for our exclusive use. Private property is a workable means for preserving land, but the needs and rights of others can override it.

384 Catholic Bishops' Conference of the Philippines. *What Is Happening to Our Beautiful Land? A Pastoral Letter on Ecology from the Catholic Bishops of the Philippines.* In Sean McDonagh, *The Greening of the Church*, 207-16. Maryknoll, NY: Orbis Books; London: Geoffrey Chapman, 1990.

This letter, approved at Tagaytay, 29 January 1988, is a message from the Roman Catholic bishops of the Philippines who remember the trees and surrounding coral reefs as their ancestors found them and declare the ecological damage to their homeland sinful and contrary to their faith. "The destruction of any part of creation, especially the extinction of species, defaces the image of Christ which is etched in creation." They call on individuals, churches, the government, and non-governmental organizations to address the ecological problems which are a matter of life and death inevitably leading to political and social unrest. Published in several sources including *CBCP Monitor 9* (January/February 1988).

385 Clobus, Robert. "Ecofarming and Landownership in Ghana." In *Missionary Earthkeeping*, edited by Calvin B. DeWitt and Ghillean T. Prance, 63-89. Macon, GA: Mercer University Press, 1992.

Clobus describes the environmental deterioration of Ghana due to natural drought cycles, population increase, overgrazing, deforestation, and overcultivation, which is occurring at the same time that traditional practices and beliefs have given way to a money economy with increasing concentration of land in state and private hands. The author urges churches to protect the independence of the small subsistence farmer and promote "ecofarming" practices such as agroforestry.

386 Cowap, Chris. "Ethical Implications of Energy Production and Use. A. The NCCC Energy Study Process and Purpose." In *Energy Ethics: A Christian Response*, edited by Dieter T. Hessel, 108-18. New York: Friendship Press, 1979.

The 1975 report chaired by Margaret Mead and René Dubos for the National Council of Churches of Christ (NCCC), Division of Church and Society, on the use of plutonium as a commercial nuclear fuel precipitated a long and heated debate on energy policy which Cowap reports. Part of this history is an approach that defines energy as a means to achieve social ends and therefore an ethical and religious as well as technical concern. Another part of the history is the preparation of "Ethical Implications of Energy Production and Use," a document which was opposed by the nuclear industry and others and was issued by the NCCC Governing Board as a Study Document rather than an agreed-upon statement of policy. Cowap summarizes the criticisms leveled at this document—that it is anti-technology, anti-growth, anti-nuclear power, and beyond the church's ability to deal with. Replying to these criticisms, she emphasizes justice for all creation. Her contributions are followed by a revised and reorganized version of the Study Document (pp. 119-31).

387 DeVos, Peter, Calvin B. DeWitt, Eugene Dykema, Vernon Ehlers, and Loren Wilkinson. *Earthkeeping in the Nineties: Stewardship of Creation.* Grand Rapids: William B. Eerdmans Publishing Co., 1991.

This, the revised edition of *Earthkeeping: Christian Stewardship of Natural Resources* (Grand Rapids: William B. Eerdmans Publishing Co., 1980) which, like the original, was written by Fellows of Calvin College's Center for Christian Scholarship, comprehensively reviews environmental ethics from an evangelical perspective. It begins with an evaluative description of "the state of the planet," and goes on to review conceptions and evaluations of nature from the ancient Greeks, through the North American experience, to present-day calls for an ecological spirituality. It critically examines the role of cosmological and ethical models in shaping thought, especially the role of ethical utilitarianism in guiding economics and technology. On the basis of Scripture, it develops a theology of dominion as responsible stewardship, attributing abuse of nature in Western Christendom to pre-Christian ideas imperfectly transformed by the Gospel. The authors regard distributive justice as applying to nonhumans and future generations as well as to living persons. They present twenty guidelines for action. Appendices include a list of "what you can do," an annotated bibliography, and factors in deciding to print the book on recycled paper. The 1980 edition discussed relations between rich and poor nations and inter-human distributive justice in more detail, and stressed that opportunities for responsible stewardship are a "good" to be more equitably distributed.

388 DeWitt, Calvin B. "Assaulting the Gallery of God." *Sojourners* (February/March 1990): 19-21.

DeWitt adds relevant Bible passages to his lists of the major degradations brought on by humanity's assault on creation—habitat destruction, species extinction, land degradation, waste production, global toxification, the greenhouse effect, ozone depletion, and human and cultural degradation. The last-named degradation results when the meek of the earth are displaced by the powerful, depriving them of land, work, self-sufficiency and stewardship; disrupting their long-standing ways of living cooperatively with the environment; and destroying their knowledge of the uses of a wide array of species.

389 Douglass, Gordon, and Jane Douglass. "Creation, Reformed Faith, and Sustainable Food Systems." In *Reformed Faith and Economics*, edited by Robert L. Stivers, 117-44. Lanham, MD: University Press of America, 1989.

"Agricultural sustainability," the authors point out, means something very different to those who define sustainability as sufficiency of food for all, those who regard it as referring to the stewardship of natural resources, and those whose primary interest is in the quality of farming communities. The authors believe, given population growth, economic restraints, and ecological limits, it is impossible to wholly belong to all three schools. Using James Gustafson as a guide, they examine the Reformed tradition for an appropriate view of sustainability, concluding that policies aimed at sustaining a future human population must be monitored and changed whenever nature's capacity for renewal is undermined. They find the Reformed tradition's historical association with cities providing few clues to the appropriateness of the community school of thought other than a general approval of its kinds of values. The authors critique several church documents on agricultural policy and end with a recommendation for a strategy of integrated rural development.

390 Evans, Bernard F., and Gregory D. Cusack, eds. *Theology of the Land*. Collegeville, MN: Liturgical Press, 1987.

These addresses from the first annual Theology of the Land Conference sponsored by the Virgil Michel Chair at St. John's University and the Catholic Rural Life Conference focus on the general dimensions of a new theology or ethic of land ownership and land use for the United States. See Austin (031), Brueggemann (035), Freudenberger (395), Hart (402), and Weber (427).

391   Everett, William W.   "Land Ethics: Toward a Covenantal Model." In *American Society of Christian Ethics, Selected Papers, 1989,* 45-73.   Newton Centre, MA, 1979.

By defining the parties (God, nature, society, persons), rights (use, income, transfer, alteration) and goods (security, expression, enjoyment, perfection) involved, Everett lays out a framework for discussing land ethics.   He examines four models of land ethics—the market model, prevalent today, limited and self-destructive; the societal model, which does not respect the claims of nature; the ecological model, associated with "bucolic utopias" that oversimplify the complexities of modern life; and the biblically-based covenantal model or God-society trust, wherein God's claims to the land are mediated through nature, persons, and societies, and in which nature provides boundaries for human lust.   He ends with a favorable examination of the land-trust movement.   The essay includes an extensive bibliography.

392   Freudenberger, C. Dean.   *Food for Tomorrow?*   Minneapolis: Augsburg Publishing House, 1984.

Trained in agronomy with years of overseas missions experience, Freudenberger provides much information on the problems of current agricultural policies and suggests possible alternatives while developing a consistently non-anthropocentric theology and ethic.   He argues that current policy does not address the magnitude of the stress of a rising demand on the global ecosystem that threatens earth's ability to provide food for tomorrow.   He finds a source for a new agricultural ethic in the biblical tradition that human beings must conform to God's will for creation and must keep the creative process going for the sake of all life.   Christ, he believes, enables us to overcome our egotism and work to preserve creation from human self-centeredness.   The purpose of agriculture is to make possible the indefinite development of the potentiality of human life within the whole community of created life.   Embracing relations with humans and nonhumans, agriculture is to be guided by the norms of justice, participation, and sustainability.   Solutions to the food crisis require much more research on sustainable forms of agriculture.   Freudenberger describes the role that the United States and the church can play in raising awareness of the problem and promoting alternative agriculture.

393   Freudenberger, C. Dean.   *The Gift of Land: A Judeo-Christian Perspective on Value and Lifestyle Change in a Threatened World.*   Los Angeles: Franciscan Communications, 1981.

Developed as background material for a five-part filmstrip exploring Judaic and Christian perspectives on value and lifestyle issues pertaining to affluent nations, this slim volume contains a selective bibliographical list of pre-1980 works relating to eco-justice.   The author's premise that the purpose of humanity is to participate with all forms of life in the on-going process of creation leads him to conclude that justice, participation, and sustainability are values of a preferred future.   The land is a gift, sustained by a covenant of Creator and creation.   Misplaced values—a narrow anthropocentrism that is the result of not seeing that nature and humanity are part of one system, the concept of human sovereignty over the rest of creation, and the reliance on military security while the needs of the world's eco-systems go unanswered—call for value change.   Such change is possible when we understand the causality of value patterns and how values change.

394 Freudenberger, C. Dean. *Global Dustbowl: Can We Stop the Destruction of the Land Before It's Too Late?* Minneapolis: Augsburg Fortress Publishers, 1990.

Freudenberger again presents his case for an alternative agriculture and an agricultural ethic, focusing on the question "Why care?" and on the contrast between modern "industrial agriculture" and a new "agroecology." He argues that agriculture has been reduced to the production of crops as market commodities, and that the "colonializing" of agriculture in the United States as well as abroad has served the interests of the powerful at the expense of the powerless, resulting in the erosion of rural communities and environmental destruction. To reverse these trends requires a new worldview focusing on relationships and the ecological values of community, harmony, beauty, cooperation, and nurture. Freudenberger sketches a land ethic based on humility, trusteeship, and concern for enhancing the land and motivated by a sense of gratitude and responsibility. He describes an agroecology in accord with this worldview that would imitate the original biotic community, enhance the natural environment, and promote the dignity, integrity, and well-being of farmers and rural communities, and he outlines a strategy for making the transition.

395 Freudenberger, C. Dean. "Implications of a New Land Ethic." In *Theology of the Land*, edited by Bernard F. Evans and Gregory D. Cusack, 69-84. Collegeville, MN: Liturgical Press, 1987.

In this article Freudenberger summarizes the position developed in his book-length works. He characterizes the land "ethic" operative in the United States as one of profit-taking, which abuses and threatens life on earth, and he advocates a theocentric "dominion ethics" in which humans promote justice and right order for the benefit of all creatures. He also proposes a regenerative agriculture modeled on original biotic communities, in which farmers are supported by quality rural human communities, and the United States works with other nations to develop a self-reliant and regenerative food system.

396 Fritsch, Albert J., and Warren E. Brunner. *Appalachia: A Meditation*. Chicago: Loyola University Press, 1986.

This juxtaposition of scriptural passages, photographs of Appalachia taken by Brunner, and lyric commentary by Fritsch conveys two realities—that of persons and land developed over time in a harmonious, reverent relationship, and that of land broken, abused, and threatened by absentee ownership, careless trashing, and economic inequities. This book is a plea for a return to land values: "Are we at home in Appalachia? While there is any injustice in the land, we are not as rooted as we'd like to be. Let this region be the place from which we spring, where we are situated, and where we'll return to the earth. And let all justice reside here."

397 Geiger, Donald R. "Agriculture, Stewardship, and a Sustainable Future." In *The Earth is the Lord's: Essays on Stewardship*, edited by Mary Evelyn Jegen and Bruno V. Manno, 89-99. New York: Paulist Press, 1978.

The author maintains that we cannot ignore the question of the long-term ecological implications of agricultural development, nor can we return to a completely undisturbed Earth; we must take a symbiotic approach that alters the earth without degrading it. His guiding idea is that of a sustainable social and biological/agronomic system in which the contradictory social structures that lead to conflicts over development versus conservation are converted into symbiotic structures. Planning and decision-making must incorporate the viewpoints and norms of each realm in the system: techno-economic structures (distributive justice), polity (common good), culture (freedom), and ecosystem (responsible stewardship).

398 Gibson, William E. "Global Warming as a Theological Ethical Concern." In *After Nature's Revolt: Eco-Justice and Theology*, edited by Dieter T. Hessel, 109-21. Minneapolis: Augsburg Fortress Publishers, 1992.

Gibson maintains that global warming shows the inherently destructive and unjust tendencies of modern civilization's anthropocentric, growth-oriented paradigm, a paradigm not fundamentally challenged by the proponents of "sustainable development." Persons of faith must respond to global warming from an eco-justice paradigm built on participation, sufficiency, and solidarity as well as sustainability.

399 Glesk, Martin, and Scott Paradise. "Fuel, Food, and Faith." In *Beyond Survival: Bread and Justice in Christian Perspective*, edited by Dieter T. Hessel, 70-90. New York: Friendship Press, 1977.

In addition to outlining the moral, social, and environmental reasons for replacing the present Western energy-intensive food system with a low-energy food system, the authors discuss the massive transformation of cultural and religious assumptions regarding work, vocation, stewardship, creation, human nature, and history required to achieve this goal.

400 Hargrove, Barbara. "The Church and the Rural Crisis." *Iliff Review* 44 (Spring 1987): 3-27.

A report on a research project funded by the Association of Theological Schools on "Theological Education for Rural Ministry in the West" which includes an analysis of the context of rural ministry, its present reality, and its theological needs. Hargrove's survey of context leaves little doubt of the seriousness of the rural farm crisis which she relates to various issues, political, ecological and social. International and national issues include global agricultural output, the lowering of farm equity, and foreclosure regulations of the Federal Credit System. Ecological issues include the lowering of the water table as a result of irrigation used to increase production, the related problem of soil salinization exacerbated by the use of fertilizers and herbicides, the health costs related to use of toxic chemicals and the location of toxic waste dumps in rural areas, the contest over water for urban development and rural agricultural use, and the buyouts of reservoir rights by cities. Social problems relate to city dwellers moving into rural communities. She finds churches in the rural West in economic decline at the same time that individual and family stress require more pastoral counseling; and she reports a general problem of rural apathy and a lack of commitment to church programs. She sees a need for rural congregations to feel tied to the rest of humanity and to all of creation, to be taken seriously by their pastors, and to feel rewarded for practices that improve the land and the general quality of life.

401 Harrison, Beverly W.. "The Politics of Energy Policy." In *Energy Ethics: A Christian Response*, edited by Dieter T. Hessel, 56-71. New York: Friendship Press, 1979.

Because a "theologically based ethic of eco-justice cannot aim at anything less than a social policy which takes special account of the effects of that policy on those already most disadvantaged in society," the author maintains that a "salvific" energy ethic based on Christian tradition alone is not adequate. An adequate policy will also consider the existing social and economic power arrangements which constitute the institutional matrix of policy formation and implementation. Christians must not only examine their life-styles, they must enter into political coalitions for just energy policies.

402 Hart, John. "Land, Theology, and the Future." In *Theology of the Land*, edited by Bernard F. Evans and Gregory D. Cusack, 85-102. Collegeville, MN: Liturgical Press, 1987.

Denying that the United States is merely "at a crossroads" between caring for and destroying the earth, Hart declares that it has passed the crossroads and chosen death rather than life, and its citizens need to turn back and redirect their steps "toward harmony with our earth, our God, and each other as children of God and of the earth." He suggests that Christian and Native American religious attitudes toward land, which are parallel and in part congruent, are bases for contradicting the prevailing ideology of greed. He finds that many traditional native peoples at the present time share "a common belief in the Creator, respect for Mother Earth, belief in the interrelatedness of all creatures, a sense of pride and sovereignty, and an activist commitment to social justice." He illustrates his belief with examples from leaders of the Navajo, Hopi, Onondaga, Muskogee, and Creek nations. Hope for the future is said to require church advocacy of land reform, land-related liturgies, and ecumenical openness toward the spirituality of native peoples.

403 Hart, John. *The Spirit of the Earth.* New York: Paulist Press, 1984.

This book is instructive of the American history of civil and religiously based agricultural movements promoting widespread and equitable land distribution and serves as a guide to the traditions which have challenged land-exploitation and concentration. Hart includes American Indian and Judeo-Christian traditions which agree that land ("Mother Earth" or "God's Earth") does not ultimately belong to its "owners" but should serve the needs of all people and generations, and that it and its creatures are to be respected and cared for. He traces an American tradition of legislation favoring equitable land distribution from the writings of Thomas Paine and Thomas Jefferson, through the Pre-Emption and Homestead Acts, to laws intended to support family-sized holdings in the twentieth century. He traces the position of the Roman Catholic church as a consistent advocate of agrarian justice. Hart maintains that the disparity between existing practice and these ideal visions must be bridged by land reform.

404 Hedström, Ingemar. "Latin America and the Need for a Life-Liberating Theology." In *Liberating Life*: *Contemporary Approaches to Ecological Theology,* edited by Charles Birch, William Eakin, and Jay B. McDaniel, 111-24. Maryknoll, NY: Orbis Books, 1990.

Though the theological section is quite brief, this is a good example of Latin American liberation theology extended to environmental issues. Hedström reviews the history of land overexploitation in Western Europe and Latin America and the current situation in Central America, focusing on the poverty and destruction caused by export-oriented cattle ranching. He proposes a "preferential option for life" over against the ideology of unlimited growth. Harmony with nature requires combining and balancing the best elements of anthropocentrism and ecocentrism, and a more just society requires respect for environmental limits. Compare with Hadsell (099).

405 Hessel, Dieter T. "Eco-Justice in the Eighties." In *Energy Ethics: A Christian Response*, edited by Dieter T. Hessel, 1-15. New York: Friendship Press, 1979.

Assuming that "social justice and environmental health occur together or not at all," and that this requires "shaping a society that has sufficient, sustainable energy systems for all," Hessel asks: "What kind of energy do we need, produced how, for what purposes, to whose benefit, at what cost to whom?" Cautioning that no direct line runs from the Bible to social policy, Hessel identifies fifteen social impact criteria, drawn from the Report of the National Council of Churches Energy Ethics Consultation 12-14 October 1977, that are "more or less consistent" with seven basic biblical eco-justice principles.

406 Hessel, Dieter T., ed. *Beyond Survival: Bread and Justice in Christian Perspective*. New York: Friendship Press, 1977.

This collection of papers resulted from the work of study-teams sponsored by a consortium of denominations and church agencies assisted by the Commission on Faith and Order of the National Council of Churches. The assumption of the anthology is that hunger education and action depend on disciplined theological-ethical reflection throughout the church. Although not explicitly stated as a purpose of the book, all but two of the papers seek to provide that reflection from a perspective that includes both social justice and stewardship of creation. See Blockwick (279), Freudenberger and Hough (288), Gibson (349), Glesk and Paradise (399), and Roodkowsky (425).

407 Hessel, Dieter T., ed. *Energy Ethics: A Christian Response*. New York: Friendship Press, 1979.

These essays, the result of deliberations of the Energy Study Panel of the National Council of Churches of Christ in the USA, offer excellent insight into how a particular policy question can be an occasion for fleshing out the theological and ethical content of eco-justice. Prophetic biblical eco-justice understandings, general criteria of the "just, participatory, and sustainable society," and the priority of basic human need satisfaction together constitute a basis for middle-level ethical norms and moral judgments regarding specific energy technologies and policies. Of special interest are essays by Cowap (386), Harrison (401), Lazareth (114), Paradise (419), and Pitcher (207).

408 Hough, Joseph C., Jr. "Land and People: The Eco-Justice Connection." *Christian Century* 97 (1 October 1981): 910-14.

This fact-driven article provides the underpinnings of what Hough calls "a clear and vital connection" of environmentalists and social-justice advocates. It develops the case against technology transfer as a solution to rural poverty, showing it to lead to increasing land concentration by the relatively wealthy while so impoverishing soil and water supplies that the land is useless for future production. Hough argues that the so-called green revolution was an attempt to solve the problems of the rural poor without the real revolution of land redistribution that is called for. He warns American Christians of the need to resist political jingoism that supports existing regimes in Third World countries in the name of anti-communism or defense of the free world. He also warns that "*no* development strategies will succeed in the pursuit of eco-justice unless they are accompanied by serious restraint on the part of those who consume the most."

409 Jegen, Mary Evelyn, and Bruno V. Manno, eds. *The Earth Is the Lord's: Essays on Stewardship*. New York: Paulist Press, 1978.

These papers from a seminar sponsored by the Bread for the World Educational Fund and the University of Dayton's Office for Moral and Religious Education have as a common theme that the earth's resources are a gift from God and should be used to meet the needs of all people now living and conserved for future generations. Part 1 contrasts the biblical stewardship tradition with current assumptions about competition, property rights, and equity. Part 2 focuses on specific issues from a stewardship perspective, and part 3 discusses the implementation of stewardship in personal, family, and community life. Each section is followed by discussion questions and suggestions for action and further reading.

410 Jung, L. Shannon. "Agricultural Technology As If God Were Involved" *Reformed Review* 41 (Spring 1988): 200-13.

Jung sees agriculture as a barometer of the way in which technology, economics, and theology intertwine and non-sustainable agricultural practices in the United States the result of ineffective theology as well as inappropriate technology. A renewed emphasis on certain aspects of Christian faith—especially the doctrine of continuing creation, the metaphor of the world as God's body, and *shalom*—could, he asserts, orient agricultural technology in sustainable and appropriate directions.

411 Jung, L. Shannon. "Ethics, Agriculture, and the Material Universe." In *The Annual of the Society of Christian Ethics, 1986*, edited by Alan B. Anderson, 219-50. Washington, DC: Georgetown University Press, 1987.

The failure of proposed solutions of the farm crisis to respect the welfare of land and farmers is attributed by Jung to the hierarchical split between spirit and nature promoted by Western philosophy, science, and neo-orthodox Christianity. He urges that theology and ethics be transformed so as to recognize the actual interpenetration of spirit and matter, which in turn should engender policies that restore the land and humanity to good health.

412 Jung, L. Shannon . "The Recovery of the Land: Agribusiness and Creation-Centered Spirituality." In *Religion in the Life of the Nation: American Recoveries*, edited by Rowland A. Sherrill. Urbana: University of Illinois Press, 1990.

Jung argues that business values have replaced agrarian values in American agriculture, depriving farmers of their dignity (and often of their farms) and the public of a healthy environment. The stewardship ethic is partly to blame: it treats nature as separate from humanity, making the health of the land secondary to money, and assumes that God is external to the world. Creation-centered spirituality, as found in Native American traditions, feminism, and the Judaic and Christian traditions, can restore a sense of God's immanence.

413 Liden, David. "Reflections on the Land Study." In *Erets: Land: The Church and Appalachian Land Issues*, edited by Davis Yeuell, 15-28. Amesville, OH: The Coalition for Appalachian Ministry, 1984.

The Appalachian Land Ownership Study is important as a case study linking environmental and social justice issues, and Liden, one of its coordinators, briefly surveys the study and then suggests practical ways the church can respond to rectify the structural problems the study uncovered. Designed and executed by persons living in the Appalachian region, the study sampled land ownership patterns and property tax patterns across six states, recording data on over 10,000 holdings. Among its findings: fifty corporate owners and ten government agencies owned 41 percent of the land; 75 percent of the surface land and 80 percent of the minerals were absentee-owned. It also found gross under-assessment of the corporate absentee-owned property. Liden points out that land control extends to encompass control over housing, community stability, environmental quality, community services, and the local power structure itself. Corporate absentee control contributes to stripping the land of its spiritual and moral qualities. He suggests specific strategies that churches might initiate in order to discourage corporate land development.

414 Lilburne, Geoffrey R. *A Sense of Place: A Christian Theology of the Land.* Nashville: Abingdon Press, 1989.

Concerned that a sense of sacred space is largely neglected by Christian theology, Lilburne turns to the Australia of his youth, finding in its Aboriginal people a religion relevant to the quest for a responsible Christian theology of the land. He differentiates theology of the land from theologies of the earth, of creation, and of nature, land being understood as a concrete historical phenomenon partaking of politics and economic power struggles. In the Aboriginal network of relationships to the land he sees similarities to early Hebrew religion, especially the notion of land as a gift to the entire community to be distributed justly, considering even the stranger in one's midst. He highlights the importance of images in Aboriginal culture; and suggests that images of local context are also important to groups such as women, blacks, and members of developing countries who have been denied a voice in theological formulation. Lilburne also distinguishes Christian religion from Aboriginal religion, the Aboriginals seeing land as a whole as sacred, while for Christians "space becomes charged with religious meaning only as we realize the stupendous truth of the Incarnation and its transforming power in our lives." Lilburne also sees parallels between Old Testament biblical stories such as that of the confrontation between Ahab and Naboth and present day land use conflicts involving Aboriginals and oil companies, black family farmers and United States tax structure, corporations and land reformers in Central America. He believes that the Christian community must support the restoration of equitable and just occupation of lands to dispossessed peoples.

415 Lutz, Charles P. "Sustainability in Agriculture: Challenge for the Church." *Church and Society* 80 (March/April 1990): 69-78.

Lutz maintains that the church's role is to be a supportive community for sustainable agriculturists. Sustainable agriculture is suitable for the local environment, economically viable, socially just, low in off-farm inputs, and respectful of cultural integrity and human interaction. It aims to improve farm health and safety, food quality, and biodiversity, and is "compatible with spiritual teachings that recognize the earth as a common heritage and responsibility." Lack of information, government policies, marketing institutions, and social pressures including the profligate use of resources by industrialized nations, are obstacles to sustainable agriculture. "The religious community is called to support people who are making and adjusting to change, to nurture people concerning biblical faith and environmental care, to advocate justice in the public policy arena, and to live its own institutional life in ways consistent with its speech."

416 McDonagh, Sean. *The Greening of the Church.* Maryknoll, NY.: Orbis Books; London: Geoffrey Chapman, 1990.

> Published four years after *To Care for the Earth* (458), this volume covers some of the same ground but focuses in greater detail on the relationship between environmental issues and the poverty of non-industrialized nations. McDonagh, a Roman Catholic priest, largely confines his examples to the Philippines where he lives and works with tribal peoples, and these lend weight to his conclusions. He highlights the problem of international debt, showing its effect on a typical Filipino farmer and the Philippines as a whole, and his discussion of population is enriched by his specifics on how population growth affects one T'boli village. He discusses the plunder of the Philippine rain forest from the period of Spanish rule to Aquino's presidency and the tendency to blame the *kaingineros* for what has a political and military cause. McDonagh is critical of the response of the Catholic church to the environment, especially to population problems, although he is hopeful of its eventual change of policy.

417 National Council of Churches. *Energy and Ethics: The Ethical Implications of Energy Production and Use.* New York: National Council of Churches, Division of Church and Society, 1979.

> Prepared for church study groups, this document is the result of a three-year study by the National Council of Churches on the ethical implications of energy production and use, and is premised on the belief that choices about production and use of energy are matters of justice that need to be addressed by the religious community. Discussed in fairly general fashion are the need for an ethic of ecological justice guided by the values of sustainability, equity, and participation; the undesirability of energy resources being developed by interests outside the community; the need for energy-conservation measures in the United States; the energy needs of non-industrialized nations; and energy measures that individual churches may undertake.

418 Owens, Owen D. *Stones Into Bread? What Does the Bible Say About Feeding the Hungry Today?* Valley Forge: Hudson Press, 1977.

> Owens maintains that the way in which the world market system of industrial agriculture produces and distributes food damages the environment, benefits the affluent, and contributes to world hunger. He interprets Jesus' refusal to turn stones into bread as signifying that bread comes from God and should be created and administered according to the will of God. To follow Jesus is therefore to recognize that industrial agriculture is under divine judgment and that we are called to new ways of food production that embody love, hope, and righteousness in our relations with all creation. He suggests three guidelines for action pursuant to an eco-justice ethic: reverence, interdependence, and stewardship. These guidelines point to the need for the affluent to voluntarily adopt simpler, less consuming life styles, and to say "no" to industrial expansion, especially oil-dependent intensive agriculture, and "yes" to such alternatives as returning garbage and sewerage to the land, organic farming, conservation, food self-sufficiency for all peoples, and the direct alleviation of world hunger.

419 Paradise, Scott. "Energy and Society: Choosing a Future." In *Energy Ethics: A Christian Response*, edited by Dieter T. Hessel, 16-32. New York: Friendship Press, 1979.

> Scott develops a fascinating explanation of history as a succession of stages limited by available power and tending toward high energy use with consequences

damaging to both humanity and nature, the result of a human psychological need for godlike power and freedom from bodily finitude. The author suggests that a light energy society can be achieved by a transition to decentralized energy production from renewable resources, energy conservation combined with an acceptance of human creatureliness and physical labor, and by seeking pleasure in nature rather than relying on energy-consuming entertainment.

420 Paradise, Scott. "Visions of the Good Society and the Energy Debate." *Anglican Theological Review* 61 (1979): 106-17.

The author maintains that the choice of an energy system is a social, moral, and spiritual decision which parallels social vision, and that, given the confluence of the energy crisis and the breakdown of the liberal consensus as to what constitutes the good society, Americans are poised to be receptive to Christian social vision. Christian axioms of stewardship, solidarity, simplicity, sin, and sanctification indicate that Christians should opt for a social vision based on the Jeffersonian model of modest population, decentralization, nonconsumptive values and energy conservation rather than a technocratic model of society with its goals of population growth, technical, industrial, and social development, and its dependence on new energy sources.

421 Pignone, Mary Margaret. "Concentrated Ownership of Land." In *The Earth is the Lord's: Essays on Stewardship*, edited by Mary Evelyn Jegen and Bruno V. Manno, 112-29. New York: Paulist Press, 1978.

Pignone argues that concentrated and unrestricted ownership of land in the United States means that food production and prices are determined by profits rather than by human needs, and that land is abused. These issues should be considered in moral terms because they are issues of "social sin," the evil consequences of unjust social structures and institutions. She recommends alternatives and policy changes to discourage concentrated ownership and land abuse.

422 Rifkin, Jeremy, with Ted Howard. *Entropy: Into the Greenhouse World.* Revised edition. New York: Bantam Books, 1989.

In this revised edition of *Entropy: A New World View* (New York: Bantam Books, 1980) Rifkin argues that the energy crisis and global warming signal our approaching an entropy "watershed" between two types of energy base—nonrenewable and solar—and their concomitant technologies, institutions, values, and worldviews. After briefly reviewing Greek, Christian, and modern understandings of the world and time, Rifkin proposes a worldview based on entropy and explores its implications for society. He argues that increasing the flow of energy through our social system (i.e., economic growth) inevitably reduces the amount of energy and matter available for use in the future and increases centralization and disorder. Thus, we must abandon our reliance upon the nonrenewable resource base and our belief in progress through accumulating material wealth. Instead, we must build a "Solar Age" society that reduces its energy flow-through in order to sustain the unfolding of all life as far into the future as possible. Rifkin proposes replacing the existing social and technological infrastructure with decentralized participatory democracy, frugality, appropriate technology, and public guardianship of land and resources. Appropriate religious responses include the Eastern practice of meditation and its ideal of unity with nature, and Christian doctrines of creation and stewardship.

423 Robb, Carol S. "The Rights of Farmers, the Common Good, and Feminist Questions." In *Covenant for a New Creation: Ethics, Religion, and Public Policy*, edited by Carol S. Robb and Carl J. Casebolt, 272-90. Maryknoll, NY: Orbis Books, 1991.

Drawing on examples from her own family of farm loss and farmer migration, Robb argues that owners of small and moderate-size farms have a right to sustain themselves through farming because their work contributes more to the common good than does agriculture based on concentrated land ownership. She believes that an alternative framework of human rights, one that defines rights as conditions for participation in community rather than as negative freedoms from impingement, warrants letting small farms exist, as does the biblical notion of justice as righteousness, which (unlike the liberal notion of justice as protection of the individual from the community) "means the fulfillment of the demands of a relationship, whether with other people, with God/ess, or, by extension, with nonhuman creation."

424 Rolston, Holmes, III. "Wildlife and Wildlands: A Christian Perspective." *Church and Society* 80 (March/April 1990): 16-40.

Philosopher Rolston looks both at biblical traditions regarding wildlife and wildlands and at the adequacy of these traditions to deal with questions of wildlife preservation in the United States today. He believes that, as biblical faith began with a land ethic, Christianity needs once again to become a land ethic to restore every living creature to the divine covenant. While both the biblical view and American society recognize private property, Rolston emphasizes that the promised land is never private property but is a landscape, a commons, which needs a management ethic achieved by consensus and enforced by law. The values that are carried by wildlife and wildlands are not primarily economic, nor do they solely concern people—wildlands carry religious values and are godly places in and of themselves. This is also true of wildness in the Bible (when it is being taken for what it is in itself rather than being used to symbolize human hopes and disappointments). Although God loves wilderness as much as culture, humans are not to treat other forms of life as they would their own neighbors. Rolston believes the Golden Rule is mistakenly applied to nature; nature should be allowed to run its course. It is, however, God's will, as expressed in the story of Noah, that each species continue. Reprinted in (106), pp. 122-43.

425 Roodkowsky, Mary. "In Agribusiness We Trust?" In *Beyond Survival: Bread and Justice in Christian Perspective*, edited by Dieter T. Hessel, 91-110. New York: Friendship Press, 1977.

This eco-justice critique of agri-business includes proposals for regulation of the food industry to enhance social justice and the stewardship of creation.

426 United States Catholic Conference. "Reflections on the Energy Crisis." *Origins, NC Documentary Service* 10 (23 April 1981): 706-19.

This statement on energy policy developed by the United States Bishops' Committee for Social Development and World Peace is a significant milestone in the articulation of an eco-justice ethic based on Catholic social teachings. Drawing on recent papal and Vatican II statements, six principles are suggested as a moral framework for energy policy: the right to life of the human person; responsibility for the welfare of the rest of creation; accepting limitations (i.e., sacrificing material possessions); striving for a more just society; special attention to the needs of the poor and minority groups; and wide participation in the decision-making process. Reviewed are alternatives to oil and natural gas; the need for a perspective on the whole energy situation including the complications associated with health, the environment, and world peace; and the need for humility and love in the energy debate. Discussion of energy distribution and control is oriented by the conviction that access to energy is a matter of justice, and that the problem of structural evil in socioeconomic systems must be taken into account.

427 Weber, Leonard. "Land Use Ethics: The Social Responsibility of Ownership." In *Theology of the Land*, edited by Bernard F. Evans and Gregory D. Cusack, 13-39. Collegeville, MN: Liturgical Press, 1987.

Weber deliberately chooses a secular mode of argument, but occasionally refers to more explicitly theological writers. He contrasts two ethical approaches to land ownership and land use policy in America—the dominant "traditional" ethic in which land is an economic resource to be used for private profit within the individualistic market system, and the "communitarian" ethic based on human sociality and the right to basic necessities. Developing the communitarian ethic, Weber argues for applying the concept of social responsibility and basic human rights to land use.

428 World Council of Churches. *Accelerated Climate Change: Sign of Peril, Test of Faith.* Geneva: World Council of Churches, [1994].

This study paper, produced by a meeting of the World Council of Churches Consultation on Climate Change in October 1993, discusses accelerated global warming, its connections to industry, transportation, population, the military, etc., and the setting and implementing of targets for slowing it. Christian response to the problem, derives from God's call "to participate with God in God's own work of stopping the degradation of Earth's protective mantle." Ethical affirmations include valuing creation for its sake and God's sake, transgenerational justice, sufficient and sustainable sustenance for all, and solidarity between humans and with other life. The paper argues that a shared vision of community is needed and suggests strategies for building community. It defines the churches' role with respect to witness, lifestyle, and collaboration with other groups. The document ends with a series of reflections linking the issue of climate change to theological affirmations (relating to God's and humanity's relationship to creation, the world's cultures and religions, male/female relations, simple lifestyles, technology, global community, and the future). Appendices give background on the churches' and the international community's response to climate change, "useful addresses," participants in the study, and the text of a statement on global warming issued by the WCC Central Committee in January 1994.

In addition to the works annotated in this chapter, readers interested in land and resource use may wish to consult the following entries located elsewhere in the bibliography: 015, 031, 035, 036, 037, 038, 118, 229, 257, 360, 377.

10

Church and Mission

Theological and ethical principles are not just abstractions, but are embodied in the lives and practices of religious communities. Works in this section relate eco-justice ethics and theology to: the nature and mission of the church, worship and sacraments, Christian education, the churches' involvement in public policy issues, and missionary activity in the Two-Thirds World.

429 Anderson, Robert. "An Ecological Conscience for America." *Social Action* 35 (September 1968): 5-20.

> In this early paper, delivered to the 1967 Faith-Man-Nature Conference, Anderson, a Congregational minister from Missoula, Montana, maintains that "what damages life in any form tends to damage us; what makes any part of existence ugly puts its blight on our soul and spirit, too." To illustrate America's need for an ecological conscience he includes examples from his home state of an egregious disregard for the quality of life. Anderson sees the ecological crisis as a religious crisis which technology will not remedy. What is needed is a revision of basic attitudes and beliefs. Addressing himself to the churches, he calls for a revision of "commitment" to include the natural order and things of existence and so become a means for human redemption. He suggests establishment of a department of conservation within the National Council of Churches; use of denominational journals, regional and state conferences, local church programming, and the church school curriculum to disseminate an ecological viewpoint; and congregational work by whatever means to solve "the biggest problem" of population explosion.

430 Baer, Richard A., Jr. "Land Misuse: A Theological Concern." *Christian Century* 83 (12 October 1966): 1239-41.

> An early call for the church to take an active role in the social/political arena to halt nature's spoilation and to confront the powers of society with an ethic of respect and care for nature. Baer gives examples of wanton ravaging of land and says that the church, though it shows no signs of having grasped the extent of the problem nor of understanding how dehumanizing the exploitation of nature is, can no longer avoid grappling both theologically and practically with it. A mature Christian position, in line with biblical witness, prevents both worship and spoilation of nature. In presenting a cogent land ethic, the church cannot afford to identify with the ethos of rural America, sports, or recreational interests, for the issues are of concern to all segments of society.

431　Barney, Gerald O.　*Global 2000 Revisited: What Shall We Do?*　Arlington, VA: Millennium Institute, 1993.

> Barney, who directed the 1980 *Global 2000 Report to the President*, prepared this volume for the 1993 Parliament of World's Religions; thus it addresses the religious faiths specifically, and gives weight to their importance.　Its several pages of questions regarding the "poverty-hunger-habitat-energy-trade-population-atmospheric waste-resource problem" or "global problematique" are challenging and worthy of careful thought; they require of each faith tradition an examination of its teachings relative to: global trends; the meaning of "progress;" relationship to persons of differing faiths, culture, politics, gender, and race; and openness to reinterpretation.　Barney asks, "Is there a faith tradition such that if everyone on Earth suddenly adopted it, the human future on Earth would be assured?" and answers that he doubts that there is a faith tradition that has adequately prepared humans for their role as co-creators of Earth's future.　Worthy of use as a study guide in churches and educational institutions, the work emphasizes global inequities and the expected needs of the world's future children with the help of numerous charts.　The issue Barney believes stands out from all the rest and parallels the breaking of life-sustaining relationships in the biosphere is the breaking of life-sustaining relationships in the human community.　He suggests actions that need to be taken and a list of reasons they may not be, including the exceptionalism of some religions, but most importantly, the fact that "we are now a people—a species—without a vision."

432　Cauthen, Kenneth.　"Eco-Justice: A Future-Oriented Strategy of Ministry and Mission."　*Foundations* 16 (April/June 1973): 156-70.

> Cauthen believes that the church must try to present the vision of a society productive of "justice and joy" for all human beings, one which can produce enough material goods for all without excessive pollution or the premature exhaustion of natural resources.　Also, the church must enable individual members to see that "eco-justice" means their liberation also.

433　Cauthen, Kenneth.　"Process Theology and Eco-Justice."　In *For Creation's Sake: Preaching, Ecology, and Justice*, edited by Dieter Hessel, 84-95.　Philadelphia: Geneva Press, 1985.

> Cauthen maintains that process theology provides preaching with the metaphors of being "midwives" for a history which is "pregnant" with the vision and morality of eco-justice—a globally sustainable society with a sufficiency of goods and services conducive to the good life within a framework of justice for all.

434　Cobb, John B., Jr.　"Afterword: The Role of Theology of Nature in the Church."　In *Liberating Life: Contemporary Approaches to Ecological Theology*, edited by Charles Birch, William Eakin, and Jay B. McDaniel, 261-72.　Maryknoll, NY: Orbis Books, 1990.

> Cobb attributes the larger church's neglect of a theology of nature to the recent proliferation of "theologies of" (liberation, women's experience, body, play, etc.), with a resulting inability to speak with a unified voice.　He proposes two strategies: conferences bringing together representatives of these different theologies for dialogue and efforts to rethink Christian theology as a whole from its central sources, using insights from a particular "theology of."　He illustrates the latter by interpreting and extending the Pauline theology of mutual immanence in terms of a philosophy of internal relations.

435 Daneel, M. L. "African Independent Churches Face the Challenge of Environmental Ethics." In *Eco-Theology: Voices from South and North*, edited by David G. Hallman, 248-63. Geneva: WCC Publications; Maryknoll, NY: Orbis Books, 1994.

The contribution of African Independent Churches (AICs) to environmental restoration in Zimbabwe is described in this article. The AICs' tradition of being healing and liberating institutions has been brought to bear on environmental degradation, and one hundred ten AICs, representing some two million members, have joined the Association of African Earthkeeping Churches (AAEC), affiliated with the Zimbabwean Institute of Religious Research and Ecological Conservation (ZIRRCON); Daneel founded both organizations. AAEC's objectives include afforestation, wildlife conservation, and protection of water resources; the organization is undergirded by the belief that, as members of the body of Christ, Christians are commanded to build new relationships with the entire creation. Earthkeeping churches have incorporated confession of ecological sins into their baptismal rites, and tree-planting into eucharistic liturgies, and they seriously attempt to expose and discipline those who continue practices that degrade Earth.

436 Daneel, M. L. "The Liberation of Creation: African Traditional Religious and Independent Church Perspectives." *Missionalia* 19 (August 1991): 99-121.

African Christian theology, according to Daneel, lacks a holistic theological concern for the liberation of creation. He describes the Association of Zimbabwean Traditional Ecologists (of which he is co-founder). AZTREC, led by former guerrilla fighters and "spirit mediums" who were active in Zimbabwe's liberation struggle, focuses on the protection of trees, water, and wildlife, and draws on Shona beliefs regarding ancestors and the creator-deity Mwari. Daneel argues that Christian churches must also participate in the liberation of creation through: "(a) vigorous programs of afforestation which become integral to church life through ecology-related sacraments; (b) a reinterpretation of the ecologically inspirational role of the ancestors in a church context; and (c) an understanding of the triune God which highlights God's mandate to humanity to liberate or sanctify creation." He suggests ways in which existing beliefs and practices of the African Independent Churches can be extended in these directions.

437 DeWitt, Calvin B., and Ghillean T. Prance, eds. *Missionary Earthkeeping*. Introduction by J. Mark Thomas. Macon, GA: Mercer University Press, 1992.

This book originated in a forum sponsored by the Au Sable Institute of Environmental Studies. The editors, acknowledging that missions have often participated in the degradation of creation, describe "missionary earthkeeping" as missions work that understands creation and its degradation and applies biblical principles to its care. The goal of missionary earthkeeping is the wholeness and renewal of creation and of people and of their relationships with each other and the Creator. Thomas's introduction surveys the book's contents and finds them to be reacting to the need for global interrelatedness and responding to environmental degradation in Asia, Africa, and South America from different Christian traditions and on the basis of encounters with those most affected by missions. See Clobus (385), Gustafson (446), Mpanya (462), Prance (464), and Testerman (022).

438 Dorr, Donal. *The Social Justice Agenda: Justice, Ecology, Power, and the Church*. Maryknoll, NY: Orbis Books, 1991.

A useful introduction to justice and peace issues as they have emerged for Christian churches in the past generation, with emphasis on the role the institutional church should play in transforming social structures. Dorr briefly surveys fourteen major social issues confronting the church today. He also reviews and compares the social teachings and agendas (including environmental issues) of both the Roman Catholic Church and the World Council of Churches (including JPSS and JPIC) and compares old and new principles of justice and peace in Catholic social teaching. Dorr's proposals for the role of the church include making a preferential option for the poor; helping explore and develop models of development more just, sustainable, and respectful of the earth; and restructuring the Church's own programs of theological education and spiritual formation.

439 Ellingsen, Mark. *The Cutting Edge: How Churches Speak on Social Issues.* Geneva: WCC Publications; Grand Rapids, MI: William B. Eerdmans Publishing Co., 1993.

Commissioned by the Institute for Ecumenical Studies in Strasbourg, France, this is a massive study of the official statements of churches and church agencies worldwide from 1964 to 1985 (and in some cases into the 1990s). The churches studied belong to the World Council of Churches and a selected number of non-member groups including the Roman Catholic Church. Their statements on nine social issues—apartheid and racism; economic development and unemployment; ecology; nuclear armaments (peace and war); divorce, remarriage, and polygamy; abortion; genetic engineering; social justice; and socio-political ideologies—are individually and collectively analyzed both for position and for kinds of theological warrants appealed to. Of particular interest for eco-justice concerns are the appendices on ecology and social justice, Ellingsen's analysis of these appendices, and his conclusions to the study as a whole.

Ellingsen finds that church statements on ecology are overwhelmingly written by churches in Western nations, although within the different denominations of the West at least one member of every denomination has issued a statement of ecological concern. He finds that a larger number of churches address the issues of ecology by theological arguments rooted in the doctrine of creation than by appeals to Christology, although they tend to make adjustments to the doctrine so as to posit a continuity between creation and redemption, to depict humans as inherently related to the environment, and in some cases, to construe creation as an ongoing process. He also finds that different theological approaches do not necessarily lead to different conclusions for ethics. Ellingsen sees the correlation of social justice with concerns of ecology or sustainability as an example of a tendency in ecclesiastical organizations to link a wide variety of social issues. He finds a significant number of church bodies authorizing social justice by appeal to the doctrine of creation, but again, their theological differences do not preclude common action or common praxis.

440 Faramelli, Norman J. "The Role of the Church in Eco-Justice: A JSAC Working Paper (May 1973)." *Church and Society* 64 (November/December 1973): 4-15.

Stating that the church must take a "pro-active" (rather than a reactive) posture regarding eco-justice by actively challenging the industrial myths of economic growth and by shaping an alternative future on the basis of criteria of self-determination, environmental responsibility, and distributive justice, Faramelli proposes specific policy responses to problems from the global to the local level, primarily dealing with pollution, transportation, and urban areas.

441 Finnerty, Adam Daniel. *No More Plastic Jesus: Global Justice and Christian Lifestyle.* New York: E. P. Dutton, 1978.

Approximately one-half of this book is a hard-hitting compendium of data on global inequalities: lopsided world resource consumption fueled by an ethos of expansion; daily life in non-industrialized nations compared to daily life in the United States; global waste; the self-serving nature of United States foreign aid; and the "myth of the middle class." The other half is a guide to strategies for correcting these imbalances, including the Simple Living movement and the Shakertown Pledge, suggestions for radical divestiture of churches, and a plan for a World Service organization of citizens who would act as designers, catalysts, and organizers of a movement for global justice. The author, one of the formulators of the Shakertown Pledge and a national organizer for it, has been active in the Philadelphia Churchmouse Collective's campaign aimed at committing churches to work actively for a better global society.

442 Forbes, James A. "Preaching in the Contemporary World." In *For Creation's Sake: Preaching, Ecology, and Justice*, edited by Dieter T. Hessel, 45-54. Philadelphia: Geneva Press, 1985.

Forbes cautions that preparation for eco-justice preaching involves heightened self-awareness of the preacher's own commitment to the cause and serious cultural analysis which recognizes forces working against the deep transformation of lifestyle and outlook that such preaching demands of listeners. Eco-justice preaching must meet persons where they are and enlist their participation; it requires technical knowledge of issues as well as a deepening of biblical and theological understanding.

443 Gibson, William E. "Theology and Ethics for a New Mission." *Church and Society* 80 (March/April 1990): 5-15.

This article, based on *Keeping and Healing the Creation* (466), repeats many of Gibson's themes as it sets out the church's mission today based on biblical faith in God the Creator and Redeemer. The church's mission today is to participate in the liberation of the human and nonhuman creation through "keeping and healing" the earth. The ethics for this new mission are defined by the norms of sustainability, participation, sufficiency, and solidarity.

444 Gomes, Peter J. "Critique of W. E. Gibson's "Eco-justice: Burning Word." *Foundations* 20 (October/December 1977): 329-32.

The author criticizes William E. Gibson's article (185) for not addressing the church's hostility toward nature, otherworldliness, and apocalypticism. Christians must "do their homework" on eco-justice issues, support needed changes, and remain faithful in the face of the inevitable crises.

445 Granberg-Michaelson, Wesley. *Redeeming the Creation: The Rio Earth Summit: Challenges for the Churches.* Geneva: WCC Publications, 1992.

Granberg-Michaelson, moderator of the World Council of Churches staff group which coordinated the Council's participation in the 1992 Earth Summit in Rio de

Janeiro (the United Nations Conference on Environment and Development [UNCED]) highlights justice issues as he reflects on what was and was not accomplished at Rio. Discussing what led to the Earth Summit, the author attends to the history of the "limits to growth" discussion, the concept of sustainable development, and the evolving relationship of environmental protection and economic justice. Appended along with the Rio Declaration on Environment and Development are four documents from delegates and observers at the concurrent WCC meeting: "Letter to the Churches," "An Evaluation of the UNCED Conventions," "Theology," and "One Earth Community."

446   Gustafson, James W. "Integrated Holistic Development and the World Mission of the Church." In *Missionary Earthkeeping*, edited by Calvin B. DeWitt and Ghillean T. Prance, 111-47. Macon, GA: Mercer University Press, 1992.

Gustafson describes the mission project in northeast Thailand with which he is associated as one of "integrated holistic development," meaning that all aspects of ministry function together to allow the grace of God to transform persons, society, and nature. The gospel's message of grace, cooperation, and other-centered concern, expressed in local idioms, confronts the local cultural value system. Rice, pig, and fish banks and ecosystem cooperative farms promote socio-economic development while furthering members' spiritual growth.

447   Hall, Douglas John. "JPIC: The Message and the Mission." *Ecumenical Review* 41 (October 1989): 492-500.

Hall applies the dialectic of law and gospel to the conciliar process of justice, peace, and the integrity of creation (JPIC), seeing it as an expression of Christian mission in today's world. The first aim of the JPIC process is to convert the churches to worldly responsibility by showing that justice, peace, and the reintegration of creation is first of all gospel—a message of hope based on God's love and action for the world. As law—a statement of what we must do—JPIC can be a forum for dialogue and cooperation with those who share the same ends but do not ground them in Christian faith.

448   Hessel, Dieter T. "Preaching for Creation's Sake: A Theological Framework." In *For Creation's Sake: Preaching, Ecology, and Justice*, edited by Dieter T. Hessel, 115-28. Philadelphia: Geneva Press, 1985.

Hessel sketches a theological framework for eco-justice preaching that begins with the good news of God's work in and for the whole creation, which in turn enables the preacher to recognize the depth of human sin and the service of human and nonhuman creation to which the preacher is called. He ends with a list of questions for preparers and hearers of eco-justice sermons.

449   Hessel, Dieter T., ed. *For Creation's Sake: Preaching, Ecology, and Justice.* Philadelphia: Geneva Press, 1985.

The Institute for Pastors on Eco-Justice Preaching, held in Stony Point, New York, 14-16 February 1984 sought to clarify the relevance of eco-justice in various cultural contexts and from several disciplines including biblical studies, systematic theology, ethics, feminist studies, and homiletics. Each of the papers from the Institute is described separately elsewhere in this bibliography. See Cauthen (433), Forbes (442), Gibson (186), Gottwald (047), Gray (234), Hessel (448), Shinn (496), and Willis (472).

450 Hutchinson, Roger. *Prophets, Pastors, and Public Choices: Canadian Churches and the Mackenzie Valley Pipeline Debate.* Waterloo, Ontario: Wilfrid Laurier University Press, 1992.

This case study involves native rights, natural resource and land use, and Christian church activism; thus it is an important work for Christian eco-justice concerns, one of a very few studies dealing with a significant, concrete issue. Project North, a Canadian inter-church coalition, aggressively promoted a moratorium, until native land claims were satisfactorily settled, on the construction of a pipeline intended to deliver natural gas to southern Canada and the United States. As described by Hutchinson, the coalition perceived its stance to be rooted in the biblical traditions of socio-economic justice and responsible stewardship of resources and they appealed to Scripture for warrant, but individual churches were divided on the issue, and members critical of the moratorium resented Project North's claim to being on the side of Christian tradition. Some church members felt that a pastoral orientation to all church members was being sacrificed in Project North's prophetic stance. Hutchinson's focus is not on the rightness or wrongness of any side; rather his concern is to analyze the debate to discover procedures that facilitate decision-making. He identifies different stages in the debate and finds particularly important the telling and hearing of individual stories as well as respect for mutually accepted procedures of argument and inquiry. He believes appeals to the Bible are both positive and negative—they create a moral ethos in which justice and stewardship issues are more easily accepted, but they tend to deepen divisions when it is assumed that they point to a particular policy decision. He found that the entry of the churches into the debate helped to expand the prevailing utilitarian/consequentialist framework in both deontological and ideological directions.

451 Jakowska, Sophie. "Roman Catholic Teaching and Environmental Ethics in Latin America." In *Religion and Environmental Crisis*, edited by Eugene C. Hargrove, 127-53. Athens, GA: University of Georgia Press, 1986.

Jakowska writes of the evolution of the Roman Catholic church toward environmental concerns as a result of its growing concern for social justice. She reviews papal documents and pronouncements by the pope and Latin American bishops on the environment (focused primarily on the protection and just distribution of natural resources) and how these have been disseminated and put into practice through church institutions and church-initiated projects in Latin America. Especially valuable are descriptions of three environmental-social initiatives in the Dominican Republic involving action on soil and water conservation, reforestation, and waste disposal.

452 John Paul II. *Redemptor hominis.* Encyclical letter "On Redemption and the Dignity of the Human Race," 4 March 1979. In *The Papal Encyclicals* 5 (1958-1981), edited by Claudia Carlin, 245-73. Wilmington, NC: McGrath Publishing Co., 1981.

Declaring that the church's way forward into the third millennium is toward Christ, the redeemer of the human race, and that proper human dominion over the earth—as a noble master, not as a heedless exploiter or slave to economic production and consumption—is essential to the dignity of the human person in Christ, Pope John Paul II says that redemption in Christ restores the world's original link to God and thus restores human dignity, value, and true dominion over the world. The church, as the guardian of the truth of humanity's eternal destiny, is concerned with both temporal and eternal human welfare in the face of pollution, war, the nuclear threat, materialism, political and economic oppression, atheism, and moral decay. Its service to humanity is to uphold the values of peace, solidarity, human rights, religious freedom, and a truly human economic order, as well as to administer the sacraments and firmly maintain divine truth.

453 Johnston, Carol. "Creation Will Be Set Free (Rom. 8:18): A Service of Repentance and Renewal for Creation." *Church and Society* 80 (March/April 1990): 104-8.

This service of repentance and renewal for creation is based on Romans 8:18, and incorporates excerpts from the report of the Eco-Justice Task Force of the Presbyterian Church (USA).

454 Joranson, Philip N., and Ken Butigan, eds. *Cry of the Environment: Rebuilding the Christian Creation Tradition.* Santa Fe, NM: Bear and Co., 1984.

This book focuses on the attempt to retrieve the biblical vision of creation, which the authors feel has been poorly grasped by the Western theological tradition. Essays deal with problems and resources of the 'Judeo-Christian' tradition; resources from the natural sciences, art, theology, and ethics; and practical expressions of creation consciousness in spirituality, worship, lifestyle, social policy, and education (four existing educational programs are described). Senior editor Philip Joranson is director of the Project on the Environment and the Christian Creation Tradition of the Center for Ethics and Social Policy at the Graduate Theological Union in Berkeley, California, which produced this book. He also chaired the pioneering Faith-Man-Nature Group in the late 60s-early 70s. See Fox (009), C. McCoy (120), M. C. McCoy (240), Miller (200), Peters (205), Stewart (021), and Weigand (025). For a review see Sherwood and Franklin (495).

455 Lechte, Ruth E. "Partnerships for Ecological Wellbeing." *Ecumenical Review* 42 (April 1990): 157-61.

Fiji resident Lechte calls on Christians to work on environmental problems alongside ecologists, ecofeminists, eco- and other economists, Greens, and bioregionalists so as to demonstrate the seriousness of their prayers for creation's sustainability.

456 Linn, Gerhard. "JPIC as a Mission Concern." *Ecumenical Review* 41 (October 1989): 515-21.

Using illustrations from a World Council of Churches' conference on mission and evangelism and from ecumenical team visits to a strip-mining area in the German Democratic Republic, landless farmers in Brazil, and refugee work in Zimbabwe and Swaziland, Linn argues that commitment to the process of Justice, Peace and the Integrity of Creation must be understood as part of the church's evangelism and mission. The church participates in God's mission to bring *shalom* to the world through pastoral care, prophetic challenge, and proclamation of hope in the context of social and global crises. The theme "the Earth is the Lord's" relates to the exploitation of nature, land reform, the pursuit of "national security," and the receiving of immigrants and refugees.

457 Massey, Marshall. "The Defense of the Peaceable Kingdom." Parts 1, 2, 3, 4. *Friends Bulletin* (San Francisco) (March 1984): 99-104; (April 1984): 115-22; (May 1984): 131-37; (June 1984): 147-56.

Addressed to the Religious Society of Friends, this series examines the power of the "collective dream" to deceive as to the seriousness of the environmental crises; details the serious disruptions of ecologic cycles that avoidable mismanagement have brought about; and proposes that the Religious Society of Friends take up the cause of the environment, not as individuals but as a group, contributing to the environmental movement their commitment to Christ's nonviolent transcendental politics. Massey believes that four teachings of Christ—the nurturing of the helpless, respect for the inter-relatedness of life, stewardship, and the cultivation of sanity—are crucial to environmentalism. He sees as counterforces to the spiritual blindness manifested in economics and ego the "three voices of God" manifested in the NIMBY ("Not In My Back Yard") syndrome, in stewardship, and in altruism.

458 McDonagh, Sean. *To Care for the Earth: A Call to a New Theology.* London: Geoffrey Chapman; Santa Fe, NM: Bear and Co., 1986.

McDonagh draws on his work as missionary to the T'boli tribes of the Philippines in this work which argues that Christians must take a more holistic approach to life and respond to the environmental destruction of life's nourishing systems. Christians need be sensitive to the fact that secularized versions of their millenial and redemption myths underlie the destructive drives of capitalism and Marxism. Humanity needs a new story, such as that presented by Teilhard de Chardin, that celebrates the evolutionary path and the spirit within all matter, beings, and cultures. The new story must include new liturgies, and McDonagh gives examples of celebrations developed among the T'boli. The sacraments also afford possibilities for ecological catechesis. Moreover, if the bond between reality and what it symbolizes is broken, symbolic possibilities are destroyed. It was, McDonagh says, in the context of famine that he understood "the eucharistic dimension" of land degradation. Christians should dialogue with other religions; missionaries and liberation theology groups should widen their vision to include a concern for Earth; and religious leaders everywhere need to respond to the moral code called for in the United Nations' *World Charter for Nature*.

459 Moltmann, Jürgen. "The Scope of Renewal in the Spirit." *Ecumenical Review* 42 (April 1990): 98-106.

Calling the theme of the Seventh Assembly of the World Council of Churches—"Come, Holy Spirit—Renew the Whole Creation"—a "mortal cry of dying creatures" and a prayer for life and freedom, Moltmann argues that creation cries out for liberation from both human injustice and the dominion of time and death, and that both of these liberations are expected with the coming of the Holy Spirit. He says that Christians need to recover a trinitarian concept of creation as not only the work of God's hands but the presence of God and God's temple-to-be. Consequences of this belief are that the adoration of God includes all things in the cosmos; that the church is not limited to human beings; that the "ecological crisis" is the crisis of the church itself; that the church must protest the suffering of weaker creatures; and that all noncorrectible assaults on the environment are sacrileges. During the fragile state of creation between its origin and its perfection a community of suffering exists among human beings and other creatures, and redemption is to be found "only in the common hope of reconciliation and the renewed creation of all things."

460 Morikawa, Jitsuo. "Evangelistic Life Style in an Eco-Just Universe." *Foundations* 18 (July/September 1975): 272-81.

Morikawa describes "Evangelistic Life Style," the denomination-wide emphasis of the American Baptist churches for 1974-76, as a lifestyle of wholeness and integrity that keeps together personal welfare and planetary survival and is empowered to change the present by hope for God's redemption of nature and history. It affirms interdependence, equitable stewardship, respect for diversity and individuality, and the need to convert communities and institutions as well as persons. It unites preaching and service, novelty and continuity, and the common calling and diverse functions of the people of God.

461 Morton, James Parks. "Environment and Religion: The Evolution of a New Vision." In *Earth and Spirit: The Spiritual Dimension of the Environmental Crisis*, edited by Fritz Hull, 119-32. New York: Continuum Publishing Co., 1993.

Morton recounts the pioneering role played by the Cathedral of St. John the Divine in New York City in response to "the sacred interrelatedness of all things" embodied in the image of earth from space. Activities of the Cathedral in the '70s included a restructuring of the seasons of the church so as to focus on the suffering and incarnation of earth, a Sun Day celebration, and a pulpit address by James Lovelock during which he unveiled his Gaia hypothesis. Since 1985, the Cathedral has held a celebration in the name of St. Francis which includes an Earth Mass written by Paul Winter that concludes with a procession and blessing of animals. In the '80s the Cathedral was instrumental in linking environmental and ecological concerns to issues of social justice. It played a role in the formation of the Joint Appeal in Religion and Science and in bringing the environmental challenge into the political arena.

462 Mpanya, Mutombo. "The Environmental Impacts of a Church Project: A Zairian Village Case Study." In *Missionary Earthkeeping*, edited by Calvin B. DeWitt and Ghillean T. Prance, 91-109. Macon, GA: Mercer University Press, 1992.

The Bwaka Mulumba village and the Kalonda mission station in Zaire are examined to show that church projects can cause severe environmental degradation. Whereas traditional subsistence methods had incorporated conservation practices, the mission made great demands on land and forests, undermined the local economy, and displaced traditional religious beliefs that protected the environment. Mpanya proposes guidelines to better relate church projects to their local environments.

463 Pitcher, Alvin. *Listen to the Crying of the Earth: Cultivating Creation Communities*. Cleveland: Pilgrim Press, 1993.

Convinced that "the Word of God cannot be heard unless we listen to what God is saying through the creation," Pitcher begins by "listening" to Earth's current ecological crisis, including global warming, ozone depletion, loss of water quality, the population explosion, soil, forest, and species depletion, and the spread of destructive technologies and economic injustices to developing nations. By examining economic, educational, and political theories and systems, he locates, in repeated failures to emphasize the connectedness of all things, the reasons why our social institutions have failed to respond to the crisis. Connectedness is also all-important as Pitcher turns to theological foundations for a more adequate response. Predicating his arguments on various biblical and theological perspectives, including liberation and Black liberation theologies, he insists on listening to the "groaning of the oppressed reality." He finds it impossible to be Christian in the modern world without radical personal change, and believes we are called to build new creation communities in which we recognize the interdependence of all humanity with each other, the earth, and the divine in a "holy triangle."

464 Prance, Ghillean T. "The Ecological Awareness of the Amazonian Indians." In *Missionary Earthkeeping*, edited by Calvin B. DeWitt and Ghillean T. Prance, 45-61. Macon, GA: Mercer University Press, 1992.

Drawing on his experiences while exploring the Brazilian Amazon, Prance, director of the Royal Botanical Gardens at Kew, gives specific examples of Amazonian Indians' knowledge and utilization of the local ecology, and of the disruption of ecologically sound practices by well-meaning but uninformed mission work. He argues that missionaries working with native peoples must appreciate indigenous ecological knowledge and practices as well as the Bible's teachings on respect for creation in order to establish a more permanent and ecologically sound Christian faith.

465 Presbyterian Church (USA). *Restoring Creation for Ecology and Justice: A Report Adopted by the 202nd General Assembly (1990) Presbyterian Church (U.S.A.).* Louisville, KY: Office of the General Assembly, Presbyterian Church (U.S.A.), 1990.

This major report draws on preparatory material in *Keeping and Healing the Creation* (466) and "Evangelicals and the Environment" (502). Defining the eco-justice crisis as the result of "tilling without keeping"—drawing sustenance from nature without maintaining its integrity—the report summarizes that crisis (adding population to the list). The theological response focuses on God's judgment on Western culture's failure to justly distribute the fruits of technology or to respect creation, on its materialism and anthropocentrism. The report affirms that nature, too, is an object of God's redemptive work, and that we must include nature as "co-victim with the poor" in our understanding of justice. The content of faithfulness—love and justice—is specified for our time by the norms of sustainability, participation, sufficiency, and solidarity. Social policies are recommended regarding agriculture, water, wildlife, waste, and atmospheric change. Commitment to eco-justice by the Presbyterian Church (USA) is given institutional form both by a new office or program group for eco-justice and by an "infusion" of existing programs throughout the church. Appendices include a history of the task force, a study guide, and an interpretive summary of the report.

466 Presbyterian Eco-Justice Task Force. *Keeping and Healing the Creation.* Louisville, KY: Committee on Social Witness Policy, Presbyterian Church (U.S.A.), 1989.

This resource paper, authored principally by William E. Gibson, is intended for use by church groups and includes a study plan. It surveys the various dimensions of the environmental problem and the realities of "eco-*in*justice," emphasizing their interconnections. Eco-justice is explained as a linkage of the plight of the vulnerable nonhuman world with the plight of poor and vulnerable persons, both subject to the forces of mistaken ideas, greed, violence, and carelessness. The eco-justice crisis is seen as requiring and eliciting fresh theological reflection, but primarily emphasized are the answers to be found in Scripture and the scriptural underpinnings of those responses deemed most necessary for positive change.

467 Przewozny, Bernard. "Integrity of Creation: A Missionary Imperative."
SEDOS Bulletin 11 (15 December 1988): 363-74.

Przewozny outlines a Catholic perspective on environmental problems in terms of
regional and global issues, biological diversity, economics, development and
underdevelopment, morality and culture, giving special attention to the issue of
demographic expansion. Missionaries with their ability to build and conduct
educational, medical, and cultural facilities in Third World countries have a role
to play in creating a new model of development, progress, and human solidarity
in keeping with Christian concern for the environment.

468 Reilly, William K. "Theology and Ecology: A Confluence of Interests." *New
Theology Review* 4 (May 1991): 15-25.

Writing as administrator of the United States Environmental Protection Agency,
Reilly urges "the joining of environmentalists and the faithful in the common
cause of responsible stewardship of creation." He lists the achievements of
environmentalists in reconciling humanity with the natural systems on which it
depends and says that these achievements are not enough. He wishes to see the
church vigorously promote sustainable development, raise questions of fairness
and equity in such areas as the dumping of hazardous and solid waste across
international borders, and come to grips with the problem of population growth in
the developing world. He also sees a role for the church in teaching the sanctity
of creation.

469 Snyder, Howard A. *A Kingdom Manifesto: Calling the Church to Live under
God's Reign.* Downers Grove, IL: InterVarsity Press, 1985.

Writing as one committed to evangelism and lacing his arguments with scriptural
references, Snyder pursues the idea of the Kingdom of God as an ecological concept that includes "the proper functioning of all elements in the environment, and
a God who "intends to redeem women and men *with* their environment, not out
of it." He understands both the Old and New Testaments to include the whole
Earth in the Kingdom of God, and to have justice for the poor as basic to the
Kingdom. Thus, the church betrays the Kingdom of God when it spoils the natural environment and when, instead of working toward reconciliation between
humanity and nature, it consumes a disproportionate share of the world's
resources. Thus also, conflict between evangelism and social action is "clearly
absurd." Snyder believes that commitment to economic justice includes working
for structural change.

470 Snyder, Howard A. *Liberating the Church: The Ecology of Church and Kingdom.* Downers Grove, IL: InterVarsity Press, 1983.

This book offers a comprehensive ecclesiology for eco-justice from an evangelical
perspective. Snyder argues that the church needs to be liberated from the self-
aggrandizing, self-protective institution it has become in affluent North America
so that it can become a liberating agent for the Kingdom of God. The purpose of
the church is to carry out God's "economy" or plan to redeem the world.
Christians are stewards, managing and upbuilding God's house—the world and
the church. Thus, both social justice and environmental responsibility are matters
of spiritual concern, and both are rooted in the idea of "economy" as the management of the household. Snyder proposes a model for the church having a social
and spiritual, as well as a physical, ecology. Problems arise when the structure
of the church fails to serve, balance, and integrate the central functions of worship, community, and witness. This ecological understanding of the church

includes seeing the church as a present sacrament of the Kingdom in the world, as a countercultural alternative community, as a servant following the example of Jesus, and as a disciple-making witness to the priorities of the Kingdom in all areas of life and society.

471 Van Dyke, Fred. "Ethics and Management on U.S. Public Lands: Connections, Conflicts, and Crises." *Evangelical Review of Theology* 17 (April 1993): 241-56.

Van Dyke argues that recent scandals in the United States Forest Service and National Park Service, revealing the political manipulation of those agencies to serve economic interests, show the need not only for reforms in law and management practices, but also for a public resource management ethic based on biblical values. The church must promote such an ethic by corporate participation in environmental policy decision-making and by developing programs in Christian colleges to train environmental professionals who will put a biblical stewardship ethic into practice.

472 Willis, E. David. "Proclaiming Liberation for the Earth's Sake." In *For Creation's Sake: Preaching, Ecology, and Justice*, edited by Dieter T. Hessel, 55-70. Philadelphia: Geneva Press, 1985.

Willis presents an eco-justice understanding of 'word' and 'sacrament'. God's liberating Word, "humanly speaking" in preaching, constitutes, corrects, and empowers the church as a community which participates in God's liberating activity in the world. The assurance of the forgiveness of sins frees oppressor and oppressed *from* the bondage of their former selves and *for* the freedom of their future selves. The liberating word also addresses the oppression of the earth, and calls us to see the earth as the equal subject of God's love, as a co-creature with whom we are bound in mutual dependence and caring. The Eucharist, also, confirms our solidarity with all creation.

In addition to the works annotated in this chapter, readers interested in church and mission may wish to consult the following entries located elsewhere in the bibliography: 010, 011, 016, 019, 041, 069, 116, 161, 185, 283, 315, 347, 376, 379, 479.

11

Institutional Forums and Organizations

The Christian eco-justice discussion has evolved through several ecumenical, denominational, and other structures: the Faith-Man-Nature group, the United Nations, the World Council of Churches, the National Council of Churches, the Board of National Ministries for the American Baptist Churches, and others. This section includes historical reviews of many of these conversations, and analyses and reports of a number of important conferences that have been held along the way.

473 Barbour, Ian. "Justice, Participation, and Sustainability at MIT." *Ecumenical Review* 31 (1979): 380-87.

> Barbour reviews discussions at the World Council of Churches conference, "Faith, Science, and the Future," on the social context of science, the relation of humanity to non-human nature, problems of developing nations, the norms of justice, participation, and sustainability (noting the much lower priority given to sustainability), and the convergence of these themes in the conference discussions on energy.

474 Best, Thomas F., and Wesley Granberg-Michaelson, eds. *Costly Unity: Koinonia and Justice, Peace, and Creation: Presentations and Reports from the World Council of Churches' Consultation in Rønde, Denmark, February 1993.* Geneva: World Council of Churches, 1993.

> This conference addressed the persistent tension in the ecumenical movement between the quest for the visible unity of the church (represented by the Faith and Order movement, now under Unit 1 of the Word Council of Churches [WCC]) and the pursuit of coordinated church action against injustice and threats to peace and creation (represented by JPIC, now carried out by Unit 3 of the WCC). While the presentations focus on the relation between ethical action and the faith and mission of the church more than on the relationship between justice and the environment, they include critiques of the Justice, Peace and the Integrity of Creation (JPIC) process and proposals that may affect future discussions of eco-justice in the WCC. Particularly challenging is Lukas Vischer, who, in "Koinonia in a Time of Threats to Life," argues that the optimistic, activist approach of the JPIC process reveals that it has not taken seriously enough the magnitude of the ecological and other threats to life, the ambiguity of the church, and the eschatological implications of the radically hidden and uncertain character of the future.

475　Coste, René.　"The Ecumenical Dynamic of 'Justice, Peace, and the Safeguarding of Creation.'"　Translated by John Bowden.　*Concilium* 4 (August 1991): 19-31.

> A Roman Catholic perspective on the European Ecumenical Assembly, "Peace and Justice for the Whole Creation," at Basel, Switzerland in 1989 and the World Council of Churches' convocation on Justice, Peace, and the Integrity of Creation (JPIC) at Seoul, South Korea in 1990.　Coste terms Basel a "splendid ecumenical experience" and notes the final document's stress on the interconnectedness of JPIC and its connection to the proclamation of the gospel.　Critical of Seoul for not deepening the analysis of social realities or theological reflection, he nonetheless values its global character and the powerful testimonies to suffering given there.

476　Engel, J. Ronald.　"Ethics."　In *The Future of the Environment: The Social Dimensions of Conservation and Ecological Alternatives*, edited by David C. Pitt, 23-45.　London and New York: Routledge, 1988.

> In a paper delivered at the Assembly of the World Conservation Union (IUCN), Madrid, 1984, Engel outlines steps being taken by the historic traditions (the religious faiths and the secular philosophies of liberal humanism and Marxism) in response to the environmental challenge.　These are: a recognition by the historic traditions of their responsibility for the environmental crisis and for environmental ethics; critical reconstruction of environmental ethics within each tradition; a consensus on eco-justice; and a readiness to expand the multi-faith dialogue on human rights to include environmental values.　Engel sees as responsible for the emerging consensus on eco-justice: the retrieval within ethics and the faith traditions of democratic and egalitarian strains and the recovery of holistic elements such as the covenantal tradition; the growing recognition that the environmental situation involves a permanent structuring of the future; analyses that point to a common origin of social and environmental oppression; and the shift away from the Western industrial paradigm of competition and individualism to a model based on interrelatedness.　He emphasizes that, while there is no evidence that this paradigm shift, or any of the steps, are wide-spread, the steps together constitute hope for more attention to ethical attitudes toward the environment in global forums.　On this basis, Engel argues that the formation of an Environmental Ethics Task Force within IUCN could contribute substantially to the implementation of the goals of the World Conservation Strategy and other international conservation initiatives.　This proposal eventuated in the founding of the IUCN Ethics Working Group which Engel chairs.

477　Faramelli, Norman J.　"Religious Reconstruction for the Environmental Future: The Great Needs and Issues As I Saw Them at the Stockholm Meetings in June."　In *Religious Reconstruction for the Environmental Future*, edited by Philip N. Joranson and C. Alan Anderson, Fa 1-Fa 29.　South Coventry, CT: The Faith-Man-Nature Group, 1973.

> In this paper addressed to the Faith-Man-Nature workshop participants and delivered several months after the United Nations Conference on the Human Environment held in Stockholm in June of 1972, Faramelli discusses candidly his perceptions of the Stockholm event.　While convinced of the seriousness of the environmental crisis, he is critical of the lack of political understanding expressed by many Western environmentalists, particularly their idea that the United Nations should eschew politics in an endeavor to save the environment; their lack of understanding of the perceived entanglement of population control and power alignments such that no program designed by the affluent can be successfully superimposed on the non-affluent; and their glib talk of redistribution and attention to ecological matters while their governments consistently vote in opposition

to these. Faramelli's remarks touch on the public stance of Barry Commoner against and Paul Ehrlich for population control, of Edward Goldsmith speaking for *Blueprint for Survival* and of the Third World's perception of *Limits to Growth*. Faramelli cautions that environmental quality must not be achieved at the expense of oppressed peoples, and that the *kind* of economic growth is more the issue than growth or no-growth. He sees religious views or fundamental values at the heart of the ecological crisis, and he enumerates the tasks of religious institutions: to understand the structural dynamics of pollution and poverty and build alternative visions of just global development, economic equality, and environmental quality.

478 Geyer, Alan F. "The EST Complex at MIT: The Ecumenical-Scientific-Technological Complex." *Ecumenical Review* 31 (1979): 380-87.

While praising the World Council of Churches' conference on "Faith, Science and the Future" as an ecumenical landmark with quality presentations, Geyer criticizes it for problems of process, participation, and make-up which prevented its making significant progress in ecumenical theology or social ethics. He pays particular attention to the discussion and reports on technology and economic justice, nuclear energy, and disarmament and militarism.

479 Gosling, David. *A New Earth: Covenanting for Justice, Peace, and the Integrity of Creation.* London: CCBI, 1992.

This multi-dimensional reflection on the response of ecumenical bodies to environmental degradation is written by the former director of the Church and Society sub-unit of the World Council of Churches, a leader in the unfolding of the JPIC (Justice, Peace, and the Integrity of Creation) process of which he writes. The book focuses on ways in which environmental degradation has developed "hand in hand" with injustice directed against particular vulnerable groups. Its treatment of justice is founded on a concern for the structural problems underlying environmental problems. For example, Gosling sees the Bhopal disaster as ultimately caused by the need for developing countries to repay international debt by producing pesticide-dependent cash crops. These themes are developed through specific examples drawn from personal acquaintance with the international history of church response to environmental problems drawn from Africa, Latin America, and Southeast Asia but also including the Western world. Gosling sees JPIC as representing a rejection of the idea of global society in favor of regional associations. In his discussion of the theological aspects of JPIC Gosling stresses the need to restructure "our entire framework of thought so that creation becomes foundational."

480 Granberg-Michaelson, Wesley. "Creation in Ecumenical Theology." In *Ecotheology: Voices from South and North*, edited by David G. Hallman, 96-106. Geneva: WCC Publications; Maryknoll, NY: Orbis Books, 1994.

The author reviews the ecumenical discussion of issues of creation/nature within the World Council of Churches from affirmations of secularization and dominion over nature in the 1960's to the issuing of a major study paper on global warming in early 1994. Granberg-Michaelson lists as points in an evolving consensus: addressing of threats to creation by churches in the South as well as the North; acceptance of the interdependence of ecology and economics, of protecting creation and justice; attention to the relationship of gospel and culture; centralizing of the theme of the relationship of Spirit and creation; and the search for new models of inter-relationship to replace the paradigm of mastery over Earth. Remaining open questions involve the place of humanity within creation; the sacredness of creation; the effect of sin on creation; God's transcendence; place versus time as central to theology; and ecological theology as a new paradigm for ecumenical theology.

481 Granberg-Michaelson, Wesley. "An Ethics for Sustainability." *Ecumenical Review* 43 (January 1991): 120-30.

Granberg-Michaelson describes the upcoming Canberra assembly as confronted by a world in which both capitalist and Marxist systems have been shown incapable of furthering justice and ecological sustainability. The search for new socio-economic and political models has precedents in the World Council of Churches' themes of "the responsible society" and "the just, sustainable, and participatory society (JPSS)" The Justice, Peace and Integrity of Creation (JPIC) program, however, has neglected questions of political and economic structures and failed to make progress in integrating environmental, justice, and other concerns. He points to ways in which Canberra can recover and advance the unfinished agendas of JPSS and JPIC.

482 Granberg-Michaelson, Wesley. "Preserving the Earth." *One World* (November 1989): 11-15.

In this helpful, nontechnical survey of the state of the ecumenical discussion at the end of the '80s, Granberg-Michaelson describes the rise in practical and theological concern for ecological issues in the World Council of Churches and by churches worldwide. He notes arguments for the priority of "integrity of creation" as an integrating concept for concerns centering on justice, peace, and the environment; environmental groups' increased attention to religion; continuing mistrust of environmentalism by justice advocates; and controversies over creation-centered spirituality and animal protection.

483 Hulley, L. D. "Justice, Peace, and the Integrity of Creation: Some Ethical Comments." *Missionalia* 19 (August 1991): 131-43.

The author, theological ethicist at the University of South Africa in Pretoria, looks at the *Act of Covenanting* approved by the participants to the 1990 Seoul World Convocation on Justice, Peace, and the Integrity of Creation (JPIC), finding it to be too global, abstract, and requiring of superhuman capacities to empower individual action. As a corrective, Hulley states his intention to discuss JPIC in terms of concrete issues faced by South Africans, but the article tends to be instead a thoughtful analysis of the terminology of the Seoul document. Hulley sees justice as a matter of human dignity and human rights rather than, as the document has it, a matter of economics; he discusses justice in terms of the history of rights and privileges withheld from Blacks in South Africa. The Seoul view of peace he finds too linked to doctrines of deterrence and national security and not enough to the concept of *shalom* defined as "peace between us and our God, us and our neighbors and also between us and our environment." Creation as set out in the Seoul commitments implies a system functioning independently of humans with which humans should cooperate, a view in which the environment and the poor humans in it are objectified—rather than what Hulley sees as more accurate—an interdependent web of relationships of which humans are a part.

484 "JPIC." [Reports on the World Convocation on Justice, Peace, and the Integrity of Creation Convocation, Seoul, Korea 5-12 March 1990.] *Christian Conference of Asia News* 25 (March 1990): 14-23.

This series of short news reports on aspects of the convocation, provide almost a day-by-day synopsis of major addresses (especially the keynote address by Frank Chikane, General Secretary of the South African Council of Churches), press conferences, worship, working group and plenary criticisms and revisions of the preparatory document, panel discussions, and special hearings. Noted are the linkages made between justice, peace, and the integrity of creation; the disagreements over priorities; and differences in perspective.

485 Kemppi-Repo, Eeva. "On the Way to Seoul." *One World* 152 (January/February 1990): 14-16.

This overview of the second draft document prepared for the World Convocation for Justice, Peace and the Integrity of Creation in Seoul summarizes the document's presentation of the issues and their interconnectedness, the idea of "covenant," and the terms of the proposed acts of covenanting for a just economic order, demilitarization, and preservation of the atmosphere. A sidebar gives the chronology of the JPIC process.

486 Kinnamon, Michael, ed. *Signs of the Spirit: Official Report; Seventh Assembly; Canberra, Australia, 7-20 February 1991*. Geneva: WCC Publications; Grand Rapids, MI: William B. Eerdmans Publishing Co., 1991.

This report shows how, in spite of the assembly's preoccupation with theological pluralism and the "inculturation" of the Gospel, the Persian Gulf conflict, Aboriginal rights, and internal problems of participatory process, the Justice, Peace and the Integrity of Creation process had begun to have a pervasive influence on theological and ethical thinking in the World Council of Churches (WCC). Environmental concerns crop up in almost all sections of the report—the assembly Message; the keynote addresses (074); reports on the sub-themes and the work of the WCC; the assembly Report; and statements on the Gulf War, indigenous peoples and land rights, and the Pacific. However, they appear alongside justice and peace concerns more often than integrated with them (and "justice and peace" often appears by itself as an encapsulation of the range of Christian social concerns). As with the Kuala Lumpur consultation (511) and the *Resources for Sections* (512), the strongest statements of the essential interconnectedness of justice and ecology are found under the sub-theme of "Giver of Life—Sustain Your Creation." The sub-theme "Spirit of Truth—Set Us Free" does note that current patterns of economic growth and world trade act against justice and sustainability alike, and the statement on the Pacific addresses regional eco-justice issues of nuclear testing, waste disposal, tourism, overfishing, and the threat of global warming.

487 Lindqvist, Martti. *Economic Growth and the Quality of Life: An Analysis of the Debate within the World Council of Churches 1966-1974*. Annals of the Finnish Society for Missiology and Ecumenics 27. Helsinki, 1975.

This study provides important background for works emerging from the World Council of Churches' (WCC) discussion, and should prove helpful for understanding and guiding other eco-justice dialogues and debates. Lindqvist analyzes the WCC debate to bring out the implicit models and to show how these models are conditioned by wider secular and theological discussions. Comparing the two basic models for relating economic growth and justice—sustainable society and self-reliant development—he finds both concerned with justice and survival but differing in structure, time- and space-frames, and geopolitical and disciplinary background. He describes three major theological approaches to human beings and nature—Western theology of history (which is predominant); process theology; and Orthodox theology. Two fundamental understandings of the relation of Christian ethics to social policy are found in the 'quality of life' debate, the one stressing the distinctiveness of Christian ideals, the other stressing Christian participation in the general social discussion of indicators of quality of life. Lindqvist identifies parallels and affinities between models in different problem areas and between groups of models and the "ethics of inspiration" or "ethics of ends." He concludes that the ecumenical discussion largely follows the secular discussion, and that the study raises central problems of concept formation and method.   ____

488 McPherson, James. "Ecumenical Discussion of the Environment, 1966-1987." *Modern Theology* 7 (July 1991): 363-71.

McPherson describes three theological perspectives on environmental issues that have emerged in the World Council of Churches' Church and Society Program. The "emancipatory theology of history," of which Derr (174) is representative, was supplanted by the "theology of hope," as set forth, for example, in Gilkey (092) and Liedke (050) around 1973. McPherson focuses on the 1987 Amsterdam consultation on "the integrity of creation," arguing that Douglas John Hall's "ontological theology of sustainability" is superior to an eschatological approach like that of A. Schloz because the latter cannot provide clear ethical guidance for an environmental ethic that must deal with the given laws and structure of the world. See Schulze (150). Compare with Lindqvist (487).

489 Morikawa, Jitsuo. "Theological Meaning of Eco-justice through Institutional Change." *Foundations* 17 (April/June 1974): 100-105.

The decision by the Board and Staff of National Ministries of the American Baptist Churches in the USA to engage in ministries to assure justice for all in an ecological context is discussed by Morikawa with a focus on the theological meaning and justification of undertaking such a task through structural change and the promotion of institutional accountability.

490 Niles, D. Preman. "Covenanting for Justice, Peace, and the Integrity of Creation: An Ecumenical Survey." *The Ecumenical Review* 39 (1987): 470-84.

Niles analyzes the few occurrences of "covenant" in ecumenical documents of 1948-1976, as well as the use of the related term "fellowship" to set the context for the 1983 World Council of Churches' Vancouver Assembly's call for "a conciliar process of mutual commitment (covenant) to justice, peace, and the integrity of creation" (JPIC). He relates the unity of JPIC to the unity of the church, as groups with different contexts and entry points are drawn together to join a common struggle and contribute to one confession, that of "faith in Jesus Christ as the Life of the World."

491 [Niles, D. Preman]. "Justice, Peace and the Integrity of Creation . . . Some Theological Perspectives." *One World* (1989): 8-9.

These extracts, from a presentation by Niles, World Council of Churches' staff member responsible for Justice, Peace and the Integrity of Creation (JPIC), to a group preparing an outline of a draft document for the Seoul Convocation, focus on questions of theological method and pluralism; the church's need to repent even as it condemns militarism, oppression, and ecological degradation; and the eschatological issues relating JPIC to the vision of the Kingdom and the elements of JPIC to each other.

492 Niles, D. Preman. *Resisting the Threats to Life*. Risk Book Series. Geneva: WCC Publications, 1989.

This book attempts to explain the World Council of Churches' program on Justice, Peace, and the Integrity of Creation (JPIC) in terms of Christian resistance to the threats to life (e.g. racism, sexism, economic exploitation, militarism, environmental deterioration). It includes information on the history and philosophy of the JPIC process, as well as stories of people involved in JPIC issues around the world. Niles characterizes JPIC as participation in the compassion of God as manifested in Jesus Christ and the martyrs of the faith. "Resisting the threats to life" begins with hearing the stories of the victims of injustice and violence (of which nature is one) and naming the powers responsible. Christians are to respond by confessing their faith, calling for repentance and proclaiming the Kingdom of God, working to unblock the future for those to whom it remains closed, and celebrating hope in the Kingdom as an alternative reality operative in the world. Niles recounts the history of the JPIC process and discusses the theological issues involved in formulating a basis for an integrated and unified response to issues of JPIC, and concludes by describing an act of covenanting to express Christians' common commitment to JPIC.

493 Niles, D. Preman, ed. *Between the Flood and the Rainbow: Interpreting the Conciliar Process of Mutual Commitment (Covenant) to Justice, Peace, and the Integrity of Creation*. Geneva: WCC Publications, 1992.

Viewpoints on the process, accomplishments, and failures of the World Council of Churches' "Justice, Peace and the Integrity of Creation" (JPIC) program, written by persons involved in the program and compiled by former director Niles. The authors' candid reflections embrace not only the impediments to ecumenical dialogue brought about by divisions existing between North and South, men and women, Protestants and Roman Catholics, but also the problems attendant to ecumenical endeavors in general—problems of definition, methodology, participation, status, trust, and the handling of conflict. A time line of key events in the JPIC process provides the reader with necessary background for the essays. The appendix includes the Final Document of the world convocation.

494 Santmire, H. Paul. "The Struggle for an Ecological Theology: A Case in Point." *Christian Century* 87 (4 March 1970): 275-77.

In a report on a 1969 conference of theologians, scientists, church leaders, and conservationists sponsored by the Faith-Man-Nature group, Santmire finds that, in contrast to the group's 1967 conference (published as *Christians and the Good Earth*), this meeting attended to the relationship between environment and social justice, was oriented toward a "theology of human responsibility" rather than a "theology of nature," and was more concerned with taking action. While the conference issued a statement urging action on population, pollution, and conservation, the participants were less clear on taking political action themselves.

495 Sherwood, Diane E., and Kristin Franklin. "Ecology and the Church: Theology and Action." *Christian Century* 104 (13 May 1987): 472-74.

The authors review attempts—such as *Cry of the Environment*, edited by Philip N. Joranson and Ken Butigan (054), Matthew Fox's *Original Blessing* (088), and Marshall Massey's "Defense of the Peaceable Kingdom" (457)—to provide a theological basis for the church's environmental concern. They note institutional forms developed within several religious bodies and ecumenical groups, including the Eco-Justice Working Group of the National Council of Churches, the United Methodist Church, the Catholic Campaign for Human Development, the World Jewish Congress, the Eleventh Commandment Fellowship, and the North American Conference on Christianity and Ecology.

496 Shinn, Roger L. "Eco-Justice Themes in Christian Ethics Since the 1960s." In *For Creation's Sake: Preaching, Ecology, and Justice*, edited by Dieter Hessel, 96-114. Philadelphia: Geneva Press, 1985.

Shinn argues that Greek and Roman culture and secular scientific and economic thought are more responsible for ecological problems than is the biblical tradition. He recounts the history of ecumenical discussions relating to economic development and the emergence of ecological concern and attempts by the churches to hold ecological and social concerns together. He sees a need for change in lifestyles and institutional structures and for preaching to recover traditional themes of creatureliness, stewardship, and dominion.

497 Shinn, Roger L. and Paul Abrecht, eds. *Faith and Science in an Unjust World: Report of the World Council of Churches' Conference on Faith, Science, and the Future*. Massachusetts Institute of Technology, Cambridge USA, 12-24 July 1979. 2 Vols. Geneva: World Council of Churches, 1980.

Volume I: *Plenary Presentations*, is edited by Roger L. Shinn. Shinn's introduction provides an overview of the conference—its goals, topics, problems, and achievements, as well as the process leading up to it. See Birch (262), Daly (341), Kurien (358), Liedke (050), and Ruether (269).

Volume II: *Reports and Recommendations*, is edited by Paul Abrecht. Abrecht's introduction provides another perspective on the planning and results of the conference. See section reports (061), (378), and (328).

498 Shoemaker, Dennis E. "Loving People, Loving Earth." *Christianity and Crisis* 47 (3 August 1987): 260-63.

Shoemaker recounts experiences showing the difficulty of keeping economic justice and environmental concerns together. He reports on an Eco-Justice Consultation at Stony Point, New York in 1986, at which poverty-level victims of environmental disasters did begin to make the necessary connections. He also notes how difficult it is for the more affluent to work to resolve, rather than to escape, such problems, and identifies the issue of eco-justice as "intensely theological."

499 Sider, Ronald J. "Justice, Peace, and the Integrity of Creation." *World Christian* (May 1990): 27-30.

Sider provides an evangelical perspective on the Seoul Convocation. He applauds the World Council of Churches' (WCC) focus on justice, peace, ecology, and interfaith dialogue while expressing concern that its witness could be marginalized by neglect of conservative economic views, disinterest in theology, and reluctance to affirm the centrality of Jesus Christ and the special status of humans. He proposes a coalition between evangelicals, confessional churches, and Eastern Orthodox Christians to help make the WCC's social action more effective by rooting it in solid biblical foundations. A slightly longer version appeared as "Reflections on Justice, Peace and the Integrity of Creation" in *Transformation* 7 (July/September 1990): 15-17.

500 Simonson, Conrad. *The Christology of the Faith and Order Movement.* Oekumenische Studien, no. 10. Leiden: E. J. Brill, 1972.

Simonson studies the progress of Christology in the Faith and Order Movement/Commission from 1910 to 1968, concluding that during this period: the arena of Faith and Order Christological discussions expanded enormously; the dynamic underlying this expansion was the search for an adequate anthropology, and the chief motif of this anthropological search has been the articulation of human beings' engagement with their social and natural world. He affirms that anthropology (and hence Christology) must be adequate to the cosmic scope of human experience and involvements in nature and history. Although this work does not deal directly with eco-justice, it provides helpful historical background for those works on this bibliography which have emerged in part from the ecumenical discussion.

501 Skoglund, John E., ed. "Ecology and Justice." Special issue. *Foundations* 17 (April/June 1974): 99-172.

The Board of National Ministries of the American Baptist Churches adopted "eco-justice" as the guiding concept for understanding and doing missions in today's world. This issue reproduces some papers which have been used for the series of consultations, workshops, and decision-making sessions in which this concept was explored. See Board of National Ministries of the American Baptist Churches in the USA (165), Faramelli (180), Morikawa (489), and Owens (307).

502 Stivers, Robert L. "Introduction: While the Earth Remains." *Church and Society* 80 (March/April 1990): 1-4.

Stivers introduces a collection of reports and resource papers generated by the Presbyterian Eco-Justice Task Force in the process of developing its 1989 report, *Restoring Creation for Ecology and Justice* (465). He also briefly describes other aspects of the study, including the issuing of *Keeping and Healing the Creation* (466); a theological symposium held in conjunction with the Evangelical Lutheran Church in America (106); and the attempt to encourage local input into the study process. Contents of this issue include Gibson (443), Rolston (424), Rush (313), Liden (413), and Johnston (453).

503 Thomas, J. Mark, ed. "Evangelicals and the Environment: Theological Foundations for Christian Environmental Stewardship." *Evangelical Review of Theology* 17
(April 1993): 115-286.

This special issue consists of papers delivered at an international consultation
sponsored jointly by the Au Sable Institute of Environmental Studies and the
Theological Commission of the World Evangelical Fellowship. Editor J. Mark
Thomas is Senior Research Fellow at the Au Sable Institute. In his guest
editorial, "Evangelicals and Environment in Process," pp. 119-21, Chris Sugden
(Resident Director of the Oxford Centre for Mission Studies) notes increasing
environmental concern among evangelicals, especially in connection with poverty
and missions in the Two-Thirds World.

504 VanElderen, Marlin. "Coverage of World Convocation on Justice, Peace, and
the Integrity of Creation." *One World* (May 1990): 4-21.

This special issue consists of a series of articles reporting on the March 1990
Seoul Convocation. Several describe the controversies over substance and procedural problems involved in discussing, amending, and adopting (and failing to
discuss or adopt) the acts of covenanting, affirmations of faith, and other agenda
items from the convocation. Among the tensions and difficulties were: criticisms
of excessively global, abstract, Western, or theological language; lack of awareness of prior World Council of Churches' discussions of the issues; the sheer
number of particular concerns brought by participants; "editing by plenary"; and
unrealistic expectations for the convocation. Some specifically eco-justice controversies included suspicions that environmental concern was a First-World ploy
to sidestep justice issues; disagreements about the human role in nature and the
scientific status of global warming; and the relatively undeveloped understanding
of "the integrity of creation." Other articles deal with South Korea as both host
country and exemplification of the struggle for Justice, Peace, and the Integrity of
Creation, and with convocation worship. Excerpts from statements by speakers
and participants are given. Also included is a "Meditation" by Kwok Pui-Lan of
Hong Kong drawing parallels between the message of Second Isaiah and the
situation of the Chinese people—their experience of national calamity, their view
of nature, and their hopes for the future.

505 VanElderen, Marlin. "Integrity of Creation." *One World* (May 1988): 11-16.

VanElderen summarizes the presentations and the report of a World Council of
Churches consultation in Gran, Norway which brought together traditional biblical and theological resources and insights from women, scientists and health
professionals, indigenous peoples, and members of various faiths to address the
term 'integrity of creation'. Despite many unresolved differences, there was consensus that creation and the healing of its brokenness is a matter of faith. Presentations by Gro Harlem Brundtland, George Tinker, Stanley Harakas, and comments by other participants are highlighted.

506 VanElderen, Marlin. "Justice, Peace, and the Integrity of Creation." *One World*
(June 1986): 12-16.

This article reports on the World Council of Churches (WCC) Executive Committee's decision to begin a five-year process leading up to a worldwide
ecumenical event at which Christians would make a common commitment to Justice, Peace and the Integrity of Creation. Recounted are how that decision: grew
out of the WCC's 6th Assembly in 1983; expresses emerging ecumenical insight

into the interconnections between injustice, war, and environmental destruction; and involves ongoing WCC programs and efforts toward church unity.

507 Vischer, Lukas. "Giver of Life—Sustain Your Creation!" *Ecumenical Review* 42 (April 1990): 143-49.

A series of insightful questions forms the foundation of this essay which addresses the preparations for the World Council of Churches' Canberra assembly on the theme, "Giver of Life—Sustain Your Creation!" Vischer asks if the assembly is asking for a *deus ex machina* to right humanly caused environmental wrongs; if by speaking of "humankind's guilt" they are obscuring the fact that guilt is greater for rich than for poor; if plans to separate the theme of "creation" from that of "liberation and justice" are not a mistake, since "liberation which does not include respect for God's creation will prove to be an illusion"; if the phrase "wholeness of creation" denies that creation is damaged and must be lived and dealt with in a damaged condition; and if the theme denies the possibility of an end to the created world.

508 World Council of Churches. *Between the Flood and the Rainbow: Covenanting for JPIC: Second Draft Document for the World Convocation on Justice, Peace and the Integrity of Creation, Seoul, Korea, 5-13 March 1990.* Geneva: World Council of Churches, [December 1989].

This document is the work of the preparatory group for the World Convocation on Justice, Peace, and the Integrity of Creation (JPIC) moderated by Marga Bührig. Its preface reviews the JPIC process, the document's development, and its planned role in the Seoul Convocation. Part 1 describes the "three great instabilities" of today: the reign of injustice (poverty, rights-violations, sexism, racism), the reign of violence (war, the nuclear threat, militarization), and the disintegration of creation. Examples of interconnections between them, their common roots in the modern quest for mastery, and the media's role in shaping awareness of them, are highlighted. A faith perspective describes justice, peace, and the integrity of creation as distinct but interrelated ways of referring to the goodness and wholeness of life intended by God—right relationships between God, human beings, and the rest of creation (*shalom*, the Kingdom of God). Christian responsibility is seen through the idea of covenant: God's choosing of humanity as a covenant partner, the failure of the churches as the covenant community to obey God, and God's forgiveness as enabling them to begin again through repentance and renewal. Part 2 lists eight theological affirmations regarding urgent JPIC issues, and part 3 presents the proposed acts of covenanting on a just economic order and foreign debt, demilitarization and nonviolence, and Earth's atmosphere and the greenhouse effect. Appendices, published as a separate document, give background papers for each act of covenanting.

509 World Council of Churches. *Fifth World Conference on Faith and Order.* Faith and Order Paper No. 164. Geneva: WCC Publications, 1993.

While not the main focus of the conference, the "Message," "Reports from Sections 2 and 4," and the "Discussion Paper" all link care of creation and working toward economic justice. The Discussion Paper asks: "What then are the connections between 'economic justice' and 'ecological preservation'?" It mentions the felt need for a Universal Declaration on the Care of the Planet. Section 2 recommends that Faith and Order dialogue with those involved with issues of justice, peace, and the integrity of creation (JPIC).

510   World Council of Churches.   *Now Is the Time: The Final Document and Other Texts from the World Convocation on Justice, Peace, and the Integrity of Creation, Seoul, Republic of Korea, 5-12 March 1990.*   Geneva: World Council of Churches, 1990.

> This booklet contains major documents, excerpts from speakers, and a liturgy from the Seoul Convocation. The introduction notes achievements and shortcomings of the convocation, and the World Council of Churches (WCC) Central Committee's recommendation that commitment to Justice, Peace and the Integrity of Creation (JPIC) continue through and beyond the 1991 Canberra Assembly (the report of Unit 2 of the Central Committee is one of the documents included). The "Final Document: Entering into Covenant Solidarity for Justice, Peace and the Integrity of Creation" parallels the second draft document (485). The "Preamble," not adopted, says little about the current threats (unlike the second draft), but presents a biblical basis for covenanting in a time of crisis (more briefly than the second draft) with reference to anxiety and hope, covenant, discipleship, repentance, conversion, community, and jubilee. Ten theological affirmations (more than in the second draft), giving basic direction for witness and action regarding poverty, racism, environment, land rights, human rights, peace, etc. were debated and passed. The preface and main points, but not the particulars, of the covenants intended to "concretize" these affirmations were passed, and a fourth covenant—on racism and ethnic discrimination—was added to the three proposed in the second draft. The "Message" adopted by the Convocation summarizes the results of the Convocation.

511   World Council of Churches.   "Implications of Sub-Theme I."   [Pre-assembly consultation on sub-theme I, "Giver of Life—Sustain Your Creation!" held in Kuala Lumpur, Malaysia, 12-20 May 1990.]   *The Ecumenical Review* 42 (July/October 1990): 313-28.

> This report urges the 1991 Canberra assembly to welcome the insights of women, the poor, and others in developing a recast theology of creation, and suggests ways of understanding the Holy Spirit's role in creation. It outlines a vision for an ethic for justice and sustainability, and claims that the biblical concept of justice helps us understand the interdependence between poverty, powerlessness, social conflict, and environmental degradation. New understandings of economic value, waste, and development are proposed. Recommended actions include joining the political struggle of indigenous peoples, a universal declaration of human obligations towards nature, and specific tasks for member churches and the World Council of Churches. An appendix by Gerald Barney explains the urgency and complexity of the social justice/eco-justice crisis.

512   World Council of Churches.   *Resources for Sections; The Theme, Subthemes, and Issues; World Council of Churches Seventh Assembly 1991.*   Geneva: World Council of Churches, 1990.

> This publication consists of resource documents for the World Council of Churches' (WCC) Canberra Assembly on the theme "Come, Holy Spirit—Renew the Whole Creation" and its four sub-themes. Each begins with the theological significance of the sub-theme, identifies major issues, suggests questions to explore, and quotes WCC and other documents. "Giver of Life—Sustain Your Creation!" (sub-theme I) asserts that protecting creation's integrity requires a Spirit-centered theology of creation, "a justice ethic for sustainability," and a new understanding of economics. Texts for the other sub-themes occasionally refer to environmental issues or to "the whole creation." "Spirit of Truth—Set Us Free" (on justice and liberation) makes only slight reference to resource use and ecosystem destruction in discussing the need for "sustainable value systems" and includes some treat-

ment of indigenous peoples' land rights. "Spirit of Unity—Reconcile Your People!" looks toward the reconciliation of all creation but says little about eco-justice issues. "Holy Spirit—Transform and Sanctify Us!" makes some connections between spirituality, affluence, and the ecological crisis. An appendix includes the "Affirmations" and "Act of Covenanting" from Seoul.

In addition to the works annotated in this chapter, readers interested in institutional forums and organizations may wish to consult the following entries located elsewhere in the bibliography: 015, 041, 043, 081, 093, 171, 209, 242, 254, 266, 305, 438, 456, 466, 474, 502.

Author Index

The Author Index references, by entry number, works annotated in the Bibliographic Survey. Authors whose works are discussed in the Critical Survey or within the annotations themselves are referenced in the Subject Index.

Title Index

The Title Index references, by entry number, works annotated in the Bibliographic Survey. Works discussed in the Critical Survey or within the annotations themselves are referenced in the Subject Index. Titles and subtitles beginning with the definite or indefinite article are arranged by the second word.

Subject Index

The Subject Index references the content of both the Critical Survey and the Bibliographic Survey. Italicized numbers refer to pages of the Critical Survey. All three-digit numbers represent entries in the Bibliographic Survey.

About the Authors

PETER W. BAKKEN is Coordinator of Outreach for the Au Sable Institute of Environmental Studies, a Christian environmental education institute.

JOAN GIBB ENGEL is a free-lance editor and writer, combining work in the fields of environment, culture, and natural history. She and her husband, J. Ronald Engel, are the editors of *Ethics of Environment and Development: Global Challenge and International Response (1990)*.

J. RONALD ENGEL is Professor of Social Ethics, Meadville/Lombard Theological School and chair of the Ethics Working Group of the World Conservation Union. He is the author of *Sacred Sands* (1983), a religious interpretation of the century-long struggle to preserve the Indiana Dunes, and has written extensively on eco-justice issues in professional journals.

ISBN 0-313-29073-3

HARDCOVER BAR CODE